YOUTH SPORT AND SPIRITUALITY

YOUTH SPORT
AND
SPIRITUALITY

CATHOLIC PERSPECTIVES

edited by

PATRICK KELLY, SJ

University of Notre Dame Press • Notre Dame, Indiana

University of Notre Dame Press
Notre Dame, Indiana 46556
undpress.nd.edu

Library of Congress Cataloging-in-Publication Data

Youth sport and spirituality : Catholic perspectives /
edited by Patrick Kelly, SJ.
pages   cm
Includes bibliographical references and index.
ISBN 978-0-268-01235-9 (pbk. : alk. paper)
ISBN 0-268-01235-0 (pbk. : alk. paper)
1. Sports—Religious aspects—Catholic Church.
2. Athletes—Religious life.
3. Sports—Psychological aspects.
4. Sports—Sociological aspects.
I. Kelly, Patrick M. (Patrick Michael), 1960– editor.
GV706.42.Y68   2015
796.01'9—dc23
2015023724

∞ *The paper in this book meets the guidelines for permanence and durability
of the Committee on Production Guidelines for Book Longevity of
the Council on Library Resources.*

Jesus said, "Let the children come to me and do not prevent them."

—Matthew 19:14 (NABRV)

CONTENTS

PART 2
PRACTICES AND PERSPECTIVES

Introduction

PATRICK KELLY, SJ

Youth Sport and Spirituality: Catholic Perspectives is a unique book that meets a pressing need at this time. The book is unique because it is the first of its kind that brings resources from Catholic cultural and intellectual traditions into meaningful conversation with scholarship on youth sport to address problems and opportunities in this domain of young people's lives. The first two chapters consider the question "What is sport?" and provide an overview of the history of Catholic engagement with play and sport. The remaining chapters are about how experiences of participation in youth sport can foster the integral development of the young person, and his or her search for meaning in life from a Christian perspective.

The book is divided into two sections. The first section contains chapters written by scholars from different academic disciplines. These chapters, while based on sound research and scholarship, are written without academic jargon or extensive footnotes. The second section of the book contains chapters written by coaches and other practitioners who work closely with young people in sport on a day-to-day basis.

The primary audience for *Youth Sport and Spirituality* is youth coaches, physical education teachers, and athletic directors who work in Catholic school and parish settings. The book will also be of interest to other groups, including youth ministers, Catholic educators and

1

administrators, parish priests and staffs, Catholic parents of children involved in sports, university students who are preparing to teach or coach in Catholic schools, Christians of other denominations, and anyone interested in the relationship between youth sport (or sport in general) and spirituality. Academics from the disciplines represented in the book, namely, philosophy, moral development, education, psychology, theology, and spirituality, will also find resources that are of interest to them. Catholic theologians and scholars of spirituality, in particular, will find that the book treats an area of human experience that has been woefully neglected in their disciplines.

Indeed, Catholic theologians and scholars of spirituality have not paid much attention to sport in the modern world. This is curious, given the Catholic sacramental worldview and emphasis on "finding God in all things," and the Catholic tendency to accept diverse cultural experiences and customs and to incorporate these into the life and even the worship of the church. The lack of attention paid to sport is even more surprising, given that sport is a "human universal," that is, it has been a part (in one form or another) of all cultures for which we have recorded histories. Sport is also pervasive in U.S. culture in our own time and in educational institutions, as well as in Catholic schools and parish settings themselves. It embodies many of the values and disvalues of the culture of the United States and plays an enormously influential role in the formation of young people. For these reasons, it is important that Catholic theologians and scholars of spirituality begin to pay attention to sport in our time.

Since this book is about youth sport and spirituality, it is important to say something about what spirituality is. Many scholars of spirituality today are trying to find a way to think about spirituality that doesn't limit it to persons who belong to a particular religious tradition. David Perrin is one scholar who has written about what this might mean. For Perrin, spirituality is a fundamental capacity in human beings. One of the first things he mentions in this regard is the human capacity for self-transcendence. As he puts it,

> Spirituality, as an innate human characteristic, involves the capacity for self-transcendence: being meaningfully involved in,

and personally committed to, the world beyond an individual's personal boundaries. This meaningful involvement and commitment shapes the way people live and allows them to integrate their lives.[1]

For Perrin, spirituality in this sense can be expressed in human experience before a person identifies with a particular religious or spiritual tradition or beliefs, rituals, or ethics.

For Perrin, spirituality also has to do with the "big questions" that all human beings ask. We try to forge meaning and find purpose and hope in the midst of our life experiences, which at times can seem disconnected or random. We attempt to "make sense of it all." And we do so in the context of what is *ultimately* important to us. As he puts it, "Spirituality stands at the junction where the deepest concerns of humanity, and the belief in transcendent values, come together in the movement toward ultimate fulfillment in life."[2]

The strength of this broad rendering of spirituality lies in its inclusiveness. It could refer to spirituality in any religious tradition. It doesn't require belief in God and so could be used with reference to nontheistic traditions such as one finds in some expressions of Buddhism. Or it could account for a spirituality that exists outside of organized religion, such as twelve-step spirituality. It is important to note that for Perrin, spirituality has to do with a "way of life." His use of the word "integrate" signals that spirituality has to do with the way a person brings together all of the dimensions of his or her life into a meaningful whole.

If this is spirituality understood in a broad sense, what is Christian spirituality? Obviously, God is the ultimate concern for the Christian. According to Perrin,

At the center of Christian spirituality is God's animating, graceful presence. It is God's Spirit alive in people's lives that moves them beyond the boundaries of their fragile selves to give their lives in many different ways to others. For the Christian, God is the foundation for all self-transcendence and for all spirituality.[3]

Sandra Schneiders, IHM, fleshes out in greater detail what Christian spirituality is when she writes:

> Christian spirituality is an explicitly religious spirituality in which the horizon of ultimate value is the triune God revealed in Jesus Christ, in whose life we share through the gift of the Holy Spirit. Christian spirituality is the life of faith, hope, and love within the community of the Church through which we put on the mind of Christ by participating sacramentally and existentially in his paschal mystery. The desired life-integration is personal transformation in Christ, which implies participation in the transformation of the world in justice for all creatures.[4]

Schneiders is a Catholic religious sister, and so it is no surprise that in her definition of Christian spirituality she emphasizes the communal dimension. In the Catholic understanding, persons are social by their very constitution—and encounter God in community. Personal transformation in Christ involves, simultaneously, a deepening experience of God's love and a deepening of our love for our brothers and sisters. Indeed, from a Christian perspective, love of God and love of neighbor are two sides of the same coin. As the first letter of John puts it, "If we love one another, God remains in us, and his love is brought to perfection in us" (1 Jn 4:12b). Because of Jesus's own example and identification with "the least of these," there is also a special emphasis on love for (and work on behalf of) those who are oppressed, poor, or in any way afflicted.

Spirituality is also an academic discipline. The discipline is relatively new, only a few decades old. And there is still much discussion and debate about what its subject matter is, how it is that scholars should go about studying it, and what its relationship should be to theology and other disciplines. For the purposes of this volume, it is enough to highlight some general areas of agreement among scholars.

As has been intimated, the subject matter that scholars of spirituality study is a person or community's *lived experience* in relationship to what is perceived as being of *ultimate concern*. As was mentioned earlier, scholars of spirituality are interested in lived experience as it is shaped into *a way of life*. In this sense, spirituality has to do with the way a person or community integrates the different dimensions of life into a meaningful whole.[5]

Scholars of Christian spirituality in our time point out that "spirituality" is not to be understood in contrast to the material or bodily dimensions of human life. It also is not concerned only with one's "interior life," especially if that is understood as not meaningfully related to life in society. According to Philip Sheldrake, Christian spirituality "is not just concerned with prayer or even with narrowly religious activities. It concerns the whole of human life, viewed in terms of a conscious relationship with God, in Jesus Christ, through the indwelling of the Holy Spirit and within a community of believers."[6]

The focus on lived experience is one of the ways the study of Christian spirituality differs from theology. The word theology derives from the two Greek words *theos,* or "God," and *logos*, or "study of." The focus of theology is thus appropriately on how Christians understand God. Scholars of Christian spirituality, on the other hand, study the lived experiences that persons or communities have of God. While they are different academic disciplines, theology is a crucial dialogue partner for scholars of spirituality. One obvious reason for this is that there is an intimate relationship between our experiences of God and our understanding of God.[7]

But other academic disciplines are also important for the study of spirituality. Indeed, in large part because scholars of spirituality are studying lived experiences and the whole of life, the method they use must be interdisciplinary. In this book, there are chapters by scholars in the academic disciplines of philosophy, psychology, moral development, and education. Using the lenses of these different disciplines helps us to understand the experiential dimension of youth sport in its full complexity.

In this book, the authors write about spirituality in its broader rendering as well as about Christian spirituality. The broader rendering makes the book accessible to persons from different religious traditions, and indeed to all people of good will. In a sense it is understandable that the authors would take such an approach. The authors who teach in Catholic universities are used to teaching diverse class-rooms of Catholic and non-Catholic students. Those teaching Catholic theology or spirituality recognize that, while they have a special ob-ligation to teach the Catholic heritage, they need to encourage *all* of their students to reflect on the way they are living their lives in the context of their own religious traditions or in the context of what is ultimately important to them. Scholars working in public universities have even more reason to take an approach that will be accessible to a broad range of students. Even in Catholic elementary and high schools, not all of the students are Catholic; hence, coaches in Catholic schools have a lot of experience coaching young people from diverse backgrounds. They too recognize the importance of having an ap-proach that is accessible to a wide range of students. Such an approach is all the more necessary for coaches working in independent or public schools.[8]

In this book the authors are writing from and reflecting on the cultural context of the United States.[9] Each author has taught in uni-versities or has coached young people, or administered youth sport programs in the U.S.[10] The United States is a distinctive context, and the authors write about the unique challenges and opportunities for youth sport associated with it in this book. The need also exists for contextual theological and spiritual reflection on youth sport by Catholic scholars in other parts of the world. The problems, issues, and opportunities of young people in relation to play and sport will be very different in the United States from those in Italy or France, let alone those in Peru or Uganda. Such theological reflection in diverse contexts will help us to understand more fully the richness of the cul-tural diversity in the still-emerging global Catholic Church.

The authors contributing to this volume, as noted, also come from different academic contexts and disciplines. Daniel A. Dombrowski and Mike McNamee are philosophers, and their chapters are located within the framework of their own academic discipline, making no at-tempt to broach theological topics or spirituality. Nicole M. LaVoi, a psychologist, teaches in the graduate school of kinesiology at the Uni-versity of Minnesota, a state university. She has been a lead researcher in two recent comprehensive studies of youth sport in the United

States. This includes one study that focuses on the experiences of girls. Her chapters provide detailed descriptions of experiences of self-transcendence in youth sport based on the most up-to-date psychological and sociological research, and so are an invaluable resource for scholars of spirituality.

David Light Shields and Brenda Light Bredemeier both teach at the University of Missouri, St. Louis, a state university. Prior to taking their current positions they worked at the Mendelson Center for Sports, Character, and Community at the University of Notre Dame. At the end of their chapter they provide an excellent definition of spirituality "in its broadest rendering," which they point out is also compatible with some of the core elements of spirituality in the religious traditions of the world.

Clark Power, Patrick Kelly, Richard R. Gaillardetz, and Edward Hastings all teach at Catholic universities. Power, who is a professor in the area of moral development at the University of Notre Dame, is also the founder of Play Like a Champion Today, which has for many years trained Catholic Youth Organization (CYO) coaches in Catholic dioceses around the country. More recently, Power is doing work with Catholic high schools. Because he understands moral and spiritual development to be integrally related, he writes explicitly about Catholic spirituality in his chapter on moral development. Kelly and Gaillardetz teach theology at Seattle University and Boston College, two Jesuit universities. Gaillardetz is a past president of the Catholic Theological Society of America. Edward Hastings teaches at Villanova, an Augustinian university. Kelly, Gaillardetz, and Hastings draw explicitly on the resources of Catholic theology and spirituality in their reflections on youth sport.

The coaches and other practitioners write from diverse contexts as well. Kristin Komyatte Sheehan works for Play Like a Champion Today (with Clark Power) at Notre Dame. As was mentioned, early in the program's development Play Like a Champion Today focused on CYO or pre–high school sports, and this age group is the focus of her chapter. Because she is working with Catholic dioceses and schools, her chapter is explicitly about Catholic spirituality. Dobie Moser is the executive director of the Youth and Young Adult Ministry and CYO office in the diocese of Cleveland. His chapter also focuses on CYO or pre–high school youth sport and is explicit in its treatment of Catholic spirituality. Jim Yerkovich and James Charles Naggi, coaches for many decades at Catholic high schools, are primarily concerned with overcoming the gap they feel exists between the educational mission of Catholic schools and how coaches understand and approach what they are doing with young people on sports teams. Sherri Retif is teaching at a private, independent high school. In her chapter, she articulates how she approaches coaching in this religiously diverse context, as someone informed by the Catholic heritage.

As you read this book you will discover that the authors, at times, articulate different points of view on topics such as the relationship between youth sport and moral development and the meaning and value of competition. As the editor, I have not attempted to resolve differences or reconcile these views to present a single perspective. My hope is that, by leaving some questions open or debated, readers will be encouraged to engage in their own reflection and discussion and think through their own positions on the topics under consideration.

While the authors differ on some issues, they also give expression to some common themes that are distinctive in the culture of the United States at this time. In some cases, the distinctiveness of the themes is owing to the fact that the authors are writing from a Catholic perspective in a culture that has been profoundly shaped by Protestant theological and spiritual traditions and more recently by the processes of secularization. I will highlight four of these themes in the comments that follow.

First, all authors are trying to articulate the *internal goods* or *intrinsic rewards* of youth sport participation. Many are critical of the tendency for parents, coaches, and even some young people to focus on external goods, such as college scholarships, pro contracts, and the fame that comes with success. In this sense, these authors are saying that we do not take sport itself and the experiences of young people who participate in sport seriously enough. The notion that we are not taking sport seriously enough is counterintuitive, given all the attention we seem to pay to it in America. But according to these authors, the connection of sport to money and the extent of media coverage are poor indicators of how seriously we are taking the activity itself. In fact, the link between sport and money can distract us from the activity itself and the experiences of young people. Dombrowski expresses a commonly held view when he writes "if the prime purpose of sport is to generate capital, then the sport activity itself has taken a back seat."[11]

The authors emphasize, then, paying attention to the *experiences* of those participating in youth sport. It is helpful, given this emphasis, that some of the scholarly contributors to this volume are from academic disciplines such as psychology, moral development, and education, whose methods involve paying close attention to the lived experiences of young people. Obviously, coaches are also in close and sustained contact with the lived experiences of young people who are participating in sport. It is only by staying close to these lived experiences and carefully reflecting on their meaning for young people that we will be able to develop a sound spirituality of youth sport.

Because they are convinced that sport has internal goods or intrinsic rewards, some authors are also critical of what they see as an overemphasis on elite youth sport in the United States today. The argument is that, if there are indeed internal goods associated with sport, then these should be available to *all* young people who want to participate. And so some authors make the case for equal playing time on elementary school teams and for a shift away from an exclusive focus on varsity sports in high schools. In this sense, they favor an approach that is reminiscent of the approach of the humanists of the Renaissance and the early Jesuits who ran the first schools primarily for lay people in the Western world. In these schools, time and space was provided during the school day for all students to play games and sports.

The second theme is closely related to the first. Several authors insist on *the human and spiritual significance of play*. In the chapter "Christians and Sport: An Historical and Theological Overview" Patrick Kelly writes about how Catholics played games and sports throughout the medieval period on feast days and Sundays. As he shows, Thomas Aquinas regarded play as important for a virtuous life. For Thomas, as for the ancients, virtue had to do with moderation. This meant that a person should not be studying or working or even engaging in spiritual exercises all the time. He or she should also take time for play and recreation. Indeed, for Thomas, *there can be sin in a lack of play*. The humanists of the Renaissance, and the early Jesuits, drew on this heritage when articulating the reasons for including time for play and sport as a part of the school day. It should be highlighted that, in this tradition, play is understood to be closely related to spiritual values. Thomas Aquinas thought, for example, that play was similar to contemplation because both activities were *enjoyable* and *done for their own sake*. Several of the authors in this book emphasize the importance of these two elements of play for youth sport in our time. While they also touch on other aspects of play, they point out that when youth sport is fun and enjoyable and done for its own sake, or for intrinsic reasons, it is related to the flourishing of the young person.

Given the U.S. context of this volume, it is worth noting that important elements of this heritage were rejected by the Puritans and later by other Protestants in the United States. The Puritans had a dislike for feast days, in particular. As the English Puritan John Northbrooke wrote in 1577:

> And where you say that holydayes (as they are termed), were invented in old time for pastimes, I think you say truth. For ye Pope appointed them (and not God in his word), and that only to traine up the people in ignorance and ydleness, whereby halfe of the year, and more, was overpassed (by their idyle holydayes) in loitering and vaine pastimes, &c., in restraining men from their handy labors and occupations.[12]

The last sentence is crucial, as it highlights that Northbrooke's concern was that playing would distract people from *work*. In large part because the Puritans associated godliness with work, they began to regard play with a new level of suspicion. They tended to see it as trivial, or even worse, as sinful. The Industrial Revolution and the full flowering of capitalism as an economic system only increased the emphasis on work and suspicion of play in the United States. These developments also made it possible for this mentality to extend beyond a particular religious community to all Americans. This heritage is still exercising its influence today, in the work orientation of U.S. culture and the tendency to regard human activities primarily from a business or monetary point of view. The influence of this heritage is felt in youth sport today as well, which has taken on the characteristics of work and (as was mentioned earlier) is commonly viewed instrumentally in relation to college scholarships, or for the more ambitious, dreams of a professional contract. Indeed, the play element is sometimes very hard to find in youth sport in our time.[13]

The third common theme is really more of a presupposition, which is that "grace perfects nature." This well-known phrase of Thomas Aquinas is one of the most basic, and consequential, presuppositions in Catholic theology. As Leo Rock, SJ, put it, "Grace does not substitute for nature, but fulfills it." From this perspective, "Healthy, sane personality development is the most fertile soil in which grace can take root and grow."[14] For this reason, the chapters that focus on moral, psychological, and social development in youth sport are very important for this volume. We have to start with an understanding of what it means to grow as a young person in the context of youth sport in order to understand how this is related to growth in the Christian life. Traditionally, "healthy personality development" has been understood as related to the development of the virtues. In his chapter, Mike McNamee provides us with a rich description of how participation in youth sport can foster the development of the virtues in an Aristotelian sense.

A fourth emphasis in this book is on *community*. Because the Catholic tradition emphasizes community, the experiences that young people have playing on a team and thereby being formed in communal values is an obvious starting point for reflection on the meaning of youth sport from a Christian perspective. (The communal emphasis of Catholicism is also likely part of the reason why Catholic schools— and universities—have often been successful in team sports. In Catholic schools there is a communal orientation that is related to transcendent values that, at least ideally, undergirds everything that happens in the school.) In this book, high school coaches Sherri Retif, Jim

Yerkovich, and James Charles Naggi write about the way their players begin to understand themselves as part of something larger than
themselves and grow in their ability to cooperate and work with
others. Retif writes insightfully about the spiritual (understood in a
broad sense) significance of such an experience for the girls on her
basketball teams. Yerkovich and Naggi show how informed and skill-
ful coaches can help their players understand the relationship between the experience of playing on a team and the experience of being
a member of the Christian community.

NOTES

1. David Perrin, *Studying Christian Spirituality* (New York: Routledge,
2007), 20.

2. Ibid., 22.

3. Ibid., 26.

4. Sandra Schneiders, IHM, "Spirituality and Religion: Strangers, Rivals, or
Partners?" *The Santa Clara Lectures*, vol. 6, no. 2 (2000): 6.

5. Some theologians, such as Hans Urs von Balthasar, are critical of the modern turn to human experience and the human subject as the starting point for
spirituality and theology. For von Balthasar, this tends to make faith too subjective
and detaches it from its foundation in revelation. As the reader will see, part of my
reason for adopting the above approach is practical: it allows academics and coaches
to invite all of their students and players to reflect on their spiritual lives, regardless of religious affiliation. When it comes to the formulation of a specifically
Christian spirituality of youth sport, however, the concerns von Balthasar and
others raise are important to keep in mind.

6. David Lonsdale, *Eyes to See, Ears to Hear* (Maryknoll, NY: Orbis Books,
2000), 10. In this sense, contemporary scholars of Christian spirituality are attempting to avoid dualist and quietist errors that have appeared in different periods in the history of Christianity and instead to put us back in touch with biblical
and more traditional understandings of Christian spirituality.

7. The relationship between theology and spirituality has been understood
in different ways throughout Christian history. For the church fathers, theology
and spirituality were not easily distinguishable, as the experience of prayer and
liturgy was the lifeblood of theological reflection. In the universities during the
scholastic period, theology and spirituality were distinguished but still understood
as related to one another in the work of the most important theologians. They became separated after medieval scholasticism, however, and this separation still im-

pacts us in our own context. The problem with this development is that theological formulations can tend to become disconnected from lived experience and hence run the risk of losing their meaning and relevance in the lives of believers.

8. The desire to appeal to all people of good will is, or should be, characteristic of a Catholic approach to this topic. The Greek word *katholikos* means "universal." The opposite of Catholic, then, is sectarian (note that it is not "Protestant"). The word "sectarian" suggests what is closed off from interaction with others who are not part of one's group, and from society more generally.

9. Of course, the culture of the United States is not monolithic. And even with respect to Catholicism in the United States, there is significant cultural diversity. Because this is the first book on this topic, we have tended to highlight basic themes that are distinctive to Catholicism. It will be important in the years to come to do more detailed study of youth sport in particular Catholic cultural contexts in the United States, such as Hispanic, Filipino, Vietnamese, and so forth. In addition, since many African American students (from different religious denominations) attend Catholic schools, it will be important in future volumes to attend to the challenges and opportunities in youth sport for young people from the African American community.

10. Mike McNamee, who is from Wales, is an exception. I heard Mike deliver his paper on "Youth Sport and the Virtues" at the first conference ever held at the Vatican on youth sport, "Sport, Education, Faith: Towards a New Season for Catholic Sports Associations," in 2009. I thought the paper was excellent and ideal for this book, and so I asked Mike for permission to include it.

11. See 21 in this volume.

12. John Northbrooke, "A TREATISE wherein Dicing, Dancing, Vaine playes, or Enterluds, with other idle pastimes, &c. commonly used on the Sabboth day, are reproved by the Authoritie of the word of God and auntient writers" (London, 1577), 44.

13. It is important to call attention to the fact that not all Protestants in the United States have been, or are, sympathetic to the Puritan approach to this topic. Indeed, prominent Protestant ministers in the nineteenth century such as Horace Bushnell and Washington Gladden were very critical of the Puritan heritage because it had led to the United States becoming a culture of "all work and no play." And in our own time, many Protestant theologians are also insisting on the importance of recovering the play element in sport and in youth sport.

14. Wilkie Au, *By Way of the Heart* (Mahwah, NY: Paulist Press, 1991), 20.

PART 1

Research-Based
and Theoretical Perspectives

CHAPTER 1

What Is Sport?
What Should It Be?

Some Definitions and Some Homeric
Remarks Regarding Moderation

DANIEL A. DOMBROWSKI

Something like the questions in the title of this chapter have been around for a long time. The first great works of literature in Western civilization, Homer's *Iliad*[1] and *Odyssey*[2] from the ancient Greek period about three thousand years ago, depict sporting events at least three times. And in each of these episodes we seem to get a different response to our questions, "What is sport?" and "What should it be?"

At one point in the *Odyssey* (book 8) the main character, Odysseus, engages in what amount to informal "pickup" games on the beach. Here sport looks very much like pure play. In partial contrast to this, in the *Iliad* (book 23) there are the much more competitive games played to commemorate the recent death of Patroclos. Although these games are competitive, they nonetheless preserve the play spirit in that the participants in effect are saying, "Patroclos is dead, but we are alive, so let's have a race!" At a third place in Homer's works (*Odyssey*, book 21) we get a still different picture. Here an archery contest turns bloody as Odysseus and his son kill many people who were plotting to take over his throne.

I posit that these three episodes from antiquity point to three different contemporary responses to the questions, "What is sport?" and "What should it be?" The first episode suggests that sport is a type of pure play, which is nonserious. The second suggests that sport is competitive play, which involves a blend of seriousness and nonseriousness, strange as that sounds. The philosopher William James had this approach in mind when he spoke of sport as the moral equivalent to (immoral) war or as a moral replacement for war.[3] But the third episode suggests that sport is ultra-serious, even warlike. As the writer George Orwell[4] urged in opposition to William James, sport *is* war by other means. We will see that a careful consideration of these texts will help us to better understand what youth sport is and what it should be.

SOME DEFINITIONS

A consideration of some basic definitions will further help us to respond in an informed way to the questions that are in this title of the present chapter. It should be noted that the word "play" comes from the Anglo-Saxon word *plega*, which originally referred to the free movement of bodily exercise as well as to the joy or delight in such movement.[5] "Sport" originally had a similar meaning. It comes from the Anglo-French word *disporter*, which meant to divert or to amuse in a pleasant pastime or recreation.

At least initially it might seem that "athletics" means something quite different from "play" or "sport" in that the word comes from the ancient Greek infinitive *athleuein*, which means to contend for a prize or to endure in a struggle. That is, there is something inherently competitive about athletics. In athletic competition one is very much concerned with who wins and who loses, which leads some people to wonder if the spirit of play is necessarily lost in competitive games. The word "game," it should be noted, comes from the Teutonic *gamen*, which refers to the amusement found in a contest engaged in according to rules.

My own view, in light of the above original meanings of some key words, is that sport is best seen as competitive play that involves some kind of test of bodily excellence. But this claim needs qualification so as to avoid the view that there is something trivial about sport. One can imagine the following list, where the generic category of play is seen to have at least three different types: (1) aimless play or frolic; (2) competitive play or sport or athletics; (3) warlike play. The first category of play is entirely nonserious (as in tossing a frisbee at a picnic), whereas the second category involves a sort of serious nonseriousness, and finally the third category involves play that is far too serious.

The goal for those who are involved with youth sport should be to foster competitive play or athletics. Everyone who is familiar with youth sport has experienced the two extremes: indifferent or lazy team members who are not competitive enough and who do not take seriously enough their games, much less practice time, on the one hand; and those team members, coaches, and parents who are too serious about athletic competition and who are too competitive, on the other. I assume that the latter is the greater danger.

The moderate position that I am defending between these two extremes can be illuminated by a consideration of the literal meaning of the word "competition." It comes from the Latin *competitionem*, which surprisingly means to strive *with* someone else, rather than *against* someone else. The word would be "anti-petition" if it meant to struggle against someone else. But this is not a word we use. The upshot of competition is that a sporting event without an opponent is no sporting event at all. One *needs* the opponent in order to have a competitive game at all. The competitors are, in effect, asking each other the question, "Which of us is better at a certain activity?" Think of how boxers congratulate each other immediately after a bout. This is competition in the best sense of the term.

Randolph Feezell, whose book *Sport, Play, and Ethical Reflection*[6] is perhaps the best in the field, helps us to understand the meanings of the above terms by asking us to consider two high school coaches, let us say basketball coaches. One coach views sport as either real life itself or as harsh preparation for the even harsher realities of real life.

At times he or she even views sport as little short of war. The sayings of some famous football coaches make us realize that this high school coach's approach is supported by the dominant culture of sport, as when Bill Parcells said that football *is* life or when George Allen said that winning *is* living. One is also reminded of the Vince Lombardi view that runs in the same direction. These attitudes have had an influence well beyond football.

In contrast to this first high school coach, who is overly serious about sport, consider a different hypothetical high school coach who exhibits a more moderate approach. This second coach encourages his or her players to be spirited competitors and to pursue victory. But this coach also encourages the players to have a sense of fair play, to respect the referees, and to understand that basketball is only one aspect of a full life.

Whereas the first coach sees the opponent as an enemy, the second coach sees the opponent as a friendly competitor, whose challenge is necessary to enhance the pleasurable possibilities of playing basketball, to use Feezell's language. Granted, it is sometimes difficult to sustain the spirit of play in the midst of intense competition, but the second coach always keeps this as the ideal. That is, his or her seriousness is tempered by the realization that, after all, basketball is "just a game."

Ultimately there ought not be any rigid distinction between "play" and "sport," on the one hand, and "athletics," on the other. That is, athletic competition in search of victory ought to retain the spirit of play and a sportive sense of lightheartedness. Think of Ernie Banks's joyful attitude toward baseball, such that his only regret on game days was when there was no doubleheader. Most young athletes share this joy. But if they do not, they should not be forced to compete, in my view. If they are not having fun, why force them to play? Indeed, there seems to be something contradictory in "forced play" in that there ought to be something liberating about play, in contrast to drudgery tasks.

The view of sport I am defending is further illustrated by a consideration of the fact that we commonly refer to youth sport participants as amateurs. It is not often noticed that the meaning of the

French word that is at the root of our word "amateur" refers to one who loves. So an amateur football player is one who plays for the love of the game. There is something bothersome in the fact that the term has come to refer to someone who does not get paid for his or her activity, as if the only activities in life that one could really enjoy are those that involve no monetary reward. *Amateur athletes* in the original senses of both of these terms know better.

Equally difficult as recovering the literal meaning of "amateur" is the difficulty in doing the same regarding "professional." This term derives from the Latin *professus*, which was originally a public declaration of the moral ideals that one hoped to sustain, as in the profession of the religious vows of poverty, chastity, and obedience, or as in the physician's profession of the Hippocratic Oath. As is well known, however, the word "professional" has come to refer to one who gets paid for his or her activity. Perhaps this debasement of the term is understandable in a culture where sport is typically not viewed as a species of play but as an integral part of the economy. Here, despite the intentions of those who prop up the sport industry, sport itself is not taken seriously enough. That is, if the prime purpose of sport is to generate capital, then the sport activity itself has taken a back seat.

MORAL EDUCATION

Given the context of the present volume dedicated to youth sport, it will be worthwhile to briefly explain the connection between the sport as competitive play thesis and the role of moral education in sport. This connection is more complex than many imagine, as is detailed in the chapter by Mike McNamee later in the present book.[7] Very often youth sport is justified in terms of its usefulness in the moral education of young people. Everyone who is familiar with youth sport is familiar with this justification. One is told that young people on sports teams develop a sense of moral agency and of moral duty right at the time that they join sports teams, such that learning how to lose gracefully, how to get along with team members (especially those that one does not particularly like), how to show proper respect for authority (such as coaches or referees), and so forth, are fostered in youth sport.

I confess that at times in the past I have enthusiastically defended this argument. Although I still defend it, I take it with a grain of salt for two reasons. First, in my experience, for every young athlete who is morally improved by participation in youth sports there is another athlete who may have been encouraged to become morally worse by athletic competition. At least we should be aware of both the moral dangers as well as the moral benefits of youth sports. In addition to teaching young people how to handle loss gracefully, youth sport also has the potential to teach youth sport participants, especially the really talented ones, how to develop a swelled head or a big ego or a sense of entitlement that is undeserved. In fact, I would go so far as to say that readers who do not know what I am getting at in the present paragraph have not been paying attention to what sport can do to the psyches of some young people. In this regard McNamee is extremely helpful in warning us that we ought to avoid the complacency found in thinking that somehow, as if by magic, the very playing of sports would instill into its young practitioners moral qualities.

The second reason why I think we should be careful not to over-emphasize the moral pedagogy of youth sports is that by reducing sport to the very serious activity of moral education we threaten to deaden the play spirit. That is, the play spirit is threatened not only by professionalization (in the sense of the undue influence of money) but also by the questionable assumption that the only (or main) worth of youth sport lies in its educational value.

I am defending the claim that sport competition is, like virtue, its own reward. The intrinsic value of competitive play, the joy of sport, ought not to be totally reduced to its instrumental value as a means to acquire capital, whether monetary capital or moral capital.

An accidental byproduct of sport competition *might* be the development of character, but this is not integrally connected to the joy of the sport activity itself nor is it guaranteed. I suspect that most or all readers of the present chapter have had the experience of losing their temper and saying things that they later regretted in the heat of the moment at an athletic event. And I also suspect that most or all readers of the present chapter have met athletes or coaches or fans (or parents!) who make losing their temper at athletic events a habit, indeed a habit that is hard to break. The moral pitfalls of athletic competition should be familiar enough to every reflective person in the world of youth sport. Here McNamee is once again extremely helpful in that he holds that the cliché that practice makes *perfect* might be profitably replaced with the saying that habitual practice makes *permanent*. That is, the habits that are inculcated into young athletes, for good or for ill, tend to have a lasting effect such that ignoring these habits is morally perilous.

Once again, I am trying to develop moderate responses to the questions, "What is sport?" and "What should it be?" To those who would respond to the first question by saying that sport is a prime means to make our young people moral I would *not* say outright that they are wrong. But I would caution them against overstatement. Youth sport *might* help children and adolescents develop into responsible citizens and into admirable adults. But it might do the exact opposite, too, especially if we adults who are in charge of youth sports allow the play spirit to evaporate altogether from competitive events.

Another book written by Feezell, along with Craig Clifford, titled *Sport and Character: Reclaiming the Principles of Sportsmanship*,[8] argues in detail in favor of sportsmanship, especially in youth sport, as a moderate stance that lies between taking sport too frivolously and taking it too seriously (once again, with the latter being the greater danger). On their insightful view, in addition to sportsmanship involving a type of moderation, it involves respect at every turn. *Respect for opponents* involves an adherence to both the golden rule (to treat others as you would like to be treated) and the silver rule (to not treat others as you would not like to be treated). It also would seem to involve an opposition to trash talking or gamesmanship. *Respect for officials* means that any discourse with referees (if there is such) should be conducted with civility. *Respect for coaches* is reciprocally related to coaches' respect for players: both are necessary in any morally defensible version of youth sports. *Respect for teammates* is obviously important, especially in team sports where coordinated activity is crucial. And finally, *respect for the game* involves a willingness to abide by the rules of the game and to pursue bodily excellence in a way that is consistent with the spirit of competition as discussed above.

RETURN TO THE GREEKS

I have worked on the assumption that in order for us to respond adequately to the questions in the title of the present chapter, one of the tasks that is required is to come to terms with ancient Greek views of sport. Their fascination with sport was so great that they actually marked the passage of time in terms of the ancient Olympic Games rather than the reverse. And this fascination with sport has conquered the contemporary world. In fact, Marxist critics of sport might see it as the new opiate of the people if it is true that sport directs our attention away from the most serious aspects of life, like premature death. But by returning to the Greeks I do not intend to replicate the romantic Olympism of Pierre de Coubertin, the figure who reinvented the Olympic Games in the contemporary period. Coubertin unfortunately continued ancient sexism and classism, and he altogether misunderstood the fact that successful ancient athletes were paid quite well for their victories and were not "amateurs" in Coubertin's sense of the term, wherein there was no financial reward for athletic activity. The Greeks do not offer us a completely pure *ursprache* that is oracular in character. Rather, we should return to the Greeks precisely because contemporary thinking about sport *is* quite unwittingly historical thinking. That is, by thinking *with* the Greeks (specifically with Homer), with both their strengths and weaknesses, we can better understand today what sport is and what it ought to be. Or again, by mining Homer what we learn from him can boomerang back to us for our contemporary edification.

It *does* matter a great deal how we talk about sport in that it makes a difference to us when we say that it is a type of competitive play that tests bodily excellence, as opposed, say, to claiming that it is primarily a locus for moral education, or entertainment, or a commodity that is bought and sold on the market, or preparation for war, and so on. Sport is complex enough that each of these ways of speaking contains a grain of truth, but it is nonetheless instructive to note that even big time sports figures started out *playing* their sports as children and stay in the neighborhood of play even when they participate in their games as adults. Just as it makes sense to be concerned about whether James Joyce's *Ulysses* (which details a day in the life of a latter-day Odysseus) is either pornography or the greatest twentieth-century novel, so also it is important to speak accurately about sport.

My defense of the thesis that sport is a type of competitive play that tests bodily excellence is consistent with the ancient view of sport found in Homer, which focuses on the key ancient Greek virtue of moderation (*sophrosyne*). The goal is to mediate between the twin dangers of not taking sport seriously enough and the more perilous tendency to take it too seriously. As Johan Huizinga, the greatest defender of the *homo ludens* hypothesis (the view of humans as players and of culture as played), puts the point: contemporary culture seems to exhibit a fatal shift toward over-seriousness.[9]

The overall method at work here is that of reflective equilibrium or Aristotelian dialectic. I am not trying to give an essential definition of what sport is or an airtight rendition of what it ought to be. Rather, I am interested in gathering together some of the most important considerations related to the questions in the title of the present chapter and in finding an acceptable fit among them. This involves both a consideration of the hypothetical decision-making devices that are popular in analytic philosophy *and* a consideration of the relevant historical (specifically Homeric) evidence. It also involves equilibrium between (Wittgensteinian) meaning as use of some key terms *and* the etymologies of such key terms from ancient Greece and elsewhere. Or again, it involves objective accounts of sport as found in biology and other disciplines *and* phenomenological evidence that comes from personal experience as an athlete, as a parent of an athlete, and as a fan. In all of these pairings, I argue, equilibrium is reached most easily when sport is seen under the umbrella of the *homo ludens* hypothesis, and disequilibrium occurs when we veer away from the idea that sport is a type of competitive play that tests bodily excellence.

THE TEXTS, AGAIN

Let us look in a bit more detail at the three depictions of athletic events in Homer so as to spell out the view of sport as moderation that I am defending. In book 8 of the *Odyssey* the protagonist, Odysseus, lands in Phaiacia after ten years at war and a disastrous trip trying to return to his home in Ithaca. He is greeted by a princess whose father, the king, eventually announces that athletic competitions will take place. At these competitions the Phaiacians declare themselves to be the greatest athletes in the world! After the games are under way, a question arises as to whether Odysseus himself has any athletic ability. This gives rise to a dilemma for Odysseus in that he could either decline to compete so as to continue working on the construction of ships that would enable him and his men to finish the trip home (but thereby miss the opportunity to show his athletic prowess) or to accept the invitation to compete (but thereby taking time away from the preparations needed for his trip). He chose the latter. In fact, because the discus throw was the event taking place at the moment, he picked up the heaviest disc (in the ancient discus, each successive throw involved a slightly heavier disc) and threw it farther than any of the previous competitors.

The reaction of the astonished Phaiacians at this point is crucial. They backed down and admitted that their real interest was the "twinkling feet" of those who took "delight in dancing." That is, after their initial boast that they were the greatest athletes in the world, they had to confess that they were not good athletes. The philosophical point that I would like to emphasize is that *if* we adopted the Phaiacians' view of sport, we would be putting into disequilibrium everything that we take seriously about it. They misunderstand the pursuit of bodily excellence and they underappreciate the pursuit of victory. Further, their approach to sport involves a mere attitudinal parsimony (to use Feezell's language): just have fun and do not worry about bodily excellence or the pursuit of victory. This story ends with the king's sons exhibiting the type of play I have called frolic by playing aimlessly with a ball. There is also an interlude involving the god

Hephaestus, who literally captures his wife in an adulterous embrace with a different god via a net constructed by Hephaestus himself. The wild laughter of almost everyone present is meant to underscore the ludic or playful tenor of this entire story.

Another sort of attitudinal parsimony is found in book 21 of the *Odyssey*. In the Penelope Games (in contrast to the Phaiacian Games) sport is depicted in an overly serious manner as competitive play morphs into warlike play. By this point in the story Odysseus has returned home, but he is not yet recognized in his attempt to regain his throne and his wife, Penelope, from the opportunistic suitors who wish to replace him on the throne and in Penelope's bed. A preliminary bout with a beggar gives an indication of the bloodshed to follow as Odysseus pummels his opponent. Once in the palace, a game has been set up by Penelope such that whoever can perform the monumental task of stringing the bow of her missing husband and then perform an incredible archery feat (to shoot an arrow through the holes in a dozen ax heads) will win her hand in marriage and also win the throne. Only Odysseus can string the bow and he shoots the arrow through the targets on the first try.

The suitors mistakenly assumed that the contest was over once Odysseus had made the incredibly accurate shot. But then Odysseus obtained more arrows and other weapons and started killing all of the suitors and the women who had entertained them in the palace. Dozens or perhaps hundreds of people were killed, including Melanthios, whose nose, ears, and testicles were cut off and fed to the dogs. Granted, Homer seems to heap approbation on Odysseus as a warrior, but as an athlete (specifically, as an archer) there is something amiss in his behavior. Once again, the key point philosophically is that *if* we accepted Odysseus's view of athletics, everything we care about in sport would be put into disequilibrium. The parsimony of his approach is obvious: simply do whatever it takes to accomplish your goal, be as ruthless as possible as long as you win. This is at odds with our usual disdain for cheating, violence, and subterfuge in sport and is too great a price to pay intellectually, hence we have to look elsewhere for a defensible view of sport. At the end of this part of the *Odyssey* the protagonist is smothered in blood and filth and is a symbol for the greater of the two dangers: that we would be overly serious about sport in that we would have the desire to win at all costs not mitigated by any sort of moderating influence. As we have seen George Orwell put the point in contemporary terms, sport in this sense can be seen as war without the shooting.

Whatever Homer's own view of sport may have been, I am arguing that in his texts can be found three major treatments of athletic competition, two of which can be seen today as extreme in that if we accepted either of them some of our most cherished beliefs about sport and the strongest intuitions we have about sport—for example, that in *some* sense the pursuit of bodily excellence and the desire for victory are important in sport, and that in *some* sense the pursuits of bodily excellence and victory have to be moderated or else we will be led to the odious results of cheating, violence—would be put into disequilibrium. But a third treatment of athletic competition in Homer points the way toward a moderate view of sport that enables us to most closely approximate reflective equilibrium.

In the *Iliad*, book 23, the Greeks had recently defeated the Trojans in battle, but one of the most important Greeks, Patroclos, was killed. The sands were drenched with blood and tears as the Greeks tried to compose themselves after the battle. In contrast to the Penelope Games, where competitive play morphed into war, in the Patroclos Games war morphs into competitive play. The ludic or playful element is alive and well in the Patroclos Games in that, as we have seen, the competitors seem to be saying, "Patroclos is dead, but we are alive, so let's race!" This is much like recess after a long morning of schoolwork in grammar school. Achilles is the Greek hero who sponsors the competitions in memory of Patroclos. Of the three athletic competitions depicted in Homer, the Patroclos Games are the closest to (although not identical with) the ancient Olympic Games. First, the competition is pacific (almost a redundancy, given the etymology of "competition" mentioned above). Second, the competition is nonetheless energetic and prizes were awarded for first, second, and third place finishers (in contrast to the Olympic Games, where only first place finishers were awarded). In the Patroclos Games we have the perfect token of the Jamesian type: the moral equivalent of war. And third, the Patroclos Games, in contrast to the Phaiacian Games

and the Penelope Games, exhibit what Feezell would call an attitudinal complexity wherein the internal seriousness of competing for
victory is moderated by the nonserious realization that nonetheless
these are merely games.

Consider a crisis event in the Patroclos Games that illustrates this
attitudinal complexity of serious nonseriousness. The event includes
a chariot race for second place where a dispute arises between the
young Antilochos and the older and venerated Menelaos. The race
was not on an oval track, but included a straight distance and then a
tight turn around a pole before a straight return to the starting point.
Antilochos was advised by his father to cut the turn around the pole
perilously close and in violation of an unwritten rule of the game: do
not endanger an opponent's horses or the opponent himself. Antilochos defeated Menelaos. However, according to the conventions of the
day, Antilochos had won not by skill but by cheating. Menelaos was
furious and confronted Antilochos after the race was over. This is a
classic case, with which we are all familiar, of athletic competition becoming especially heated and on the verge of a major conflagration.
A blowup was avoided when Antilochos was led by Menelaos to see
his hubris and apologized. Heated emotions were cooled and the light-
hearted spirit of the Patroclos Games was restored. This lightheartedness was amplified in one of the contact sports when Epeios helped his
defeated opponent to his feet after having pummeled him moments
before. It is also amplified when Aios falls in a footrace and has his
face splattered with mud and offal, to the amusement of those present.
The latter case exhibits a rather low level of humor, but it does put a
ludic punctuation mark on the Patroclos Games not found in the
Penelope Games. The fact that in each of the events the competitors
strenuously tried to win also provides an instructive contrast to the
Phaiacian Games.

SOME FURTHER IMPLICATIONS FOR YOUTH SPORT

There are two further implications for youth sport that follow from
the Homeric texts that I have considered. As a result of Friedrich
Nietzsche's nineteenth-century criticisms, it is today widely assumed

that "asceticism" refers to a body-hating attitude and a loathing of anything physical like competitive play. It is worthy of note, however, that the etymological root of the word "asceticism" is athletic in origin, as the ancient philosopher Plotinus notes.[10] *Askesis* referred to something positive, specifically to the training that is required in order to participate in an athletic event. Further, not only is the training that is required for athletic competition something positive, it is related to the etymological origin of ethics itself. That is, the ancient Greek word *ethos* referred to habits, in general, as well as to good habits that were admirable, in particular. It is not so much the case that once we get clear regarding what ethics is we can then apply ethical principles to athletic activity. Rather, the reverse can equally make sense and historically it did make sense. The athletic life *is* an ascetic life that requires the sort of discipline that enables good habits to be formed and endure. Asceticism and ethics are difficult to disentangle.

The philosophical point I would like to make in this regard is related to my thesis in the section above on moral education. *If* participants in youth sport are to be morally improved as a result of athletic competition, such improvement would be the result of literal *askesis* and *ethos*: positive training and the formation of good habits, as McNamee again emphasizes. For example, the Phaiacians were not trained, hence there is something flabby about them both physically and in terms of their psyche. By partial contrast, Antilochos was morally improved as a result of the training he received from his elders (if not his father), especially Menelaos, who encouraged him to take the first step along the path of the development of good habits, like the avoidance of cheating.

The second point helps to clarify the first. We should not despair if youth sport competition does not morally improve the participants, so long as it does not lead to moral regress. If sport is a type of competitive *play*, there is an intrinsic value to the activity that is worthy of our consideration quite apart from its possibility to morally improve its participants. As before, there is a danger in instrumentalizing youth sport by seeing it as a mere stepping stone to either money *or* moral improvement. The danger is that the very joy of sport, rightly emphasized by Michael Novak,[11] would be lost. In this regard there is a strong analogy between aesthetic pleasure and sport in that there are reasons to read novels, say, that are quite different from their conduciveness to moral improvement. As before, I am more confident that youth sport *reveals* moral character (or lack thereof) than I am that it *builds* it, although the latter is not impossible. Menelaos *is* an admirable character and Antilochos *might* be on the way to becoming one.

I would like to sum up my responses to the questions that are the subjects of the present chapter in the following way. What is sport? Sport is a type of play, specifically a type of competitive play that can synonymously be called athletics. It tests bodily excellence in its participants (hence checkers is not a sport, even though it is a type of competitive game) through competition. But competition, it should be remembered, involves struggling *with* an opponent rather than *against* an opponent, in that without the opposition no sporting event could occur. Further, competitive play, even at the youth level, should guard against the corrosive effects of related phenomena like commercialization, professionalization, and specialization. Further, and counterintuitively, youth sport in particular needs to guard against the assumption that its prime purpose is moral education. This is because overly serious sport activity runs the risk of extinguishing the play spirit. But to the extent that sportsmanship is exhibited by all involved, it *is* possible to be morally improved by youth sport activity.

At the beginning of this chapter I suggested that we might better understand contemporary sport by appeal to the ancient Greeks (also see a book of mine titled *Contemporary Athletics and Ancient Greek Ideals*).[12] In this regard we can agree with the American philosopher Josiah Royce, who once urged the following: "Whenever I have most carefully revised my moral standards, I am always able to see . . . that at best I have been finding out, in some new light, the true meaning that was latent in old traditions."[13] The "old tradition" of the ancient Greeks to *both* compete for prizes *and* to do so nobly might still be instructive today in the dual effort to descriptively understand what sport *is* and to prescriptively urge what it *ought to be*.

NOTES

1. Homer, *The Iliad*, 2 vol. Loeb ed. (Cambridge: Harvard University Press, 1954). See also Homer, *The Iliad*, trans. W. H. D. Rouse (New York: Signet Classics, 1970).

2. Homer, *The Odyssey*. 2 vol. Loeb ed. (Cambridge: Harvard University Press, 1960). See also Homer, *The Odyssey*, trans. W. H. D. Rouse (New York: Signet Classics, 2007).

3. William James, "The Moral Equivalent of War," in *The Essential Writings*, ed. Bruce Wilshire (Albany: State University of New York Press, 1984).

4. George Orwell, *Collected Essays, Journalism and Letters* (London: Harmondsworth, 1970), 4:61–64.

5. As is well known, eventually the word had many applications, including a theatrical performance being called a play and the playing of musical instruments.

6. Randolph Feezell, *Sport, Play, and Ethical Reflection* (Chicago: University of Illinois Press, 2004).

7. Mike McNamee, "Youth Sport and the Virtues," chap. 4 in this volume.

8. Randolph Feezell and Craig Clifford, *Sport and Character: Reclaiming the Principles of Sportsmanship* (Champaign, IL: Human Kinetics, 2010).

9. Johan Huizinga, *Homo Ludens: A Study of the Play Element in Culture*, trans. R. F. C. Hull (Boston: Beacon Press, 1955).

10. Plotinus, *Enneads*, trans. A. H. Armstrong, 7 vol. Loeb ed. (Cambridge, MA: Harvard University Press, 1966–88), 1.1.10; 1.3.6; 6.8.6; 2.9.15; 3.2.8, for example.

11. Michael Novak, *The Joy of Sport* (New York: Basic Books, 1976).

12. Daniel Dombrowski, *Contemporary Athletics and Ancient Greek Ideals* (Chicago: University of Chicago Press, 2009). For further readings, see also Daniel Dombrowski, "Homer, Competition, and Sport," *Journal of the Philosophy of Sport* 39 (2012): 33–51, and "Review of Randolph Feezell, *Sport, Philosophy, and Good Lives*," *Sport, Ethics, and Philosophy* 7 (2013): 479–82, which is a review of Randolph Feezell, *Sport, Philosophy, and Good Lives* (Lincoln: University of Nebraska Press, 2013).

13. Josiah Royce, *The Philosophy of Loyalty* (New York: Macmillan, 1908), 11.

CHAPTER 2

Christians and Sport

An Historical and Theological Overview

PATRICK KELLY, SJ

It is common for historians of sport to assume that there is something fundamental to Christianity that is antithetical to sport. This "something" has to do with negative Christian attitudes toward the body. Indeed, a recurring narrative in the writing of the history of sport tells how Christians up until the time of the Reformation viewed the body only in negative terms, as associated with sin or evil. As one scholar put it: "Early Christianity gradually built a foundation based on asceticism, which is a belief that evil exists in the body, and therefore, the body should be subordinate to the pure spirit. . . . Nothing could have been more damning for the promotion of active recreation and sport."[1] According to the recurring narrative, it was only after the repressive regime of the Puritans in England and America that people began to have more enlightened views about the body. In the nineteenth century reasonable people started accepting games and sports, and they began to have a more prominent place in society. And Christians and theologians have only recently, and somewhat reluctantly, embraced sports.

This way of looking at things, however, has difficulty accounting for some basic things we know about the daily lives of people during the medieval and early modern periods. In fact, Christians participated in games and sports during these periods on Sundays and on the feast days of the church year. William Baker describes the medieval period in his book *Sports in the Western World*:

No puritan pall hovered over Sundays. After the sermon and the sacraments in the morning, villagers lounged or played on Sunday afternoon. For youths, especially, re-creation meant recreation. Nor was recreation confined to Sunday afternoons. The church calendar of holidays, aligned with ancient seasonal patterns, granted festive occasions at Easter, during harvest season, and at Christmas. Throughout Europe this basic pattern was followed. . . . Blessed by church leaders, accepted by landlords, and sanctified by tradition, some of these seasonal breaks in labor ran for several days. Wine or ale, music, and dance accompanied the peasant games and frolic.[2]

It is significant that the holy days were so numerous that they typically accounted for around one-third of the calendar year. The games and sports were also depicted on stained glass windows and woodcuts in churches and in prayer books. People of all ages—boys and girls and men and women—participated in the games and sports of this period. Women's place was not yet exactly in the home, given that they participated in the labor of the agrarian economy, which "made them a hardy lot."[3]

When Catholic humanists of the Renaissance began running schools primarily for lay students in the fifteenth century, they included time in the daily schedule for the students to play games and sports. They were influenced in this regard by the medieval traditions just mentioned and also by what the classical authors of Greece and Rome had to say about the importance of the body and sports in the educational process. The early Jesuits followed the humanist lead and incorporated time and space for games and sports in the first schools they opened in the late sixteenth century—and all of their subsequent schools. These developments would have a significant influence on education because the Jesuits were running nearly eight hundred schools in Europe and in other parts of the world by the mid-eighteenth century.

The ease with which games and sports were incorporated into medieval and early modern Catholic cultures and educational institutions was supported by several factors, including the Christian understanding of the material world as good and of the human person as a unity of body and soul (or body, soul, and spirit); an understanding of the relationship between faith and culture, which tended toward the acceptance of non-Christian customs and cultural traditions that were good in themselves (or at least not objectionable on moral grounds), and their inclusion in the religious tradition; and the view that a virtuous person should be moderate in his studies or work and take time to engage in play and recreation. For some theologians, such as Thomas Aquinas, play was even understood to have spiritual significance.

Catholics brought these earlier cultural traditions with them to the United States, where they engaged in play and sport routinely (and without anxiety) and incorporated them in their schools as a matter of course. This approach was very different from that of the Protestant majority in the United States, and it was a part of what made lay Catholics seem alien and unusual to this majority when Catholics first arrived in the United States in large numbers in the nineteenth century.

THE MATERIAL WORLD AND HUMAN BODY

It is true that one can find examples of theologians and spiritual writers in the early church, and the medieval period, who encouraged flight from society, and who seemed to regard the body—and sexuality—primarily as an obstacle or problem in the Christian life. Some of this is owing to the fact that most, if not all, theologians and spiritual writers were monks or celibate priests. Such emphases often served a rhetorical purpose in their writings about the spiritual life and were possibly even helpful with regard to living out their particular vocation. But this was not the only, or even the dominant, perspective in the longer tradition.

Indeed, early and medieval Christian theologians spent much of their time criticizing Gnostics and Manicheans, precisely because these groups associated the material world and the human body with evil. One of the complaints of Christian authors was that Gnostics and Manicheans did not include the Old Testament as a part of the Christian scriptures and therefore did not accept the account of the creation of the world in the first chapter of Genesis. On the contrary, the Gnostics and Manicheans constructed elaborate mythological accounts of the origin of the material world, which associated it with a *fall* or an *evil principle.* Thus, they regarded the material world as antagonistic to what is truly spiritual. From this perspective, progress in the spiritual life had to do with extricating oneself from the material world and, indeed, from the body itself. It will come as no surprise, then, that they denied the resurrection of the body.

In response to such views, Irenaeus and other early Christian theologians pointed out that, if one reads the first pages of the Old Testament, one learns of a God who created all things in the world and pronounced them "very good." As Augustine put it,

> After each of God's works, is added, "And God saw that it was good," and after the completion of the whole series we have, "And God saw all that he had made, and, behold, it was very good." The meaning of this is that there is only one cause for the creation of the world—the purpose of God's goodness in the creation of good.[4]

Christian theologians emphasized that if the material world as created by God was good, then it was not possible to regard the human body as a mistake or to associate it with evil. Rather, the body was constitutive of the human being as created by God. And Christians, as Irenaeus put it, "hope for the . . . salvation of the whole person, that is, of soul and body."[5]

These theological sensibilities influenced Catholic religious practices, which engaged the material world and involved the body in an integral way. In the thirteenth century, Thomas Aquinas wrote about the sacraments:

> That one might not believe visible things evil of their nature . . . it was fitting that through the visible things themselves the remedies of salvation be applied to human beings. Consequently, it would appear that visible things are good of their nature—as created by God. . . . Thus, of course, one excludes the error of certain heretics who want every visible thing of this kind removed from the sacraments of the church.[6]

When a controversy arose at the end of the eighth century about whether it was appropriate to use images in worship, John of Damascus convincingly argued in favor of their use based on an understanding of the material world as good and the person as a unity of body and soul. As he put it to his opponents:

> The apostles saw the Lord with bodily eyes; others saw the apostles, and others the martyrs. I too desire to see them both spiritually and physically and receive the remedy by which the ills of both soul and body (for I am composed of both) may be healed. . . . You, perhaps, are superior to me, and have risen so far above bodily things that you have become virtually immaterial and feel free to make light of all visible things, but since I am human and clothed with a body, I desire to see and be present with the saints physically. Condescend from your heights to my lowly state of mind.[7]

An argument similar to John's was necessary for the emergence of medieval drama, an enormously important aspect of medieval societies in which the gospel stories and lives of the saints were "played out" by ordinary citizens. Such dramas later occupied a prominent place in the schools of the Jesuits, where they were attended by people from all segments of European society.

The understanding of the person as a unity of body and soul also influenced the humanist approach to education. In an essay on education, Michel de Montaigne wrote: "We are not bringing up a soul; we are not bringing up a body: we are bringing up a person. We must not split him into two."[8] In Montaigne's vision, the young person would not be "split into two" because games and sports would be an integral part of the activities the students engaged in during a typical day. "The games and sports themselves will form a good part of his studies: racing, wrestling, music making, dancing, hunting and the handling of arms and horses. I want his outward graces, his social ease and his physical dexterity to be molded step by step with his soul."[9]

FAITH AND CULTURE

Christians' attitudes toward games and sports also had to do with their understanding of the relationship between faith and culture. One of the most important decisions made by the leaders of the early church was that the Gentiles did not need to undergo circumcision and adhere to other prescriptions of the Mosaic Law—that is, become Jewish—before they could be baptized as Christians. Theologically, this decision was based on the doctrine of creation—on the teaching that, as St. Paul put it, God created "all nations to inhabit the whole earth" (Acts 17:26). For Paul, just as all people were created by God, so too all people were affected by the sin of Adam. Most important, all who believed in Jesus Christ were likewise redeemed through this faith. This theological position was confirmed by the experience of the outpouring of God's grace in the lives of Gentiles, which the leaders of the early church themselves had witnessed. As the author of Acts put it, "The circumcised believers who had come with Peter were astounded that the gift of the Holy Spirit had been poured out even on the Gentiles, for they heard them speaking in tongues and extolling God" (Acts 10:45–46). The decision to accept Gentiles into the Christian community without requiring them to adhere to Jewish law would have a significant influence on future developments in the Christian church. For one thing, it was an important statement about the universality of the salvation that was offered to people in Jesus

Christ. The decision also set a precedent—recorded in scripture—for accepting peoples from diverse cultures, along with their traditions and customs, into the Christian community.

One of the more immediate consequences of this decision was that Christian theologians began to think through the various aspects of their faith in dialogue with, and sometimes in opposition to, Greek philosophical thought. This is a well-known phenomenon about which much has been written. But not much has been written about the relationship between Greek athletic culture and early Christian spirituality. This relationship is evident in the writings of Paul himself—a Greek-speaking Jew—who used athletic imagery as a matter of course to describe the Christian life in his letters to the Greeks living in places like Corinth and Philippi.

According to Paul, one similarity between the life of an athlete and that of a Christian was that both needed to exercise self-control. He writes in a letter to the Corinthians:

> Do you not know that in a race the runners all compete, but only one receives the prize? Run in such a way that you may win it. Athletes exercise self-control in all things; they do it to receive a perishable wreath, but we an imperishable one. So I do not run aimlessly, nor do I box as though beating the air. No, I drive my body and train it, for fear that, after having preached to others, I myself should be disqualified. (1 Cor 9:24–27)

Paul draws a contrast in this quote between the athlete's pursuit of a "perishable wreath" and the Christian's pursuit of an "imperishable" wreath—that is, the resurrection. In other letters, he uses imagery from athletics as a metaphor for the resurrection itself. His letter to the Philippians is characteristic:

> This one thing I do: forgetting what lies behind and straining forward to what lies ahead, I press on toward the goal for the prize of the heavenly call of God in Christ Jesus. . . . He will transform the body of our humiliation that it may be conformed to the body of his glory, by the power that also enables him to make all things subject to himself. (Phil 3:13b–14, 20–21)

Theologians in the early church continued to make use of athletic metaphors to describe the dynamics of the Christian life. John Chrysostom (347–407), bishop of Constantinople, in an address about "The Right Way for Parents to Bring up Their Children," exhorted parents to remember that "we are raising an athlete, let us concentrate our thought on that."[10]

> Raise up an athlete for Christ! I do not mean by this, hold him back from wedlock and send him to desert regions and prepare him to assume the monastic life. It is not this that I mean. I wish for this and used to pray that all might embrace it; but as it seems to be too heavy a burden, I do not insist upon it. Raise up an athlete for Christ, and teach him that he is living in the world to be reverent from his earliest youth.[11]

Chrysostom went beyond the use of athletic metaphors, however. He also saw participation in sport itself as important for the growth of the young person in the Christian life. A young boy could learn valuable lessons about the importance of controlling his passions by wrestling with members of his own household, for example.

> And let there be many on all sides to spur the boy on, so that he may be exercised and practiced in controlling his passions among the members of his household. And, just as athletes in the wrestling school train with their friends before the contest, so that when they have succeeded against these they may be invincible against their opponents, even so the boy must be trained at home. . . . Let someone in wrestling stand up to him and defend himself so that the boy may try his strength against him. So, too, let the slaves provoke him often rightly or wrongly, so that he may learn on every occasion to control his passion. If his father provoke him, it is no great test; for the name of father . . . does not permit him to rebel. But let his companions in age, whether slave or free, do this, that he may learn equability amongst them.[12]

Historians of sport who characterize early Christians as having disdain for the body (and therefore little regard for games and sports) often point to writings associated with martyrdom or monasticism to make their argument. But it is precisely in these most arduous and challenging contexts that the images of the athlete and the athletic contest are used most often. This is evident in the writings associated with the experience of the early Christian martyrs. Ignatius, bishop of Antioch, used such imagery when writing to Polycarp, bishop of Smyrna, during the persecutions of Christians at the beginning of the second century. He exhorts Polycarp, who would eventually experience martyrdom, to "bear the infirmities of all, like a master athlete."[13] After all, he wrote, "it is like a great athlete to take blows and yet win the fight." He encourages Polycarp, "as God's athlete," to be levelheaded and calm, for the stakes are immortality and eternal life.[14]

The account of the martyrs of Lyons and Vienne depicts the persecution and suffering of a woman named Blandina and tells how she, "like a noble athlete," renewed her strength in her confession of faith.[15] For the author of this account, it is what Blandina endured in her body that makes it fitting to call her an athlete and is most important for understanding her experience as having significance from a Christian perspective. The way she endured the persecution and suffering enabled others to see "through their sister Him who was crucified for them."[16]

> But Blandina was hung on a stake and was offered as food for the wild beasts that were let in. Since she seemed to be hanging in the form of a cross, and by her firmly intoned prayer, she inspired the combatants with great zeal, as they looked on during the contest and with their outward eyes saw through their sister Him who was crucified for them.[17]

According to the author of this account, when none of the wild beasts touched Blandina she was taken down from the stake and put into prison, "being saved for another contest" so that by conquering through more trials she would make the condemnation of the "crooked Serpent" irrevocable. In the end, although small and weak and greatly despised, she had put on the great and invincible athlete Christ, and in many contests had overcome the Adversary and through the conflict had gained the crown of immortality.[18]

The athlete and athletic competition were also used as analogies and metaphors to describe the life of a monk. In the fourth century John Cassian, one of the most influential spiritual writers in Western monasticism, regularly used such images. In his book *The Institutes*, Cassian often quotes St. Paul's letters that contain references to athletic competition. For Cassian, it is "only by comparison" that one can know what St. Paul wanted to teach Christians by the example of this world's games. And so it was important to understand the games themselves if one wanted to understand the meaning of the comparison. This is why Cassian gave his fellow monks a detailed explanation of the Olympic Games, with a special focus on the training of the athletes.

Cassian pointed out that aspiring Olympians were tested to see whether they deserved to be admitted to the games in the first place. When a man had been thoroughly examined and found to be worthy and to have a good reputation, it was still necessary to find out whether he had demonstrated sufficient skill and had achieved enough success to warrant admitting him to the Olympic Games.

If he offers appropriate proof of his skill and his strength, and in contests with his juniors and his peers, has demonstrated both his proficiency and his strength as a young man; and if he has gone beyond boyish contests and, with his strength now honed by lengthy practice, has, after the presider's trial, received permission to join those who have been approved; and if by his unremitting efforts he has not only shown that he is their equal in strength but has also frequently obtained the palm of victory from among them—only then will he deserve to participate in the noble contests, in which the right to compete is given to none but victors alone and those who have been adorned with the tributes of numerous crowns.[19]

"If we have grasped the example taken from fleshly combat," Cassian wrote, "we ought also, by comparisons with it, to understand the discipline and the order of the spiritual contest."[20] For Cassian, one of the most basic comparisons was that the person who wanted to engage in the "Olympic struggles with vice" that were characteristic of the monastic life must have already shown himself to have lived a life of discipline and training and to have been successful in the struggles against the lesser vices. If he had done so, he would be ready for the more advanced contests.

> And when the examination of him who presides over the contest has found us unbesmirched by the notoriety of any base lust, and he has not judged us to be slaves of the flesh, ignoble and unworthy of the Olympic struggles with vice, then we shall be able to do battle against our peers—that is, against the desires and movements of the flesh and the disturbances of the soul. For it is impossible for a full stomach to undertake the struggles of the inner man, nor is it right for someone to be made trial of by more violent battles if he can be overcome in a less important conflict.[21]

When the monk was more advanced, the contest would become more challenging, involving struggles against such vices as pride. For Cassian, "the athlete of Christ, who is lawfully engaged in the spiritual contest and desires to be crowned by the Lord, must also and in every respect strive to destroy this most savage beast (pride), since it devours all the virtues."[22]

Most of the Christian authors we have considered so far, starting with St. Paul, made use of athletic imagery as an analogy or metaphor to help explain the dynamics of the Christian life. Of course, athletic imagery only works as analogy or metaphor if some legitimate points of connection exist between the experience of participation in sports and the experience of living the Christian life. It is these points of connection that also make possible the present volume on youth sport and spirituality.

By the medieval period, Christians had moved from being a per-secuted minority into a position of influence in Europen society. At this time theologians began thinking about the proper place of play and sport in society. Hugh of St. Victor (d. 1142) was one theologian who did so, in his book the *Didascalicon*. Hugh's book, written in Paris in the 1120s, appeared at a time when education centers had moved from the mainly rural monasteries to the cathedral schools of the newly emerging cities. In this different context, a new overview was needed regarding the subjects that should be studied and the manner in which they should be taken up. Hugh of St. Victor's book provided just such an overview.[23]

The course of studies described by Hugh was ambitious, given that, in his view, philosophy deals not only with the nature of the things of the created world and the regulation of morals, but also with "the theoretical consideration of all human acts."[24] All human acts would have included the enjoyable activities people engaged in for recreation and entertainment. And so the "science of entertainments" was included in the curriculum of the newly emerging cathedral schools as one of the mechanical arts.[25] He also calls this science "the-atrics" because the theater was the most popular place for such enter-tainments for the ancient Greeks. But it was not the only place.

> Some entertainments took place in theatres, some in the en-trance porch of buildings, some in gymnasia, some in amphi-theaters, some in arenas, some at feasts, some at shrines. In the theater, epics were presented either by recitals or by acting out dramatic roles or using masks or puppets; they held choral processions and dance in the porches. In the gymnasia they wrestled; in the amphitheaters they raced on foot or on horses or in chariots; in the arenas boxers performed; at banquets they made music with songs and instruments and chants, and they played at dice; in the temples at solemn seasons they sang the praises of the gods.[26]

Hugh points out that the ancients reflected upon these activities and gave an explanation of their human and social significance.

Moreover, they numbered these entertainments among legitimate activities because by temperate motion natural heat is stimulated in the body and by enjoyment the mind is refreshed; or, as is more likely, seeing that people necessarily gathered together for occasional amusement, they desired that places for such amusement might be established to forestall the people's coming together at public houses, where they might commit lewd or criminal acts.[27]

The significance of Hugh's treatment of "entertainments" is primarily in his insistence that they have a legitimate place in society and therefore also among the arts to be studied. His arguing for their inclusion in educational curricula is important because of the level of influence his work would have on education throughout medieval Europe.[28]

Thomas Aquinas was another theologian of the medieval period whose writings would carry even more influence than Hugh of St. Victor's with respect to play and sport. Because he is the most influential theologian who wrote about the relevance of play in a virtuous life, I will treat his thought in the next section.

MODERATION AS CENTRAL TO VIRTUE

In the ancient world, and in particular in the writings of Aristotle, moderation was regarded as central to a life of virtue. Living virtuously involved trying to find the "mean" between excess and deficiency. The virtue of courage, for example, lay somewhere in the middle between foolhardiness (excess) and timidity (deficiency). This way of understanding virtue influenced how Christian theologians thought about play and sport. According to Thomas Aquinas, there can be a "virtue about games," because a moderate person should not be spending the whole of his or her life working or worrying about work. As he puts it:

I pray, spare thyself at times: for it becomes a wise person sometimes to relax the high pressure of his attention to work.

(Augustine) Now this relaxation of the mind from work consists in playful words and deeds. Therefore it becomes a wise
and virtuous person to have recourse to such things at times.
Moreover, the Philosopher [Aristotle] assigns to games the virtue of eutrapelia, which we may call *pleasantness*.[29]

For Thomas, while play does relax the high pressure associated
with work, playful activities do not have their significance in relation
to work. That is, he does not view them merely as the "pause that re-
freshes" so that people can return to their work and be more produc-
tive. Rather, playful activities are engaged in for their own sake. As
we will see later, this is one of the reasons that he views play as similar
to contemplation.
　According to Thomas, if one's play exceeds or is less than what is
reasonable, then this is sinful. A person's play exceeds what is reasonable if during play he employs indecent words or deeds that cause injury to his neighbor. A person's play can also exceed what is reasonable
if there is a lack of concern for circumstances, as when a person makes
use of fun "at undue times or places, or out of keeping with the matter
in hand, or persons."[30]
　In Thomas's view, *it is also possible to sin by having less play in
one's life than is reasonable.* For him, a person who is always serious
and does not participate in any activities that provide relaxation or
enjoyment would be sinning.

In human affairs whatever is against reason is a sin. Now it is
against reason for a person to be burdensome to others, by offering no pleasure to others, and by hindering their enjoyment.
Wherefore Seneca says "Let your conduct be guided by wisdom
so that no one will think you rude, or despise you as a cad."[31]

The humanist educators of the Renaissance made use of this way
of understanding virtue when they deliberated about the amount of
time students should devote to their academic pursuits. They emphasized that students should not be excessive in their studies, which
would lead them to regard school as a burden. Rather, they should

take a break from their studies from time to time and engage in re-
laxing activities that would rejuvenate them. Ball games and other
sports were understood to be these kinds of activities. Aeneas Sylvius
Piccolomini, the future Pope Pius II, wrote in a treatise about education for the still very young King Ladislaus of Austria, Hungary,
and Bohemia, for example:

> I approve of and praise your playing ball with boys your own
> age. . . . There is the hoop; there are other perfectly respectable
> boyish games, which your teachers should sometimes allow
> you for the sake of relaxation and to stimulate a lively disposi-
> tion. One should not always be intent on schooling and serious
> affairs, nor should huge tasks be imposed upon boys, for they
> may be crushed with exhaustion by such labors, and in any case
> if they feel overcome by irksome burdens they may be less re-
> ceptive to learning.[32]

The humanist educator Pier Paolo Vergerio was of the same mind
as Piccolomini. For Vergerio, the student should not always be engaged in serious school work, "but must from time to time indulge in
relaxation."[33] He refers to Quintus Mucius Scaevola, a Roman jurist
of the first century and later proconsular governor of Asia and pon-
tifex maximus, who used to take a break from the practice of law by
playing a ball game.

> He is said to have been an excellent ball player, a recreation he
> used to take up particularly to restore his powers and strengthen
> his chest when tired from the law courts and from his labors in
> interpreting civil law. A devotion to hunting, fowling and fish-
> ing also falls into this category; such activities refresh the spirit
> with great delight and the movement and effort they require
> strengthen the limbs, "with zeal gently deceiving severe labor,"
> as Horace says.[34]

The students in the humanist schools could learn from this example
that taking time for recreation was important during their school days
and during their adult lives as public servants as well.

As we have seen, for Aristotle, virtue lay in the middle—in what he called the mean—between excess and deficiency. But for him there was a mean with respect to the object and one with respect to the person. He gives the example of ten being too many and two being too few of some object. In this case, six is the mean with respect to the object itself, arrived at by arithmetical reasoning. But there is also a mean in relation to the person, which might very well be different. This mean is decided upon by taking into consideration the person in question and all of the details of his or her situation in life. As he puts it, "In this way, then, every knowledgeable person avoids excess and deficiency, but looks for the mean and chooses it—not the mean of the thing, but the mean relative to us."[35]

The humanists made use of this way of thinking when making decisions about the manner and extent to which their students should engage in physical exercises and sports. They emphasized that physical exercises should be introduced gradually so that they corresponded to the natural dispositions and the physical capacities of each student, which would differ at different ages. Vergerio wrote in his treatise on education, for example:

Those exercises, then, should be undertaken which preserve good health and render the limbs more robust; here the natural disposition of each student must be kept in mind. . . . [A]ge must be taken into account, so that up until the age of puberty they should be subjected to lighter burdens, lest the sinews be worn down, even at this age, or the growth of the body impeded. But after puberty they should be broken to heavier tasks.[36]

According to Philippe Aries, the early Jesuits also played an important role in introducing games and sports as a part of the school day in the Western world. In the first schools they ran starting in the late sixteenth century, the Jesuits made use of buildings that had been intended for other purposes and that did not have any space for the students to play games and sports. In the school buildings the Jesuits themselves built, however, they included a courtyard in the middle of the structure that opened out onto the classrooms. They did so to encourage students to play games and sports. Originally they thought this space would be used primarily by the students who boarded at the school. But they discovered that students who commuted were using the space a great deal of the time as well.

The Jesuits provided ample time for recreation in their schools. An hour of recreation was introduced after the noon meal, and other shorter periods for recreation were introduced in between classes. On one free day in the middle of the week students would take a walk into the countryside and play games and sports. In the summer months, students would walk to a villa owned by the Jesuits and play board and card games and less vigorous sports. Students had vacation days on most feast days and longer vacations at Christmas, Easter, and in the summer.

The approach of the early Jesuits can be traced back to their founder, Ignatius of Loyola. The third part of the "Rules of the Colleges" that were written for the first colleges where young Jesuits lived and studied is dedicated to "Conserving the Health and Strength of the Body." One part of the document pertains to:

> *Some honest bodily recreation.* There will also be some hours for honest bodily recreation, as after lunch or dinner for a while; between the hours of study some relaxation is as useful for the body as for the studies, to which one returns with more of a disposition to make progress, when preceded by some honest bodily exercise.[37]

In the Constitutions of the Society of Jesus as well, Ignatius emphasized the importance of moderation in studies for young Jesuits, writing that "it is not good to continue to work for a long time without some proper relaxation or recreation."[38]

This emphasis on moderation in one's studies found its way into the detailed instructions regarding recreation and vacation days in the *Ratio Studiorum* of 1599, the formal education program for the Society's schools. "A nice balance should be maintained," the authors of the *Ratio* wrote, "between study time and recreation periods."[39] Because the *Ratio* was the plan of studies for all Jesuit schools, it became common to set aside time for recreation and sports in the vast network of Jesuit schools throughout Europe and in other parts of the world.

PLAY AND SPIRITUAL VALUES

With respect to our topic of Christian attitudes toward play and sport, it is important to recognize that, for some theologians, play itself was closely related to spiritual values. Thomas Aquinas, for example, points out that play is very similar to contemplation. For him, the two activities are similar because they are both enjoyable and done for their own sake. As he put it:

> There are two features of play which make it appropriate to compare the contemplation of wisdom to playing. First, we enjoy playing, and there is the greatest enjoyment of all to be had in the contemplation of wisdom. As Wisdom says in Ecclesiasticus 24:27, "My spirit is sweeter than honey."
> Secondly, playing has no purpose beyond itself; what we do in play is done for its own sake. And the same applies to the pleasures of wisdom. . . . [T]he contemplation of wisdom contains within itself the cause of its own enjoyment, and so it is not exposed to the kind of anxiety that goes with waiting for something which we lack. This is why it says in Wisdom 8:16, "Her company is without bitterness" (the company of wisdom, that is) "and there is no boredom in living with her." It is for this reason that divine Wisdom compares her enjoyment to playing in Proverbs 8:30, "I enjoyed myself every single day, playing before him."[40]

In a commentary on a text from Ecclesiasticus, Thomas even refers to contemplation itself as a kind of play. The text from Ecclesiasticus he is commenting on reads, "Run ahead into your house and gather yourself there and play there and pursue your thoughts."[41] In contemplation, Thomas writes, "it is . . . necessary that we ourselves should be fully present there, concentrating in such a way that our aim is not diverted to other matters." Accordingly the text goes on, "and gather yourself there, that is, draw together your whole intention. And when our interior house is entirely emptied like this and we are fully present there in our intention, the text tells us what we should do: 'And play there.'"[42]

CATHOLICS AND SPORTS IN THE UNITED STATES

Catholics brought these cultural, theological, and spiritual traditions with them to the United States. In the latter part of the eighteenth century, John Carroll, the first Catholic bishop of the United States (in Baltimore), started an academy—to which Georgetown Preparatory School and Georgetown University trace their roots—on which he placed all his "hopes of permanency, & success of our H[oly] Religion in the United States."[43] Carroll was a former Jesuit. The Society of Jesus had been suppressed in 1773, and Carroll and several other Jesuits in the early colonies were left without a religious community with which to be affiliated. These former Jesuits continued the educational traditions of the Society of Jesus, however, which were well known among former members of the order who were living in Europe and the colonies. And one of these traditions had to do with the incorporation of games and sports into the school curriculum.

The public advertisement for the "College of George-Town" of 1798 states that the college is dedicated to "the improvement of youth in the three important branches of *Physical, Moral,* and *Literary* education." After pointing out that the college is situated on one of the healthiest spots in the United States, the advertisement states, "A constant and scrupulous attention to cleanliness, wholesome and regular diet, moderate exercise, and a due proportion of application and relaxation are the means adopted and unwearily pursued, in order to preserve the health of youths, especially those of a tender age."[44] In 1809, the public advertisement points out that "the garden and court adjoining, where the young gentlemen play, are very airy and spacious. The situation is very pleasant and healthy."

Sports were a part of the rhythm of the school day at Georgetown from the time of its founding, as they had been at the earliest Jesuit schools in Europe. As Joseph Durkin writes:

Dinner (the midday meal) was followed by "recreation" or playtime for an hour and a half. Spacious playing fields were available. The popular sports were handball, a rudimentary kind of football that was probably more like present-day soccer, and gymnastic exercises. Fencing and boxing also had their devotees.[45]

To accommodate the large numbers of Catholics arriving in the United States in the nineteenth century, the Jesuits started colleges in many regions of the country. These colleges had extensive playgrounds for the students and incorporated ample time for recreation. The description in the 1857–58 Catalogue of St. Joseph's College in Bardstown, Kentucky, is typical. It reads, "The situation is healthy and beautiful: the buildings are spacious and commodious; the refectories and dormitories are large and well ventilated. The play-grounds are extensive and handsomely set with trees." In the "Collegiate Regulations," one reads that "each division has its own play-ground, Study-Hall, Dormitory and Refectory" and that "every Thursday of the Academic year is a general recreation-day."[46] The 1878–79 Catalogue of Santa Clara College is more descriptive and reads under the heading "Play-grounds":

These occupy nearly four acres of ground, gently sloping and sandy, so that very soon after the heaviest rain, they are dry enough for recreation. On three sides are numerous shade trees and seats. Verandas of aggregate length of a thousand feet extend along the building, affording shelter and exercise in rainy weather. There are besides two large gymnasiums and play-rooms supplied with chess and checker games, &c. Athletic games, however, receive more encouragement than others. On Thursday and Sunday those who wish, may go out walking in the country in company with some of the Fathers.[47]

A very similar approach was followed at other Catholic colleges in the United States in the nineteenth century. The program of studies that Fr. Edward Sorin outlined for the students at Notre Dame in 1843 alternated between study, religious exercises, and recreation just as the Jesuit schools had done. John Theodore Wack, a doctor on his way from Detroit to Chicago, stopped at Notre Dame's campus in the 1850s and saw what he described as a "scene that filled me with admiration." Along with a Gothic church, clusters of buildings, and two lakelets, he mentions seeing "a large playground with gymnastic apparatus."[48] A great distance in another direction he saw "a crowd of boys at play in the college-grounds; a group of them was bathing in a secluded cove of one of the lakes, watched by a man in a long black robe."[49]

He was taken to the religious superior, who walked him over a causeway between the two lakelets to the islands where the Holy Cross seminarians lived. "While we remained, the hour of recreation sounded on the bell," he wrote. "Then study, devotion, and work were laid aside, and the whole community of priests, and nuns, lay-brothers and lay-sisters, students and apprentices, enjoyed their hour of innocent and sometimes boisterous mirth." After the midday meal, there was a brief thanksgiving, "and the well-ordered boys filed out of the room; and we soon heard their glad hurras in the playgrounds, while the Superior and several clerical and lay professors gathered under a shady piazza, to enjoy the leisure after-dinner hour."[50]

When interscholastic athletic competitions began at the end of the nineteenth century, Catholic schools joined right in. And, as happened in schools all across the United States, the varsity teams generated enthusiasm and feelings of loyalty toward the schools from just about everyone associated with them. This was true at both the high schools and the universities (which were becoming separate institutions around this time). One Jesuit prefect at St. John's College in New York City noted in his diary in 1904 that "from the day the boys returned in September till Commencement Day and after, keen interest is taken in the Varsity Team by every boy in the house from seniors down to tots . . . by the Faculty and even by the workmen."[51]

And, as they had traditionally been, the sports were intimately connected to religious practices. Christa Klein describes, for example, "the blending of baseball and piety at Fordham," which was "nowhere clearer than during Holy Week" during the years the students remained on campus.

> All day long students alternated between the chapel and the playing field. After mass in the morning they went to their respective division ball fields. . . . Although no other mail was distributed, "baseball letters" concerning intervarsity games were made available. After lunch the teams practiced until "Way of the Cross" at 2 p.m. After Tenebrae they played a ball game.[52]

Catholic traditions associated with play and sport also continued in the Catholic parishes in the United States. For well over a century the Catholic Mass had been outlawed in the English-speaking world, including the colonies of the New World. Thanks to William Penn and the tolerance of the Quakers, however, Catholics were able to celebrate their first Mass openly in the colonies at St. Joseph's Parish in Philadelphia in 1733. The Jesuit Felix Barbelin became pastor at St. Joseph's after the restoration of the Jesuits in 1814, for a tenure that would last from 1838 to 1869. Barbelin continued the Jesuit traditions of religious drama at the parish and encouraged as many parishioners as possible to be involved in the plays there. He also took the children who were involved in the various confraternities on daylong excursions during which they would play games and sports.

In a letter to the editor of the *Catholic Herald*, a parishioner named Paul writes about a delightful rural excursion to "Point Pleasant" that members of one sodality took under the care and direction of Barbelin in 1845.

> The day was spent in all the sports and convivialities which enliven such excursions. Sweet solitude and calm repose, that day at least, took their flight, and the groves of Point Pleasant resounded with the merry shouts of joyous youth, with music and with song. Where shall I find language sweet enough to

describe the unrestrained hilarity and innocent mirth of those dear youth, who compose the "Angel's Sodality"? The sparkling eye, the rosy glow of health, the cherub smiles and merry shouts of that sweet-angel band would have driven care and sadness from any heart.[53]

According to Gerald R. Gems, the kinds of experiences described in this letter were common in Catholic parishes in the nineteenth century, where young people participated in recreations and sports as a matter of course on feast days and Sundays. And these activities alternated in a very easy way with traditional religious practices.

Such activities were becoming more organized in parishes by the end of the nineteenth century. The Knights of Columbus sponsored recreational activities and athletic clubs that were thriving in Catholic parishes by the 1890s. By 1910 Chicago Catholics were operating the largest religious baseball league in the United States. Bishop Bernard J. Sheil founded the Catholic Youth Organization (CYO) in Chicago in 1930. In Sheil's own words, the CYO was to be "a recreational, educational and religious program that will adequately meet the physical, mental and spiritual needs of out-of-school Catholic boys and girls."[54] Other archdioceses around the country established their own CYO programs in subsequent years. The CYO has continued to be very important up to the present time as the context in which elementary school children participate in sports in Catholic parishes all across the United States.

"CATHOLIC LEAGUES" FOR CATHOLIC HIGH SCHOOLS

In the early part of the twentieth century, Catholic high school athletic leagues were established in some of the larger cities in the United States to provide Catholic schools with opportunities to compete in sports against other Catholic schools. In Chicago, the Catholic League was founded in 1912. Prior to World War I, the Chicago Catholic League was a part of an attempt to set up a "separate society" within a predominantly Protestant country. By the 1920s, however, it had grown too big to be ignored by outsiders, and debates were common about the virtues of the Catholic and public systems of education. The Chicago newspaper *Herald and Examiner* proposed a football game— to be called the "Prep Bowl"—between the Catholic League and Public School League champions at the end of the 1927 season. In the first Prep Bowl, Mt. Carmel surprised everyone and defeated Schurtz—a school ten times its size—6–0, before 50,000 spectators. Subsequent Prep Bowls were witnessed by as many as 90,000 to 120,000 fans and remained a major cultural event in Chicago until the 1970s.[55] According to Gems, football played an important role in acculturating Chicago's Catholics into the mainstream of American society, while at the same time allowing them to take pride in their difference.

Football represented for Catholics their coming of age in American society. As interleague games acculturated Catholics into the mainstream athletic structure, they also manifested their separate religious identity, and football remained a means to oppose the intrusion of the dominant ideology and glory in Catholic difference. Catholic victories brought pride, a measure of acceptance, and the reinforcement and celebration of an alternative culture, yet one that came to be more closely aligned with the other in its values, aspirations, and sense of American patriotism.[56]

Catholic educators and administrators started "Catholic Leagues" independently in different cities in the United States. And there was variation as well with respect to when girls' schools joined these leagues. The Archdiocese of Philadelphia seems to have been in the forefront in this regard, especially with regard to basketball. In Julie Byrne's book *O God of Players: The Story of the Immaculata Mighty Macs* she points out that, thanks largely to the influence of Monsignor John Bonner, Catholic all girls' schools were playing basketball in the Catholic League by the 1920s. This was at a time when the prevailing wisdom in the United States was that girls should not be participating in varsity high school sports. Byrne points out, "In the late twenties—years when a formidable Catholic League rivalry developed between the Hallahan and West Catholic girls' teams—most physical educators, women and men, considered girls' competitive play, particularly in basketball, 'an acute problem of national significance.'"[57]

Catholic high school girls' teams in Philadelphia consistently sold out city venues starting in the 1940s, however.

> Catholic league girls did not play for a Philadelphia high school championship, because the public schools did not have squads that could even come close to measuring up. Instead, starting in the forties, crowds of Catholic folk packed Convention Hall for Friday night all-girls double-headers for the entire regular season. As the years went on, tickets for the girls' Catholic League championship, played at the Palestra, and event tickets for big duel matches sold out weeks in advance. "We'd be four thousand girls in that building screaming our heads off," remembered Mary Frank McCormick '50, who played at Convention Hall with her team from Notre Dame Academy.[58]

Byrne points out that the system set up by the Archdiocese of Philadelphia, which encouraged girls to play basketball and provided intense competitions at the high school level, was crucial for the success of the basketball program at Immaculata College, which won the first three women's national championships in college basketball, from 1972 to 1974. Immaculata was run by the IHM sisters. Nearly all of the 1,800 IHM sisters in the local community were from the Philadelphia archdiocese and so were typically "city born-and-bred basketball players and fans themselves," according to Byrne. With a reputation for educating working class girls at low cost, Immaculata attracted many Catholic League players. All six starters of a storied 1946 team, which defeated city rival Temple, were captains of their Catholic high school teams. Five of the eleven players from the 1972 national championship team came from Catholic League powerhouse Archbishop Prendergast, where a former Immaculata player had been head coach. "Throughout the years," Byrne writes, "the tradition of girls basketball in the Archdiocese of Philadelphia largely explained the success of the Immaculata program."[59]

Contrary to a recurring narrative in the writing of the history of sport, Christians prior to the Reformation did not have an unremittingly negative attitude toward the body. Rather, they emphasized the goodness of the material world as it had been created by God and that the body was constitutive of human personhood. The human person, in this understanding, was a unity of body and soul or body, soul, and spirit. These emphases were related to the emergence of a religious culture in which the body was integrally involved in religious practices, such as the sacraments and the use of images in worship. They were also a part of what led Christians to adopt an accepting attitude toward play and sport.

Another reason that Christians tended to be accepting of play and sport had to do with the way they understood the relationship between faith and culture. The original opening of the church to the Gentiles played an important role in this regard. As we saw, St. Paul routinely made use of references from Greek athletic culture to describe the dynamics of the Christian life. Following St. Paul's lead, later theologians and spiritual writers used athletic imagery as an analogy or metaphor to describe the experience of martyrdom and the monastic life. In the medieval period, Christians tended to accept and even "baptize" the ball games and other sports of cultures that were converting to Christianity. These games and sports were engaged in on Sundays and feast days and depicted in the religious art of the period. The original opening to the Gentiles made it possible centuries later for the humanists and early Jesuits to draw inspiration from ancient Greek schools with respect to including physical exercises and sports in their schools.

Medieval theologian Thomas Aquinas was influenced by Aristotle's ethics, which emphasized that moderation was central to a life of virtue. With respect to our topic, this meant that a person should not be studying or working all the time. Such a life would be immoderate. He or she also needed to have time for relaxation and recreation. Thomas's approach provided a rationale for play and sport on Sundays and the feast days of the medieval period. The humanists and early Jesuits were also influenced by the classical emphasis on moderation as central to a life of virtue. They argued on this basis that it was important for their students to take breaks from their studies from time to time and engage in play and recreation. This heritage also influenced Catholics in the United States, who incorporated play and sport into their educational institutions and parishes as a matter of course.

NOTES

1. D. Stanley Eitzen and George H. Sage, "Religion and Sport," in *Religion and Sport: The Meeting of Sacred and Profane*, ed. Charles S. Prebish (Westport, CT: Greenwood Press, 1993), 84.

2. William J. Baker, *Sports in the Western World* (Totowa, NJ: Rowman and Littlefield, 1982), 45.

3. Allen Guttmann, *Women's Sports: A History* (New York: Columbia University Press, 1991), 47–48.

4. St. Augustine, *City of God*, trans. Henry Bettenson (New York: Penguin Books, 2003), 455.

5. Irenaeus, "Against Heresies," in *Irenaeus of Lyons*, ed. Robert M. Grant (New York: Routledge, 1997), 172.

6. Thomas Aquinas, *Summa Contra Gentiles, Book 4: Salvation*, trans. Charles J. O'Neil (Notre Dame, IN: University of Notre Dame Press, 1975), 247.

7. John of Damascus, *On the Divine Images: Three Apologies against Those Who Attack the Divine Images* (Crestwood, NY: St. Vladimir's Seminary Press, 2000), 58.

8. Michel de Montaigne, *The Essays: A Selection*, ed. and trans. Michael Screech (New York: Penguin Books, 1987), 59.

9. Ibid.

10. John Chrysostom, "An Address on Vainglory and the Right Way for Parents to Bring up Their Children," in *Christianity and Pagan Culture in the Later Roman Empire*, ed. and trans. M. L. W. Laistner (Ithaca, NY: Cornell University Press, 1967), 112.

11. Ibid., 95.

12. Ibid., 113–14.

13. Ignatius of Antioch, "To Polycarp," in *The Epistles of St. Clement of Rome and St. Ignatius of Antioch*, trans. James A. Kleist, SJ, Ancient Christian Writers 1 (Westminster, MD: Newman Press, 1961), 96.

14. Ibid., 97.

15. Eusebius, *The Ecclesiastical History*, trans. Roy J. Deferrari, The Fathers of the Church (New York: Fathers of the Church, Inc., 1953), 277.

16. Ibid., 282.

17. Ibid., 282.

18. Ibid., 282–83.

19. John Cassian, *The Institutes*, ed. Dennis McManus, trans. Boniface Ramsey, OP, Ancient Christian Writers 58 (New York: The Newman Press, 2000), 124.

20. Ibid.

21. Ibid.

22. Ibid., 272–73.

23. *The Didascalicon of Hugh of St. Victor: A Medieval Guide to the Arts*, trans. Jerome Taylor (New York: Columbia University Press, 1961).

24. Ibid., 51. For Hugh, philosophy is the "discipline which investigates comprehensively the ideas of all things, human and divine."

25. Hugh divides philosophy into four categories, "the theoretical, which strives for contemplation of truth; the practical, which considers the regulation of morals; the mechanical, which supervises the occupations of this life; and the logical, which provides the knowledge necessary for correct speaking and clear argumentation" (*Didascalicon*, 60).

26. Ibid., 79.

27. Ibid.

28. Jerome Taylor writes that a crude index of the influence of the *Didascalicon* on its own and later ages is that it was found in nearly one hundred different manuscripts of the twelfth through the fifteenth centuries, preserved in some forty-five libraries throughout Europe from Ireland to Italy, Poland to Portugal (*Didascalicon*, 4).

29. Thomas Aquinas, *Summa Theologica*, vol. 2, trans. Fathers of the English Dominican Province (New York: Benziger Brothers, Inc., 1947), Pt II–II, Q. 168, art. 2.

30. Ibid., art. 3.

31. Ibid., art. 4.

32. Aeneas Silvius Piccolomini, "The Education of Boys," in *Humanist Educational Treatises*, ed. and trans. Craig W. Kallendorf, The I Tatti Renaissance Library 5 (Cambridge, MA: Harvard University Press, 2002), 143.

33. Pier Paolo Vergerio, "The Character and Studies Befitting a Free-Born Youth," in *Humanist Educational Treatises*, ed. and trans. Kallendorf, 83.

34. Ibid., 85.

35. Aristotle, *Nichomachean Ethics*, trans. J. A. K. Thomas (New York: Penguin Classics, 1984), 100.

36. Vergerio, "The Character and Studies Befitting a Free-Born Youth," 77.

37. *Monumenta Paedagogica Societatis Jesu: Penitus retractata multisque textibus aucta*, ed. Ladislaus Lukacs, vol. 92, nos. 107–8 (Rome: Institutum Historicum Societatis Jesu, 1965), 68–69.

38. *The Constitutions of the Society of Jesus and Their Complementary Norms: A Complete English Translation of the Official Latin Texts*, ed. John Pad-

berg, SJ, Series I: Jesuit Primary Sources in English Translation 15 (St. Louis: Institute of Jesuit Sources, 1996), 127.

39. *The Jesuit Ratio Studiorum of 1599*, trans. by Allan P. Farrell, SJ (Washington DC: Conference of Major Superiors of Jesuits, 1970), 12.

40. *Albert and Thomas: Selected Writings*, trans. and ed. Simon Tugwell (Mahwah, NJ: Paulist Press, 1988), 527–28.

41. Ibid., 527.

42. Ibid.

43. Joseph T. Durkin, *Georgetown University: First in the Nation's Capital* (Garden City, NY: Doubleday, 1964), 5. It is important to point out for the purposes of this book, which is about *youth* sports, that the first "colleges" that the Jesuits and others started in the nineteenth century were educating young boys and adolescents. John Carroll had set the minimum age for admission to the "College of Georgetown" at eight, and this was raised to twelve years of age in 1870. In the early part of the twentieth century the "colleges" separated into two different institutions, our present-day high schools and universities.

44. "College of George-town, (Potomack) in the State of Maryland, United States of America, 1798," Georgetown University Archives, Lauinger Library, Georgetown University, Washington DC.

45. Durkin, *Georgetown University*, 12.

46. "Catalogue of the Officers and Students of St. Joseph's College, Bardstown, KY, 1857–1858," Archives of the Detroit Province of the Society of Jesus, University of Detroit-Mercy Library, Detroit, MI.

47. "Descriptive Catalogue, Santa Clara College, 1878–1879," Santa Clara University Archives, Orradre Library, Santa Clara, CA.

48. John Theodore Wack, "A Description of Notre Dame du Lac in the 1850s," Appendix II, p. 1. The work is available at http://archives.nd.edu/wack/wack.htm.

49. Ibid., 2.

50. Ibid., 2–3.

51. Christa Klein, "The Jesuits and Catholic Boyhood in Nineteenth-Century New York City: A Study of St. John's College and the College of St. Francis Xavier, 1846–1912" (Ph.D. diss., University of Pennsylvania, 1976), 255.

52. Ibid., 254–55.

53. "Excursion of St. Joseph's Sodality," *Catholic Herald*, September 4, 1845; Parish Archives, Old St. Joseph's Parish, Philadelphia, PA.

54. Roger Treat, *Bishop Sheil and the CYO* (New York: Messner, 1951), 55.

55. Gerald R. Gems, "The Prep Bowl: Football and Religious Acculturation in Chicago, 1927–1963," *Journal of Sport History* 23, no. 3 (Fall 1996), 293.

56. Ibid., 295–96.

57. Julie Byrne, *O God of Players: The Story of the Immaculata Mighty Macs* (New York: Columbia University Press, 2003), 18.

58. Ibid., 23–24.

59. Ibid., 24.

CHAPTER 3

Youth Sport and Psychological and Social Development

NICOLE M. LAVOI

Youth sport is an important and salient social institution for millions of children and their families. Through sport participation, youth have the potential to reap a host of positive outcomes from well-run programs, including psychological, social, and physical assets. A body of emerging research from scholars in diverse fields including but not limited to sport and exercise psychology, child development, pediatric medicine, and public health has developed a framework that outlines the context by which positive youth development through sport and physical activity is more likely to occur and flourish.

A POSITIVE YOUTH DEVELOPMENT APPROACH

Positive youth development (PYD) emphasizes the potentialities and capacities of young people, rather than their supposed limitations—including young people from the most disadvantaged backgrounds and troubled histories.[1] Recently, the PYD approach has been mapped onto the context of sports and physical activity. Some scholars use the term "positive youth development through physical activity" and others use the term "sports-based youth development"—essentially both terms encompass the same concepts and can be used interchangeably.

The following definition summarizes a sports-specific youth development approach:

[It] is a methodology that uses sports to provide the supports and opportunities youth need to be healthy contributing citizens now and as adults. A sports-based youth development program offers youth an experience in which they learn and master sports skills along with life and leadership skills in a safe, fun, supportive, and challenging environment. This experience involves caring relationships, facilitated learning, experiential learning, and vigorous physical activity.[2]

This definition combines recommendations of the National Research Council and Institute of Medicine with the work of various scholars.[3] Existing positive youth development models have traditionally treated *physical assets* in a somewhat minimal and generic way,[4] but sport-specific frameworks make explicit the importance of sport for developing physical assets simultaneously with psychological and social assets. Two evidence-based reports, the 2007 *Tucker Center Research Report, Developing Physically Active Girls* and the President's Council on Physical Fitness and Sports' *Promoting Positive Youth Development through Physical Activity*,[5] lay out a framework and summarize the research on positive youth development and sports participation. Much of what is outlined in this chapter can be found in elaborated form within these two evidence-based reports and the resources in the chapter reference list.

ASSET DEVELOPMENT THROUGH SPORT AND PHYSICAL ACTIVITY

Table 3.1 summarizes the array of assets that can potentially, but not automatically, be attained when life skills are intentionally and systematically taught and incorporated into the teaching of sport skills and competencies within structured environments. Social assets are gained via social experiences and the social climate (e.g., connectedness, support, empowerment, boundaries, and constructive use of time), psychological and emotional assets are generated through positive experiences (e.g., emotional regulation, commitment to learning, positive values, social competencies, positive identity, and spirituality), intellectual assets accrued via learning opportunities (e.g., critical thinking and reasoning, decision making, and academic success), and physical assets developed through physical activity and education (e.g., good health habits and risk management).[6] Having more assets is associated with increased likelihood for positive and successful youth development.

Social Assets

Sports are a social activity and provide an opportunity for youth to develop social assets that may transfer into other domains. Participation in structured sport opportunities also leads to the development of social assets such as teamwork, conflict management, cooperation, character, decision making, social capital, leadership, and the ability to make meaningful, close friendships. Sports participation increasingly appears to be a source of popularity and social capital for girls, as it has always been for boys, but gender stereotypes pertaining to femininity that limit girls' participation are unfortunately alive and well.

Psychological Assets

Participation in sport can result in higher levels of self-efficacy, confidence, self-esteem, physical competence and self-worth, and more favorable body esteem. In turn, favorable self-perceptions and feelings of well-being and enjoyment created by participation can increase the likelihood of initiating and sustaining sport participation. Youth with high self-perceptions in sport contexts are more likely to initiate participation and less likely to drop out. Creating sport climates that foster favorable self-perceptions and build physical competencies is essential.

Table 3.1. Assets framework for positive youth development through physical activity

PHYSICAL ASSETS

Physical health
Health- and performance-related physical fitness
Physiological capacities
Motor skill competencies and movement literacy
Physical activity competencies
Physically active lifestyles
Knowledge about physical activities, sports, and games

PSYCHOLOGICAL ASSETS

Commitment to physical activity
Positive values toward physical activity
Interpersonal competencies, teamwork, cooperation
Positive body image and physical identity
Mental health, positive affect, and stress relief
Cognitive functioning and intellectual health
Self-determined motivation pertaining to physical activity

SOCIAL ASSETS

Support from significant others (e.g., coaches, parents, peers)
Meaningful and close personal relationships and friendships
Social capital
Learning, life skills, and empowerment
Boundaries and expectations
Constructive use of time for active living
Healthy gender identity

Adapted with permission from D. Wiese-Bjornstal and N. M. LaVoi, "Girls' Physical Activity Participation: Recommendations for Best Practices, Programs, Policies and Future Research," in *The Tucker Center Research Report, Developing Physically Active Girls: An Evidence-Based Multidisciplinary Approach,* ed. M. J. Kane and N. M. LaVoi, 63–90 (Minneapolis: The Tucker Center for Research on Girls & Women in Sport, University of Minnesota, 2007).

Physical Assets

Positive youth development can occur in a variety of contexts, but sport and physical activity uniquely offer the potential to develop physical assets simultaneously with psychological, social, and emotional assets. Learning physical skills and motor competencies are critical to sport participation for youth but are also essential for maintaining an active and healthy lifestyle into adulthood. Based on the data, physical activity plays a role in decreasing the risk of coronary heart disease, obesity, hypertension, depression, osteoporosis, and Type 2 diabetes. If physical assets are not developed in childhood and adolescence, an active adult life is less likely—thereby increasing the risk for chronic and acute health conditions later in life.

NEGATIVE OUTCOMES THAT CAN RESULT FROM SPORT PARTICIPATION

The evidence suggesting that positive outcomes can result when youth participate in sports is compelling. But scholars have also noted positive outcomes are not an automatic byproduct of sports participation, and some argue participation can have detrimental effects on youths' health and well-being. Overtraining or excessive sport participation can, for example, lead to negative psychological and physical outcomes such as burnout, chronic or acute injury, depression, stress, anxiety, eating disorders, and dropout. Something called the "female athlete triad" occurs when an eating disorder, amenorrhoea (absence of menstruation), and osteoporosis (decreased bone mineral density) are present. Negative outcomes such as poor sportsmanship, low levels of intrinsic motivation, and lack of enjoyment can also result when adult leaders focus too much on winning or outperforming others, rarely allow athletes voice or choice, punish mistakes, or give special attention to the more talented. Development, whether negative or positive, is a process that is facilitated by the actions of people who also create contextual features of the sport environment.

CONTEXTUAL FEATURES

The body of research produced by scholars highlights the importance of contextual features in promoting positive youth development through sport—especially positive social relationships, skill-building activities, and caring and supportive climates.[7] Features of positive social relationships and caring and supportive climates include opportunities to develop caring, warm, close relationships with adults and peers, to belong, to foster prosocial norms, autonomy, appreciation and inclusion of individual differences, valuation of diverse opinions, and expression of those opinions. Features of skill building include opportunities to learn and improve relative to one's self rather than in comparison to others, a clear developmentally appropriate structure with consistent rules and expectations, and adult supervision, and psychologically and physically safe health-promoting facilities. These features in combination with social influences help promote positive youth development through sport.

SOCIAL INFLUENCES

Development occurs in social contexts—such as sport—as youth interact with significant others. Figure 3.1 outlines specific actions that youth sport stakeholders—including youth athletes—can take to facilitate positive youth development. In the following section, the actions of parents, coaches, and peers will be elaborated on, as they are arguably the most important and central social influences in the lives of youth athletes.

The Role of the Parents

Parents greatly influence the sport participation and experiences of their children as they provide opportunity and resources, interpret experiences, appraise abilities, assign value, and encourage and support

Figure 3.1. An evidence-based multidisciplinary model for developing physically active youth

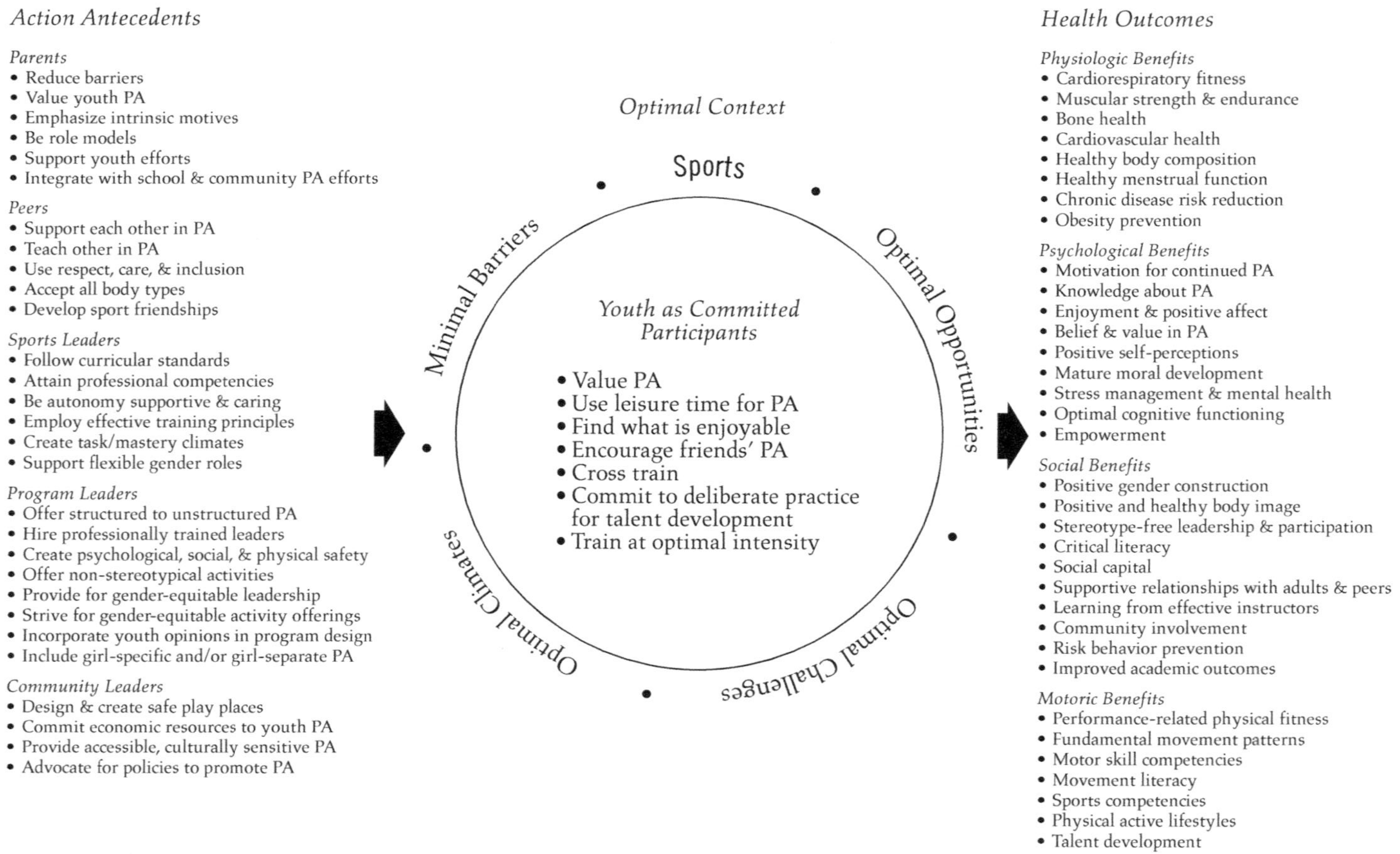

Action Antecedents

Parents
- Reduce barriers
- Value youth PA
- Emphasize intrinsic motives
- Be role models
- Support youth efforts
- Integrate with school & community PA efforts

Peers
- Support each other in PA
- Teach other in PA
- Use respect, care, & inclusion
- Accept all body types
- Develop sport friendships

Sports Leaders
- Follow curricular standards
- Attain professional competencies
- Be autonomy supportive & caring
- Employ effective training principles
- Create task/mastery climates
- Support flexible gender roles

Program Leaders
- Offer structured to unstructured PA
- Hire professionally trained leaders
- Create psychological, social, & physical safety
- Offer non-stereotypical activities
- Provide for gender-equitable leadership
- Strive for gender-equitable activity offerings
- Incorporate youth opinions in program design
- Include girl-specific and/or girl-separate PA

Community Leaders
- Design & create safe play places
- Commit economic resources to youth PA
- Provide accessible, culturally sensitive PA
- Advocate for policies to promote PA

Optimal Context

Optimal Opportunities

Sports

Youth as Committed Participants
- Value PA
- Use leisure time for PA
- Find what is enjoyable
- Encourage friends' PA
- Cross train
- Commit to deliberate practice for talent development
- Train at optimal intensity

Minimal Barriers

Optimal Challenges

Optimal Climates

Health Outcomes

Physiologic Benefits
- Cardiorespiratory fitness
- Muscular strength & endurance
- Bone health
- Cardiovascular health
- Healthy body composition
- Healthy menstrual function
- Chronic disease risk reduction
- Obesity prevention

Psychological Benefits
- Motivation for continued PA
- Knowledge about PA
- Enjoyment & positive affect
- Belief & value in PA
- Positive self-perceptions
- Mature moral development
- Stress management & mental health
- Optimal cognitive functioning
- Empowerment

Social Benefits
- Positive gender construction
- Positive and healthy body image
- Stereotype-free leadership & participation
- Critical literacy
- Social capital
- Supportive relationships with adults & peers
- Learning from effective instructors
- Community involvement
- Risk behavior prevention
- Improved academic outcomes

Motoric Benefits
- Performance-related physical fitness
- Fundamental movement patterns
- Motor skill competencies
- Movement literacy
- Sports competencies
- Physical active lifestyles
- Talent development

Adapted with permission from D. Wiese-Bjornstal and N. M. LaVoi. "Girls' Physical Activity Participation: Recommendations for Best Practices, Programs, Policies

participation. Facilitative actions parents can take to increase the likelihood that positive development through sport will occur for their
children include: value, enjoy, and model participation in physical activity, emphasize intrinsic reasons for participation (e.g., fun, making
friends, love of the game, learning new skills), avoid a primary focus
on winning or "win at all costs" attitude, include family dialogue
about sportsmanship, encourage a focus on what can be controlled
(e.g., effort, self-referenced improvement), provide tangible support
(e.g., transportation, time, money), reduce barriers, partake equally in
active (e.g., coaching) and logistic (e.g., bringing snacks, organizing
equipment) sport roles, and convey a belief about a child's sport
abilities.[8]

In addition to beliefs, values, and actions parents foster at home,
parental behavior on youth sport sidelines is also important to facilitating positive experiences. Children's perceptions of their parents'
sideline behaviors is the factor most predictive of poor sport behavior
of the child. When a parent yells at or argues with the referee, the
child will perceive that this behavior is acceptable and normative.
Therefore, parents should refrain from commonly reported "negative" behaviors that children and youth report they do not like and
don't prefer, such as yelling at the referee, coaching from the sidelines,
acting like a crazed fan, and distracting athletes from performance.

The Role of Peers

As youth transition from childhood to adolescence, peers and the
peer group become the most important social influence and can
greatly influence and affect the sport experience. Best practices that
should be encouraged for peers of youth athletes include: support and
encourage sport participation, teach sport skills to each other, demonstrate care, respect, and inclusion for everyone regardless of age, gender, ability, sexual orientation, race, or socioeconomic status, refrain
from teasing, bullying, and hazing, invite others to participate, develop diverse groups of friends both in and outside of sport, and recognize and affirm the sport accomplishments of others. Perceived

support for sport participation from peers is associated with enjoyment of sport, and youth who perceive their peers provide social support for their physical activity report higher activity levels and greater participation rates.[9]

The Role of the Coach

Over twenty-five years of research in sport psychology supports the salient role of the coach in facilitating positive youth development. Best practices coaches should strive to emulate include: focus on self-referenced learning and skill mastery, teach skills, give positive reinforcement for effort and improvement (rather than punishment for mistakes), use behavior-contingent praise and informational feedback that will help the athlete learn, refrain from defining success only in terms of winning, encourage supportive and cooperative peer relationships, demonstrate care toward all athletes regardless of skill, role, gender, ability, sexual orientation, race, or socioeconomic status, practice consistent and clear communication pertaining to the unique and valued role of each athlete, seek input and allow youth developmentally appropriate choices, support flexible gender roles, foster participatory and athlete-centered decision making and problem solving, embrace two-way communication, develop caring and warm relationships with athletes, and provide instructive and specific feedback following errors.[10]

Based on the evidence, coaches who embrace these best practices are more likely to have athletes with higher levels of sport enjoyment and satisfaction, self-esteem, intrinsic motivation, and sportsmanship, and lower levels of anxiety, stress, burnout, and drop out. Effective coaches who possess high levels of both technical and relational expertise are more likely to meet athletes' universal human needs for competence, belongingness, and autonomy (sense of self-control and determination). When essential needs are met, optimal functioning and performance, growth, social development, and personal well-being are more likely to flourish. Effective, caring, and well-trained adult leaders who create a safe, cooperative, mastery-focused climate are critical for ensuring that positive development occurs in and through sports.[11] The coach independently and in combination with parents and peers greatly influences the development of athlete assets. The role and responsibility of the athlete, however, should not be overlooked.

The Role of the Athlete

At the center of figure 3.1 is the role of the athlete in the development of assets. Youth possess agency to value and take responsibility for sport participation, and be committed sport participants. However, a sole focus on the individual fails to acknowledge that values, choices, expectations, effort, interest, and enjoyment of youth are shaped by the cultural and societal values and beliefs and social and physical environments in which youth live. Framing lack of sport participation as an issue of commitment, making "the right" choices, discipline, self-improvement, and self-responsibility—rather than structural factors such as racism, sexism, and poverty—can be problematic. A solely individual-based focus places judgment, responsibility, and blame on the individual, which can in turn reinforce participation, developmental, and health inequalities, and maintains the many barriers that also influence sport participation.

BARRIERS TO POSITIVE YOUTH DEVELOPMENT THROUGH SPORT

Many youth fail to achieve their full potential due to a multitude of barriers that impede or prevent their participation in sport or physical activity—and this is particularly true for girls. A clear gendered gap in sport participation exists, but geography, class, disability, and race intersect with gender in complex ways that prohibit or make it challenging for underserved youth to be physically active.[12] Girls of color and girls from low-income communities are some of the least active populations in the United States and become increasingly inactive as they move from childhood through adolescence. An individual's positionality (e.g., gender, class, race) influences their access to sport participation, which can create health and developmental disparities.

Barriers to sport participation can be individual, social, structural, or societal. A broad but not exhaustive overview of potential barriers to sport participation follows. Individual barriers may include lack of perceived competence, dislike of sport, fear of injury or embarrassment, anxiety about participation, or perception that available sport opportunities are not interesting or culturally relevant. Social barriers are people related and stem from individuals such as coaches, peers, parents, and siblings. Common social barriers may include lack of social support from peers, peer teasing, criticism, or bullying due to lack of sport competence, lack of parental value in and support of sports, family expectations to work outside the home, care for siblings, or contribute to domestic chores, and lack of a caring and competent coach. Structural barriers may include lack of space, unsafe space, facility proximity, cost, and lack of programming. Societal barriers may include outdated gender stereotypes about femininity that place ideas about what it means to be a "real girl" and a "real athlete" in opposition, and ideals about masculinity and what it means to be "a real man" that place boys at risk for injury.

Based on the evidence, the contextual features and best practices needed to increase the likelihood that positive youth development will occur through sport are clear. Using the evidence, parents, coaches, and decision makers in youth sport must strive together to implement what is known to "work" while simultaneously reducing barriers that may limit or prevent sport participation. Striving to do so is not only good for *everyone* in the sport community—most importantly it is good for the millions of children and youth who have much to gain from a positively constructed sport experience.[13]

NOTES

1. William Damon, "What Is Positive Youth Development?" *The ANNALS of the American Academy of Political and Social Science* 591, no. 1 (2004): 13–24.

2. Daniel Perkins, Kristine Madsen, and Cory Wechsler, *Sports-Based Youth Development* (Boston: UP2US Center, 2008).

3. National Research Council and Institute of Medicine, *Community Programs to Promote Youth Development* (Washington DC: National Academy Press, 2002). Available via http://www7.nationalacademies.org/dbasse/DBASSE _Publications .html.

4. Diane Wiese-Bjornstal and Nicole LaVoi, "Girls' Physical Activity Participation: Recommendations for Best Practices, Programs, Policies and Future Research," in *The Tucker Center Research Report, Developing Physically Active Girls: An Evidence-Based Multidisciplinary Approach*, ed. M. J. Kane and N. M. LaVoi, 63–90 (Minneapolis: The Tucker Center for Research on Girls & Women in Sport, University of Minnesota, 2007). Online version available at http://www .cehd.umn.edu/tuckercenter/library/docs/research/2007-Tucker-Center -Research-Report.pdf.

5. Maureen Weiss and Diane Wiese-Bjornstal, *Promoting Positive Youth Development through Physical Activity*, Research Digest Series 10, no. 3 (Washington DC: President's Council on Physical Fitness and Sports, 2009). Online version available at https://www.presidentschallenge.org/informed/digest/docs /september2009digest.pdf.

6. Wiese-Bjornstal and LaVoi, "Girls' Physical Activity Participation."

7. Weiss and Wiese-Bjornstal, *Promoting Positive Youth Development through Physical Activity*.

8. Wiese-Bjornstal and LaVoi, "Girls' Physical Activity Participation," 85.

9. Ibid.

10. Ibid.

11. Ibid.

12. Ibid.

13. Also see these sources for further information: Daniel Perkins and Gil Noam, "Characteristics of Sports-Based Youth Development Programs," *New Directions for Youth Development* 115 (2007): 75–84; Daniel Perkins and Cory Wechsler, *Quality Components of Sports-Based Youth Development* (Boston: UP2US Center, 2008); Don Sabo and Phil Veliz, *Go Out and Play: Youth Sports in America* (East Meadow, NY: Women's Sports Foundation, 2008); and Jessica Fraser-Thomas, Jean Cote, and Janice Deakin, "Youth Sport Programs: An Avenue to Foster Positive Youth Development," *Physical Education and Sport Pedagogy* 10, no. 1 (2005): 19–40.

CHAPTER 4

Youth Sport and the Virtues

MIKE MCNAMEE

SPORT, VIRTUE, AND THE MODERN WORLD

In medieval Europe, the Roman Catholic Church was the dominant social and political institution as well as the seat of learning. The vast majority of the populace, however, were illiterate, and so the possibility of their following or even understanding its principal ceremony, Holy Mass, conducted in Latin is unthinkable. One fairly widespread way of reducing the mysteriousness of religious morality was the enactment of morality plays. The precise details of this cultural practice are unknown, so I offer here the merest sketch to make the point I wish to make at the beginning of this chapter on the ethics of sports.

Around this time, traveling circuses not only brought entertainment to the masses, but typically included in their show a morality play. Here good and evil were played out on a stage where what was at stake was the very soul of the principal character: Everyman.

Though crudely analogous, it is my contention that sports, among other things, now fulfill this role or function on a global scale. In a world where the Enlightenment myth of shared morality is assaulted on every side by anthropologists, cultural commentators, and philosophers alike, sports offer a cognitively simple canvass of good and evil writ large in the everyday contexts of the arena, the court, the field, and of course the back pages of our newspapers and the screens of our televisions. Just as the moralizing point of the medieval plays was not dramatically dense, one needs neither complex cognitive nor moral vocabularies to understand cheating and courage, nor fair and foul play, in the varied fora of sport. Sports thus offer one of our best vehicles for moral education in the light of the clash of moral cultures that the present world throws up. I can indicate what that large thesis might look like in this short essay.

SPORTS AND VIRTUE ETHICS

I maintain that in and through sports we can develop, promote, and ramify the virtues. They have sometimes been referred to, rather aptly, as moral laboratories. I do not mean to say that sports are some kind of universal panacea as sports lovers sometimes maintain, merely that they are social sites rich in opportunities for ethical development. This sounds like a noble but nostalgic belief. But what does it mean? Virtue-based theories are commonly described as *arētaic* since their exposition is often traced back to the ancient Greeks for whom virtue, or excellence, is translated as *arēte*. Its first substantial expression is found in Socratic philosophy, but it is Aristotle who couches his writings on living well (or flourishing, to use the standard interpretation) in terms of practical wisdom supported by the well-disposed and relatively settled set of character traits that are typically called "virtues." After him, as is well known, St. Thomas Aquinas developed his specifically theological account of the virtues, the confluence of which largely forms our understanding of Christian virtues.

    Why, it might be asked, ought youth sports coaches reach back to antiquity in an effort to understand how they should coach or teach better, or to better mold the action and character of young athletes? An answer to this question is partly revealed by a consideration of the nature of virtue as well as a consideration of the nature of sports contests. Let me take the former here, and only make passing reference to the latter. And even with this restricted aim I will discuss almost exclusively the coach and athlete in relation, largely ignoring other social and political institutions that are clearly implicated in the development, organization, and promotion of sports.

Sports talk is littered with reference to the achievement of excellence. So too is virtue ethics. *Arēte*, in ancient Greek, meant just that: excellence. *Arēte* could mean the excellence of anything. A standard example often used to explain this is that of a knife. A knife is an excellent one when it fulfills its purposes of cutting. A good knife should be sharp; its sharpness should be consistent over time; it should not be too flexible or it may cut the user as well as their food; it should not be so small or so large that it cannot be gripped firmly in the hand of its user; and so on. In human terms, a virtue, then, is a way of being humanly excellent. We do not think of people as being born with excellence but rather of learning to become an excellent human being. A human virtue, then, is an acquired human quality. And sports, as I have said, present a rich arena for such acquisition. The Oxford literary scholar, author, and Christian educator C. S. Lewis has given an excellent account of the nature of virtue and he used sports as the context for the purposes of illustration:

> What you mean by a good player is the man whose eye and muscles and nerves have been so trained by making innumerable good shots that they can now be relied upon. . . . They have a certain tone or quality which is there even when he is not playing. . . . In the same way a man who perseveres in doing just actions gets in the end a certain quality of character. Now it is that quality rather than the particular actions that we mean when we talk of virtue.[1]

What Lewis offers is a dispositional account of virtue. A wine glass is brittle by disposition, so it will smash if I drop it; its nature is fragile. Human dispositions are more complex. We say that the courageous person seeks to achieve a valuable end in the face of danger or fear. And to call a person courageous is to say that they are *typically* so, that they are by nature disposed to courageous action in normal circumstances. Well, that is not quite accurate. It is better to say that a courageous person is by *second nature* disposed to act courageously. Now if we are to say that virtues like courage are *acquired* human qualities, we must say at least a little about how they are acquired. Here are but a few points that can be surmised from Aristotle regarding concepts such as habituation, emulation, and initiation.

In the early stages of the development of ethically sound character, habit formation is critical. Practice does not make perfect, as parents and grandparents are apt to say. Rather, practice makes permanent, a point observed by Aristotle long before the psychologist's remark became a commonplace. He writes: "It makes no small difference then, whether we form habits of one kind or of another from our very youth; it makes a very great difference, or rather *all* the difference."[2]

Richard Peters put this point beautifully when he remarked that "the palace of reason is entered through the courtyard of habit."[3] Now the end point of secular moral education within a liberal framework is the development of rational autonomy, which will entail moral autonomy, that is, reasoning one's way to the right course of action free of external influences. Yet it scarcely takes an educator to point out that rational autonomy is not in the possession of the young, and takes more than enough time to flower in adulthood. It is, therefore, the acquisition of good habits that we are crucially after in general, and in particular in youth sport.

The pedagogical potential of sports as a moral laboratory rests *precariously* on habituation, however. I say this because the habits that are fostered by the sports coach are as good and as bad as the coach him- or herself. Children perceive quickly the dissonance between word and action. "Do as I *say* not as I *do*" is a poor—though not entirely useless—moral dictum often used by parents, educators, and coaches. As the Duc de la Rochfoucauld once remarked, hypocrisy is the tribute that vice pays to virtue. The coach with bad habits who exhorts his or her young athletes is to be preferred to the coach who demands his or her players to cheat, foul, or be spoilsports. But children fasten upon other habits of the coach: who they praise or chastise, or who they select or put on the bench. More than this they focus on adverbial qualities too: *how* the coach praises or chastises, the *language* that they use, the *manner* in which they select and pull players from the field of play, and so on. These habits, sometimes accompanied by deliberate choice, sometimes not, also have an influence on habit formation of youths who have a keen eye on the distribution of reward and punishment. So, for example, long before children can theorize justice they can exclaim with righteous indignation "That's not fair!" at the privileging of a teammate over them for no perceived good reason.

It is true that youths model their behavior, language, choices, postures, and so on, on the coach or sports star, emulating them within and beyond the contexts of sports. These processes of emulation (loosely: following role models) and identification (whom do we see ourselves in the light of) are not a fully rational affair. The beginning of moral education in general, or moral apprenticeship in sport in particular, is necessarily heteronymous. Children are literally at the mercy of those who are entrusted with their care and development in and through sports.

It is important to note that the process of initiation into a practice occurs over time. There may be Gestalt shifts—where learners make a moral leap in their progress—but the general picture is slower and less dramatic. The British philosopher of education Ray Elliot once gave a beautiful account of the phenomenological character of initiation and personal development within a practice that is richly suggestive for sports:

(A) child at school finds a subject attractive, takes delight in it, and begins to look forward to the lessons in which it is taught. The subject seems to welcome his [*sic*] attention, his work pleases his teacher, and he comes to think of himself as "good at" the subject. It becomes "his subject." During its lessons time passes with a strange swiftness. He believes it to be "better" than other subjects, and is prepared to give up other pleasures because absorption in his subject pleases him still more. Perhaps he develops a passion for it, and begrudges time spent on anything else. In due course it dawns on the student that his enthusiastic interest in his subject is not enough. There are standards which have to be met, and to meet them he has to develop skills and abilities which he did not originally associate with his subject. He also has to do a good deal of work which seems to be commonly like drudgery. Pleasures do not come easily now, but he finds fulfilment in trying to satisfy the demands his subject makes upon him. He has become devoted to its disciplines and feels at times that he has been enlisted in its service.[4]

This story is very much in keeping with Aristotelian ideas of good living: first we pursue and repeat that which is pleasurable, coming to pursue the honorable only later, after (as it were) one has been enlisted or initiated into a certain virtue-laden conception of the practice as a worthwhile activity.

A key point of the ethical development of children as they become youths (in what we might call the intermediate stage between heteronomy and autonomy), when they attempt to explore the limits of their bodies, identity, and values, is the exemplars they choose to emulate. Clearly at this time their character is in transition. In the right circumstances children and youths learn to adopt attitudes less egoistically driven and come to care as well as to reason for others' interests and needs. Here the knowing acceptance of the rules of sport can play an important role in curbing excessive egoism. Games are contracts, and the players must fulfill their role as contestants. Crucially youth is also a time for the formation of emotional sensibilities that are cognitively grounded. In this stage of development, moral emotions such as regret, shame, guilt as well as pride and loyalty come to be thought of as appropriate or inappropriate responses to situations and acts. Typically, these responses come to form patterns of more or less stable perception, emotion, and deliberation. They ought always to be grounded in right reasons of course. To act virtuously is indeed to act from a settled character that sees and judges things properly.

But this is not the whole story. As Aristotle remarked, to be virtuous is to feel the right emotions at the right time, to the right degree, and in relation to the right objects. Thus emotional sensibility is part of the fuller model of virtue development, and it can only come with time and immersion into sports contexts where there is a strong moral atmosphere or ethos, where ethical considerations are a basic ingredient and not merely the icing on the cake.

In formal terms, moral exhortation and instruction will of course be critical in youth sports. Nevertheless, we should not underestimate the value of the things learnt while we are not explicitly coaching or teaching, that is, in the locker room, the parking lot, and so forth. Children are learning all the while, by such basic things as *how* we stand, *how* we address others, what *language* we use, and what examples we choose. The *modes* of interaction are as much a part of their learning about how to conduct themselves in and out of sport as the explicit skills, techniques, and strategies we teach them. The sociologists of education refer to this phenomenon as the "hidden curriculum," and it is a powerful shaper of the values and attitudes of young learners.

Two further points are particularly noteworthy. The first relates to the powerful, though old-fashioned, notion of a role model I noted above. In Aristotelian thought, understanding the right thing to do, feel, and see is a product of our learning from wiser souls (the *phronimos*), those whose grasp of practical judgment (*phronesis*) or wisdom is more reliable and sure-footed than our own. But the adverbial quality of our action (how we do what we do in and out of instructional modes) is crucial for it (and ourselves) to be considered virtuous and not merely a simulacra or false veneer of such:

> Actions, then, are called just and temperate when they are such as the just or the temperate person would do; but it is not the person who does these that is just and temperate, but the person who also does them *as* just and temperate people do. It is well said, then, that it is by doing just acts that the just person is produced, and by doing temperate acts the temperate person; without doing these no-one would have a prospect of becoming good.

But most people do not do these, but take refuge in theory and think they are being philosophers and will become good in this way, behaving somewhat like patients who listen attentively to their doctors, but do none of the things they are ordered to do. As the latter will not be made well in body by such a course of treatment, the former will not be made well in soul by such a course of philosophy.[5]

This is why philosophers have stressed that sports can be an important arena for the development of virtue: sports provide, in a very public way, occasions for good and evil. Creating relatively controlled, and sometimes contrived, situations, we can afford opportunities not merely for sporting youths to "try out" moral action, but to think and feel it out too. It is rare, in sports at least, that one does not know the right thing to do. Doing it out of the right motivation and emotional states is what is to be aimed for.

But we cannot swallow Aristotle hook, line, and sinker, as they say. Some points of caution need to be registered here. First, we must acknowledge the situatedness of Aristotelian thought. It is clear that the practices of ancient Greece would be misogynistic by modern lights. For sports to become sites of moral education, no naive revival project is required. Aristotle talks of the good and wise "man" and often of the "great-souled man" when he is referring to acts of manly courage and nobility. Of course, our interpretation needs to be revisionist in this regard. The Athenian society of his day was class and ethnically biased (and he knew this well being an outsider: a Macedonian) and it is no historical insight to say that it was deeply sexist too.

Nonetheless, his emphasis upon the absolute necessity of habituated action in the moral development of the young is as apt today as it was then. Often, perhaps mostly, we act according to our early habituation and only thereafter according to our reflective appreciation of what good people would do in such situations. Blind rule-following observance is in a clear sense not the same thing as following a rule wholeheartedly, where one's actions are predicated on a conception and dedication to do the right thing by being the right kind of person. But behavior in youth sport is characterized by uncertainty and unreliability. Children and youths come gradually to resist their egoistic motivations and values under the appropriate guidance and support. Developing mature and reflexive attitudes in relation to their evolving value-scheme is a task that must often take place in relation to success or failure in spaces on and beyond the field of play. Some refer to these instances, rather beautifully I think, as "teachable moments" to be seized upon as precious opportunities.

Character training in this intermediate phase of ethical development, characteristic of youth sports, helps our evolving moral agent to reliably (re)produce the right acts at the right times while coming to feel appropriately about them. It is a mistake, however, to think of this habituation as mere rote learning in the way that early skill-psychologists believed we learned a particular motor skill by constant repetition. Rather, like a schema, one learns the generalized responses to situations and then one must refine them, becoming ever more sensitive or fine-tuned to the particularities of each situation.

This youthful stage of life and moral development is often summed up by the phrase that one has learnt "the that" of moral action. One appreciates that one must act according to the dictates of virtue. In order fully to mature, to reach the final stage of Aristotelian moral development, moral agents must also comprehend "the why." As Tobin puts it: "Acquiring the why in ethics will help [those in the intermediate stage] to overcome the gaps, unclarities, and straightforward mistakes in his moral awareness."[6] But that of course is the project of a lifetime, not merely one for youth sport.

Now although the talk of virtue in sport may feel somewhat anachronistic, I maintain that it is not. I have elsewhere developed a sustained account of the virtues and vices in sports.[7] In doing so I have drawn on a variety of authors including Nussbaum, Rorty, and Pincoffs. I shall now draw on these authors—without respecting important differences in their positions—and develop a framework for a virtue ethics of sport here.

A CATALOGUE OF VIRTUES IN SPORT

While I cannot offer here a completed scheme or catalogue of the virtues, I think it would be an advance on bland exhortations to virtuous conduct to at least begin to delineate the different sorts of virtues that could instantiate sports ethics in athletic conduct.

First, the catalogue of all virtues is functionally various,[8] but here I merely distinguish the non-instrumental virtues from the instrumental virtues; the latter relate specifically to elite sports where the sphere is essentially instrumental, goal-oriented, action. In speaking of non-instrumental or moral virtues we might want to insist on a range of virtues that secure no more than minimally reasonable interpersonal conduct based loosely upon a core human value of not harming others. It may seem reasonable to claim that these moral virtues are most likely to have a transcultural reach. Such a list would include fairness, honesty, integrity, and trustworthiness. In elaborating the virtues of, say, an Olympian or a great professional sportsperson, we might wish to incorporate much higher than moral minimalism, however. The persisting ideal of sportspersons as honorable heroes would be sullied were they to take on so callous or cavalier an attitude to the constitutive and regulative rules of sports, the best traditions of those sports, and the standards of honesty and integrity we properly expect of (handsomely paid) professionals.

Without attempting to vilify unjustifiably any of the many sporting villains whose vices have corroded the ideals of sports, one thinks readily of the disgraced American sprinters Marion Jones and Justin Gatland and cyclist Lance Armstrong. One difficulty for Olympic athletes is to be publicly held to account for higher standards of conduct and character. A corresponding philosophical difficulty would be the precise philosophical content given to the moral virtues that would underwrite the idea of positive, perhaps heroic, role models.

One of the chief moral educational powers of sport is, I suggest, in the role modeling of elite sportspersons, such as Olympians, who engage in the kinds of behaviors where, against the grain of direct competition, they act in ways that are selfless (such as assisting fellow athletes who are injured, or deliberately eschewing easy opportunities to win at the expense of incapacitated opponents) or super honest where they indicate to the official that they have broken a rule where the official had not realized it. I recognize that this is setting the bar rather high and asking of athletes more than might be expected of others. But it is precisely because of their high profile, and the enormous financial endorsements or social prestige, that expectations of higher standards are justified. And the expectation is hardly a new one. Even at its roots in ancient Greek athletic struggles or contests (*agon*) we are aware of the myth of champions winning only laurel wreaths. To the contrary, we know that they were paid handsomely and were expected to behave honorably. Clearly many and perhaps most people would seek to gain unfair competitive advantages under such circumstances. The fact that, with so much to win and lose, the vast majority of athletes ignore opportunities to cheat is one reason that we properly think of them as above everyday folk.

It is often said that it is sports' focus on competition that fosters egoism. Logically speaking, this simply cannot be the case. Even the etymology of the word tells us that competition is a coming together to test each other. And one can only share a test when one has agreed to cooperate. What is playing sport if not an appeal to suspend all differences of creed or color in order to strive together for victory? The demonstration of superiority requires cooperation. Sporting contests cannot survive without this shared spirit we often call fair play. This point flows from the very structure of sports and places demands on the very characters of sportspersons. Note, I am not saying that the presence of contrary vices is not everywhere to be seen in sport, but that to reach the ideals captured in sport at its best, the virtues thus must be cultivated. Indeed the point can be distilled from a most general level. Nussbaum puts it thus:

The point is that everyone makes some choices and acts somehow or other in these spheres: if not properly then improperly. Everyone has *some* attitude and behaviour toward her own death; toward her own bodily appetites and their management; toward her property and its use; towards the distribution of social goods; toward telling the truth; toward being kindly or not kindly to others; toward cultivating or not cultivating a sense of play and delight; and so on. No matter where one lives one cannot escape these questions, so long as one is living a human life.[9]

Nussbaum's claim here is the noble and expansive one of unifying all good human living under the same canopy of virtues. I am staking out a claim of much more modest scope. I am merely claiming that sport, because of its very nature and purposes, places demands on all players. Their responses are obligatory in nature through rule structures and conventions. Observing them, and doing so not only because of a fear of penalty or sanction, still challenges us because of our weakness of will and the ready availability of (more or less substantial) external goods that incentivize the ends of victory over the means of playing fair and well. The seriousness of the competition within and between individuals and teams heightens the stakes. The virtues, in their variety, are a response to this problematic.

As was noted, there is little difficulty setting out the kinds of virtues that we might expect to cultivate in sports and sports teams. While it is fairly obvious that one would need virtues such as discipline, determination, persistence, and tenacity, as sportspersons whose endeavors are focused on a specified goal, one would also need "courage" and "prudence" in knowing when which levels of risk were really worth taking in one's sporting life. This period, often in our teens and early adulthood, is usually only a microcosm of a life fully and wholly lived over the course of one's allotted years. Choosing wisely just how much to risk of one's future health by downplaying injuries or training excessively in one's adolescent years (say, for example, by using off-label anabolic steroids or other illicit performance enhancing substances) represents a challenge that demands great prudence and moral imagination. It might also be important to recognize again the potential competitiveness of different virtues in addition to the heterogeneity even within virtues such as courage (both active as in the Greek *andreia*—whose context is military—and the Latin *fortitudino*, which might be understood as withstanding pain or suffering and still holding on or keeping going).

There may be many pointers that we can take from this examination of the functional variety of the classification of virtues relevant to the assignation "sporting." I shall note merely two. First, it would be unreasonable to select a catalogue from the non-instrumental virtues and expect all sportspersons to instantiate them. Just as the virtues are functionally various, we must also recognize the enormous variety of sports and the radically different challenges they pose to contestants. Archery, basketball, hockey, judo, sailing, swimming, and track and field all share a competitive logic and a certain winning mindset. But this mindset is surely not a virtue but a compendium of virtues that is open textured. We can expect a much greater shared approach in relation to the instrumental virtues, but even here there will be some context specificity that may lead to alternative interpretations of those virtues.

Secondly, a pedagogical point follows this philosophical one. Relatively few, if any, of these virtues have ever been targeted specifically in the policy documents and curricular outlines of coaches, physical education teachers, and sport pedagogues in my limited experience. Yet in the UK at least, home to the Victorian legacy of moralistic sports, and what is known as muscular Christianity, which so inspired the founder of the modern Olympics, Baron Pierre de Coubertin, it was always thought that somehow, magically, the very playing of sports would inculcate in its practitioners moral qualities we think of as virtues. Nothing, it strikes me, warrants such confidence in amateur sport let alone professional or Olympian encounters.

It could be said that the philosopher or pedagogue, in attempting to establish a singular ethics of sports based upon the cultivation of virtues, is suffering from excessive nostalgia. There may be some truth in this claim. The shared identities, norms, and purposes of the *polis* (or city-state) are long gone and inapplicable to the modern multicultural world. Yet without some kind of conserving traditions it may be difficult to foresee the kind of sport whose best traditions we try in our coaching and teaching to preserve. And if sports, with their explicit rules and implicit ethos of fair play, cannot model human behavior in all its glory (warts and all), it is difficult to see what modern practices can.

FINAL REMARKS

I have tried in this brief discussion to share with you a condensed and simplified ethics of youth sport based upon Aristotelian thinking.

I have not attempted to develop any of its more subtle points, its moral psychology, the doctrine of the mean, the relationship to his metaphysical biology, nor many other interesting ideas in his philosophy. Instead I have tried to show a little of what moral educational prospects there might be in sports conceived of as an arena of human excellence, where virtue-ethical considerations are central to a conception of both sports performance and pedagogy.

NOTES

1. C. S. Lewis, *Mere Christianity* (New York: Macmillan, 1979), 63.
2. Aristotle, *Nichomachean Ethics*, book II.I; 1103b22–25.
3. R. S. Peters, *Ethics and Education* (London: Routledge and Kegan Paul, 1966), 314.
4. R. K. Elliott, "Education, Love of One's Subject, and the Love of Truth," *Proceedings of the Philosophy of Education Society of Great Britain* 8, no. 1 (1974): 135–53.
5. Aristotle, *Nichomachean Ethics*, book II.V; 1105–21.
6. Bernadette Tobin, "An Aristotelian Theory of Moral Development," Journal of Philosophy of Education 23 (1989): 195–211, at 203.
7. M. J. McNamee, *Sports, Virtues and Vices: Morality Plays* (Abingdon: Routledge, 2008), esp. 69–86.
8. E. L. Pincoffs, *Quandaries and Virtues* (Lawrence: University Press of Kansas, 1986), 150–74.
9. M. C. Nussbaum, "Non-Relative Virtues: An Aristotelian Approach," *Midwest Studies in Philosophy* 13, no. 1 (1988): 32–53, at 32.

CHAPTER 5

Playing Like a
Champion Today

Youth Sport and Moral Development

CLARK POWER

Two decades ago coach education programs focused on teaching sports specific skills and strategies. Little attention was paid to deliberate character education per se. Today, all of the major youth sport coach education programs in the United States have a character education component, and "Character Counts Sports" places character at the center of its educational programming. This is a welcome development prompted by concern that youth sports were getting out of control. The problem with youth sports appears to be not so much the children but their elders, whose antics are increasingly captured on handheld video cameras and publicized through the internet. An examination of the most popular youth sport education programs, such as the American Sport Education Program (ASEP), Positive Coaching Alliance (PCA), and Character Counts Sports, suggests that we focus less on building the character of children than on improving the behavior of their coaches. Of course the two are related. Research on youth sports indicates that children's misbehavior correlates with their parents' and coaches' misbehavior.[1] If coaches and parents scream at officials, taunt opposing players, and even belittle their own players, what can we expect our children to learn from their sport experience?

As important as it is for coach education to address adults' character flaws, the Play Like a Champion Today educational program that we have developed takes a different approach to character education. We shift the focus from the adult to the child in identifying ways in which informed coach-ministers can help children to grow morally and spiritually. I will argue in this chapter that a child-centered approach to coaching differs in important ways from the traditional character education approach espoused by most coach education programs today. Although I applaud the efforts that other coach education programs are making to call attention to the importance of building character and improving the quality of children's sports experiences, I believe that the conventional character education model has limited potential to foster children's moral development.

THE COACH-MINISTER MODEL OF MORAL AND SPIRITUAL DEVELOPMENT

In this chapter I will offer an overview of the Play Like a Champion approach to character education within the ministerial framework that we use in working with Catholic sponsored youth sport programs. This chapter is meant to complement the approach that we take in chapter 9 to foster spiritual development. Christian spirituality is more than having "peak experiences" or moments of intense awareness or happiness. Christian spirituality involves discipleship, which means following the "way" of Jesus and trusting everything to God. The way of Jesus is one of ministry, of service to others. For the Christian, spiritual development is bound up with moral development. There can be no love of God whom we do not see without love of neighbor whom we do see. For the Christian, the human to God relationship can never be isolated from the human to human relationship. Dorotheus of Gaza, a sixth-century monk, helps us to see the way in which these two relationships are related to one another with a simple spatial metaphor. Imagine a circle with all of humanity at the circumference and God at the center. The only way for the people to come close together is for them to come closer to the center, which is God.[2]

There can be no authentic Christian spirituality that focuses on God in isolation from others. Nor can there be a Christian morality that focuses exclusively on love of neighbor. God is love, and the most powerful experience of God is to be found in human love. For the Christian, morality flows directly out of spirituality and "unmasks" pseudo-spiritualities, which preach a love of God disconnected from a true love of neighbor. No self-proclaimed Christian can read Matthew 25:31–46, the parable of the sheep and the goats, without some trepidation. In that parable of the Day of Judgment, Jesus tells his followers that eternal happiness will be given to those who care for him by caring for the poor. On the other hand, eternal damnation will be given to those who failed to care for him by failing to care for the poor. Jesus says nothing about adhering to religious beliefs, praying regularly, or taking time for meditation. Religious belief and devotion surely has its place, but it is worthless without love of neighbor.

The Play Like a Champion approach reminds coaches that their ministry to children involves fostering children's moral and spiritual development. Children are not miniature adults. They are growing as persons made in the image and likeness of God. Coaches are called to help children to grow by establishing a nurturing environment that meets children's needs. When coaches become self-centered or fail to take into account that children are growing and not fully mature, they introduce toxic elements in the sports environment that stunt and in some cases even distort children's development. Play Like a Champion calls its approach GROW, to emphasize that coaching youth sports is fundamentally different from coaching sports at the professional, college, or even high school level. At the youth level, which extends as early as age four to as late as the eighth grade or age fourteen, coaches need to do more than give moral direction and model moral behavior. They need to provide children with the opportunities and support necessary to persons of faith and responsible moral agents.

CHARACTER EDUCATION: A FLAWED MODEL?

There is little solid research evidence that demonstrates that sports foster character development. In fact, despite popular belief that sports teach values, some research suggests that sports may undermine character development.[3] Perhaps the general public harbors some skepticism about the character-building potential of sports as well. How else might we explain the popularity of Heywood Broun's line (often attributed to John Wooden), "Sports do not build character, they reveal it"? Although, it is certainly true that sports reveal character (or the lack of it), those of us who have played and coached know that sports influence character in different and complex ways.

Whenever we give a Play Like a Champion Today workshop to coaches of Catholic-sponsored sports teams, we ask early on, "Do you think sports build character?" Not surprisingly, coaches resoundingly answer "yes." When we inquire into what they mean by character, they invariably list virtues such as hard work, perseverance, and courage. These are virtues that have to do with achievement. Coaches far less frequently mention social virtues, such as friendship, teamwork, and cooperation, although they sometimes bring up selfishness as a problem. Rarely do coaches refer to fairness or sportsmanship without prompting.

Coaches witness incidents of unsportsmanlike conduct and unfair play all the time, but they usually think that the best way to respond to such incidents is through good officiating or personally reprimanding players when they get out of hand. They rarely, if ever, talk about the need to teach their players about morality. When it comes to matters of good sportsmanship and justice, coaches seem to focus more on responding to incidents of undesirable behavior than on cultivating virtues or moral judgment.

Perhaps coaches implicitly believe that character is "caught" not "taught." Character educators typically note that setting a good example or being a good role model is the best way to teach character. Unfortunately, research conducted at Notre Dame indicates that many youth sport coaches give children a "bad example."[4] Over one quarter of children between the sixth and eighth grades reported that their coaches encouraged retaliation after an opponent's dirty play, angrily argued with a referee, angrily yelled at a player for making a mistake, and bad-mouthed an opponent during their most recent sports season. Imagine what these children witnessed over the course of several sports seasons!

If children learn simply through imitating role models, our children would clearly be in bad shape. Not only do children witness coaches misbehaving, but also their parents. The same research study reveals that spectator behavior is even worse than coach behavior.[5] Approximately 40 percent of the children in the sample report that fans teased them and fellow players and were embarrassed by the behavior of a fan. Over two-thirds of the children report seeing fans angrily yell at an official. Given that this study focused only on the previous sport season, we can only imagine what youth sports subject children to over several seasons and several years.

THE ROLE OF AUTHORITY

Fortunately, research on child development demonstrates that children are not sponges who soak up whatever they experience.[6] Children bring a moral awareness to their sports experiences, and they know when adults are behaving well or poorly. Children know that it is wrong to yell at someone for making a mistake, whether that person is a child or a referee. They also know that it is wrong to tease or humiliate another person. For example, during a Little League baseball game, with the bases loaded, a ball was well hit to left field. The left-fielder caught the ball on one hop and tried to make a long throw directly to the plate. The ball bounced off the roof of the dugout and caromed out past the pitcher's mound as the runners rounded the bases. When the chaos ended, three runs had scored and the batter was on third. Mr. Cooper, the manager of the fielding team, was beside himself. Fuming, he waddled out of the dugout past the pitcher's mound screaming at the left-fielder while jabbing his index finger into his temple, "What were you thinking?" "How many times have

I told you to hit the cut-off man?" The center-fielder, Jimmy, the oldest on the team at age nine, yelled back, "Lay off, coach, he is only seven years old." Mr. Cooper just glared at Jimmy, until the inning ended. Waiting until Jimmy took a seat on the bench, Mr. Cooper confronted him, "You are done for the afternoon, Jimmy; and don't you ever talk back to a coach again, do you understand?"

Chastened, Jimmy learned a tough lesson that day. His coach could say whatever he wanted even if he was being unkind, but Jimmy was to keep his mouth shut, even if he was standing up for a "little kid." Children know that belittling another person is wrong and that adults, who are bigger and stronger than children, ought to know better. Children do not need adults to point out right from wrong. They do not need adults to preach to them. They do need adults to listen to them and to guide their understanding. We have all had our "Mr. Cooper moments" of losing our temper when athletes, even seven-year-olds, make mistakes. Rather than setting ourselves up to be models of perfection, we would be better moral educators if we opened ourselves up to criticism, even from a child. After all, adults frequently complain about children acting like they are "know-it-alls" and not taking correction. Mr. Cooper no doubt felt threatened by Jimmy's "talking back." Perhaps Jimmy could have handled the situation in a more sensitive and respectful way. Yet Jimmy had a point, which Mr. Cooper failed to understand or acknowledge.

Mr. Cooper failed to be a moral educator in this situation not because he did not want to assume the role of being a moral educator, but because he misunderstood what being a moral educator means. His authority as the manager of the team interfered with his effectiveness as a teacher. Mr. Cooper put obedience and compliance ahead of fairness. He discouraged Jimmy from thinking on his own about what was right and from acting responsibly.

WHAT IS CHARACTER?

Our experience in working with over 40,000 coaches now at both the youth and high school levels has taught us that before we undertake the enterprise of character education, we have to pay attention to what we mean by the term character. In his very helpful book, *Positive Coaching: Building Character and Self-Esteem through Sports,* Jim Thompson describes character as made up of the following traits in the following order: (1) mental toughness, (2) having fun, (3) winning and losing with class, (4) courage, (5) setting and committing to goals (defined in terms of sports skills), and (6) effort and determination.[7] Like the majority of the coaches who attend our workshops, Thompson tends to equate character with the achievement side of sports. The only social or moral virtue that he mentions is "class." Thompson notes that playing with class means displaying sportsmanship and refusing to cheat to win. Why call this playing with class? When we speak of a person showing class, we mean that that person displays elegance or style. There are social class connotations to this. Playing with class demonstrates a kind of nobility. A person without class is a person of lesser rank or worth.

The appeal to "class" as a motive for playing fairly and as a good sport goes back to the ancient Greeks. Aristotle, for example, uses the word *kalos* with reference to virtue and character. *Kalos* connotes beauty, high social standing, and being upright. A difficulty with the term "class" is that it is directed toward the outer more than the inner and invites social comparison (those who have "class" are superior to those who do not). Although we applaud Thompson's inclusion of moral content into his list of character traits, his inclusion of moral content within the frame of "class" is at best a limited one.

Does Michael Josephson do any better when he subsumes morality and sportsmanship under the rubric of honor? His Character Counts Sports Program has as its motto "Victory with Honor." The connection between honor and virtue also goes back to the Greeks. To be a person of honor is to be judged by others as having admirable qualities. Honor, like class, is based on a judgment of one's worth. Honor like class is displayed. To be concerned about class and honor is to be concerned with one's social standing.

Thompson and Josephson make an important contribution to character education by trying to establish a connection between actions and self-worth. In sports, we typically earn worth by winning and achieving. Clearly children need to learn that playing with respect and fairness is valued as well. Yet is the respect to be earned through effort and high achievement the same kind of respect to be earned by practicing sportsmanship?

CHARACTER AND CONDUCT

What sense do we make of the highly publicized college soccer game, in which New Mexico junior Elizabeth Lambert kicked, punched, and even pulled a BYU player to the ground by her ponytail? Cameras caught it all, and even though Lambert received only a yellow card, she was suspended for the game. Later the University of New Mexico suspended her indefinitely. Predictably Lambert apologized. She excused her bad behavior as due to the intensity of game: "I let my emotions get the best of me in a heated situation. This is in no way indicative of my character or the soccer player I am."

Lambert did not just blow up once. She played recklessly throughout the game and could well have caused a serious injury. On at least two occasions, however, she was clearly retaliating. Once, she struck back after being elbowed in the chest. She yanked her opponent down by the ponytail after being grabbed in the crotch. Although she may well have been provoked, we may still judge Lambert's rough play to be a violation of what Thompson calls "class" and Josephson calls "honor." Some believe, however, that such a criticism may reflect gender bias. Lambert may not have met our standards for "ladylike behavior," but some of her defenders allege that such a judgment is gender-biased and naïve. Class and honor may reflect relative standards of respectability. Lambert's antics, some soccer fans contend, would have gone unnoticed in the men's game.

Some of Lambert's internet fans go so far as to praise her for playing aggressively and sending a strong message that neither she nor her teammates would be taken advantage of. Her bio allegedly says that she "is fearless when making a challenge." Perhaps Lambert was right in defending her character. Even if she did not exhibit the trait of winning with class, she appears to have exhibited all of the others. Displaying five out of six character traits does not appear too bad.

In our view, Lambert's refusal to admit that her dirty and dangerous play reflected poorly on her character reveals the weakness of conventional approaches to character education. These approaches break character down into a set of discrete, socially desirable traits or virtues with no serious attempt to prioritize among them. For example, Thompson puts "winning and losing with class" in the middle of his list. Although Thompson puts "class" ahead of "winning," he does not put it ahead of the virtues that contribute to winning, such as effort and mental toughness. Moreover, as we have pointed out, subsuming the moral virtues under the label of "playing with class" seems to imply that morality is a matter of meeting social expectations. If that is all that morality is, then Lambert should be puzzled by those who accused her of having bad character. She was a first team all-conference player in her junior year of high school and a Who's Who Scholar Athlete. She was even praised for her "aggressiveness" as a defender in her sophomore year of college. In other words, Lambert has been singled out for praise through her achievements in soccer and the classroom. When did she first learn to play dirty? What kind of feedback did she receive from her coaches, teammates, and fans over her rough play? Why was no fuss made until the media turned Lambert's play into a sideshow? Why was Lambert singled out for punishment?

In our view, Lambert was the victim of a flawed approach to character education. That approach not only blurred the distinction between achievement and morality but also put the emphasis on achievement and social acceptance. Lambert did all that she was asked to do and won accolades along the way. No one took responsibility for addressing her style of play until there was a public outcry against her lack of class. "Class" and "honor" are uncertain guides in moral matters. They are judgments based on shifting standards of what is offensive to the public rather than on principles of fairness.

What is the relationship between morality and public opinion? Why is it that Jesus, who epitomizes the moral person for the Christian, was condemned by both the civic and religious authorities of his community? Why was Socrates, the most moral of all the moral philosophers, put to death for heresy and corrupting the youth of Athens? And why was Martin Luther King Jr. reviled for his prophetic stance toward our nation's institutionalized racism? We have to be careful not to define good character as compliance with social expectations. Such a view reduces character to upholding the *status quo*. Christians should be especially suspicious of such a definition. The Kingdom of God involves a radical transformation of the existing economic and political order. Here is what Isaiah has to say about the coming Christ in a passage read during the first week of Advent: "He humbles those in high places, and the lofty city he brings down; He tumbles it to the ground, levels it with the dust. It is trampled underfoot by the needy, by the footsteps of the poor" (Isaiah 26:5–6). To be a moral person is not to conform to social expectations but to be an agent of justice and compassion.

Instead of joining the chorus in condemning Lambert's dirty play, we should be taking a hard look at our whole approach to sports, and what we might do to change a culture that is becoming increasingly toxic. Lambert is not the problem; she is the product of a culture gone awry. Those of us working in Christian sponsored organizations ought to take a hard look at what role we might play in today's sports culture. By all accounts, we are no different from the rest. In fact, my own re-analysis of the data from the Shields, Bredemeier, and Power study suggests that athlete, coach, and spectator behavior in Catholic sports programs is worse than in public ones.[8] Perhaps we might reclaim our prophetic tradition in undertaking an approach to youth sports that puts morality first.

EDUCATING FOR MORAL DEVELOPMENT

Although most approaches to coach education highlight the values of sportsmanship and fairness, none draw directly on Kohlberg's moral development theory or moral education research.[9] As we have illustrated, conventional approaches to character education have major shortcomings. First, they do not adequately distinguish moral from achievement virtues. Second, they confuse morality with social acceptance. Third, they mistakenly assume that children are passive receptacles of moral instruction and not active moral agents with developing notions of right and wrong. Even preschool children will declare,

"It's not fair," when they think that they are getting the short end of the stick. As Damon showed, children's views of fairness have their shortcomings but develop as children understand that morality means considering perspectives in addition to their own.[10] Damon also found that even preschool children understand that moral claims cannot simply be asserted but must be justified with reasons that others would find compelling. The "Einstein" of contemporary child psychology, Jean Piaget, claimed that children develop their morality not by internalizing the morality given to them by their parents and other significant adults but by constructing their own morality through cooperating with each other.[11] Studying how children at different ages mastered the rules of popular games, Piaget found that children developed from an early phase of mechanically imitating the actions of older peers to modifying and even making up their own rules.

Notice how young children play board games. They enjoy rolling the dice, moving their pieces around the board, and reaching the goal of the game, but they have no understanding of the rules or of the competitive strategies that make the game fun. Young children play sports in the same way. They have fun kicking the ball in soccer or running after hitting the baseball, but have no idea of what the rules are and why the rules are even important. By the time they get into middle school, children not only know the basic rules and strategies of the sport they play, but they devise their own ingenious rules and strategies. For example, look at how children play wiffle ball in the backyard. Some of the younger children may get an extra strike and help running the bases. There will likely be an elaborate set of "ground rules," such as a ball hit into the neighbor's rose garden is an automatic out, a ball hit over the garage roof is a home run, and a ball that lands in the gutter over the porch roof is a ground-rule double (provided someone can retrieve it). Piaget found that by the time they reach twelve, children with a lot of experience playing a game become highly developed democratic legislators. They are as capable as any adult of modifying rules or making up new ones to make their games more fair and fun. He also found that they did not need the help of adults to do this. In fact, Piaget claimed that adults tended to get in the way of children's moral development because adults invariably acted as bosses who expected to be obeyed. When adults take the role of authorities, children are no longer expected to think for themselves and solve their own problems. Adults create what Piaget called a moral climate of "constraint." On the other hand, when the children are by themselves, they establish a morality of cooperation.

The world of organized youth sport promotes this morality of constraint. Instead of letting children choose teams, assign positions, set up rules, work out strategies, and do their own officiating, adults do it all for them. When adults take control of youth sport, Piaget would say that they rob sports of their educational potential. Children do not learn the sport as well, and they are blocked from having the democratic experiences that would foster their moral development.

In the Play Like a Champion clinics, we address the problem of the adult domination of youth sport in several ways. We start by noting that adult domination transforms play into work. Play starts from the heart and is self-directed. Adults can facilitate children's play and even play with children, but when adults try to rule children's play, they ruin it. We then identify three areas in which adult facilitation can be genuinely helpful. These areas make up the GROW approach discussed by Sheehan in chapter 9. First, coaches can help children to define personal and group goals and to derive confidence and esteem as they progress toward those goals. Second, coaches can help children to develop their relationships with one another and with the team as a whole. Third, coaches can assure that children experience a sense of ownership of their "play" by asking for their input and by making decisions in democratic team meetings. As we noted earlier, without ownership, there is no play. We try to extend that insight further by helping coaches to understand that without ownership there can be no genuine motivation or moral development. Moral development requires conscience and agency.

BROADENING THE CONSTRUCT OF MORAL DEVELOPMENT

The GROW approach draws on a number of theories in developmental psychology and ethics. The pioneering contributions of Gilligan[12] and Noddings,[13] among other feminist ethicists, to an ethic of care have had an important influence on how Play Like a Champion instructs coaches to guide athletes in their relationships with teammates and opponents. Although philosophers, psychologists, and educators provide different perspectives, all see care as a selfless concern for the well-being of another. In her early work, Gilligan presented care and justice as distinctive moral orientations and criticized Kohlberg's stage theory as biased toward a male justice orientation.[14] Research evidence, however, has not supported her criticism.[15] Care and justice are not distinctive female and male virtues but interrelated human virtues. Nevertheless, Gilligan's articulation of psychological dynamics of care and responsibility in the moral life led Kohlberg and others to develop a fuller and more nuanced description of moral functioning with an emphasis on the relationship of the self to the other.[16] Although Title IX has led to a dramatic increase in girls' participation in sports at all levels, sexist and homophobic attitudes unabashedly predominate in sports. Such attitudes are especially harmful for children and adolescents who are developing their gender identities. As the Lambert example shows, the emphasis given to the "manly" virtues, which focus on strength and dominance, obscures and often undercuts the importance of care and responsibility.

James Fowler's research on faith development provides another significant resource for the way in which we approach moral education in sports.[17] Fowler helps us to recognize that the shared meaning and values conveyed through significant others, especially coaches and parents, mediate an abiding sense of trust in others and hope for the future. For Fowler, faith is an implicit knowing that underlies all human activity. Like all kinds of knowing, faith develops and requires a nurturing environment to support that development. Faith has particular relevance to sports insofar as sports are play. As Kelly points out in his introduction to this volume and in chapter 7, play expresses human freedom, transcendence, and solidarity. When children play sports like soccer and basketball, they connect not only with their teammates and opponents but with a wider, intergenerational, and international community of athletes and fans. Through participation in sports, they experience the fleeting but exquisite exhilaration of victory as well as the crushing and often devastating blow of defeat. Sports confront children with the never-ending cycling of life, death, and resurrection. Coaches, parents, and friends can help children not only to cope with the challenges of everyday life but also to develop a deep sense of hope and trust in the ultimate goodness of creation and the promise of the future. The simple phrase "Play Like a Champion Today" is an exhortation rooted in faith. It has a clear moral dimension because playing like a champion means playing to the best of one's ability as a caring teammate, a fair opponent, and a responsible leader. The exhortation has an important temporal dimension. Play Like a Champion Today expresses a faith in the importance of the now or *kairos*. It means that we must take a God-like perspective on our activity and focus not on our past failures and successes but on what we are about to do.

YOUTH SPORT COACHES AS MORAL EDUCATORS: POSSIBILITIES AND CHALLENGES

Although character education approaches have been proliferating in classrooms and sports fields, we continue to have precious little information about their success in fostering meaningful moral development. Moral and character education literature going back to early moral discussion studies led by Colby, Kohlberg, Fenton, Speicher-Dubin, and Lieberman[18] to the present, such as that by Selman,[19] indicates that the effectiveness of any moral education program, no matter how well designed, depends on the competence of those who teach it. Teachers play an important role in any educational program, but because of the interactive nature of moral education, their expertise is indispensable. What is the nature of such expertise and how can it be acquired? How successful have we been in preparing coaches, or teachers for that matter, as moral educators? Although we do not as yet have satisfactory answers to these questions, we have reason to be cautious about the effectiveness of coach education.

For example, in the "Stone Study" undertaken by Colby, Kohlberg, Fenton, Speicher-Dubin, and Lieberman, only half of the social studies teachers trained to lead moral discussions actually employed the methods that they were taught.[20] Even more disappointing was the finding that a year after the end of the research study, only a handful of the teachers continued to use the moral discussion approach in their classes. In the thirty years since this study, we have, I believe, made some progress in addressing the failures of the Stone Study. Those of us in the field of education are far more aware today than ever before that "teacher-proof" curricula are a fiction. We are also aware that coaches and teachers come to moral education with their own set of assumptions about how children learn to become moral. We cannot help anyone to become an effective moral educator without meeting them where they are and inviting them into a long journey of self-examination and personal growth.

As Sheehan notes in her chapter in this volume, we place a special emphasis on the role of the coach as a minister in the Play Like a Champion workshops. Coach-ministers are to serve children by being child-centered. That means most basically that they should put their athletes' enjoyment and growth ahead of their own interests. The role of coach-minister is counter-cultural in the world of contemporary youth sports. Few, if any, observers of youth sport today would deny that youth sports leagues from about age seven on up are dominated by adult-centered coaches and parents, who with little reflection or inhibition turn what should be children's play into their own. As we noted in our discussion of Piaget's research, once children lose control of their own play, they lose not only enjoyment but a precious opportunity for social and moral development. Once a morality of constraint takes the place of a morality of cooperation, children become like Jimmy in our example. They tune out morally and comply in order to please the coach.

The coach-minister approach aims at recapturing sports as play and, in the process, to foster a morality of cooperation. The approach is based on the insight at the core of Piaget's cognitive developmental theory that children actively construct knowledge through interaction with their environment. Coaches should promote children's moral development by respecting their freedom and active intelligence. In this way, coach-ministers treat children as made in the image and likeness of God. The conventional character education approach, employed in most coach training programs, emphasizes the role of the coach, who is to teach through direct instruction (e.g., by using trait or virtue labels) and by role modeling. This approach assumes that children are passive receptacles of adult wisdom. Jimmy's comment to his coach illustrates that the opposite is the case. Research now shows that children can and do make moral judgments beginning in toddlerhood. The task of moral educators, whether they are parents, teachers, or coaches is to establish a moral atmosphere conducive to children's development. Such an atmosphere provides children with ample opportunities to grapple with age-appropriate moral problems and encourages children to relate to one another in ways that are fair and caring. Coaches need to realize that children are endowed with a natural desire for justice. It is far more effective for coaches to encourage children to discover moral ideals than to tell children how to behave.

EQUAL PLAYING TIME: A FOUNDATIONAL PRINCIPLE?

The coach's role as a moral educator is thus to create a moral environment that encourages children to be moral. The first step in creating such an environment is to guarantee all children equal playing time. In our view, this is simply a matter of justice. All children have a right to play. The fact that organized sports have taken the place of the pickup game places an extra burden on adults to assure that organized sports are really play experiences for all of the children. Sometimes adults lose sight of the fact that play is good for children. Play brings children happiness and helps children to develop socially and morally. Playing sports gives children an invaluable opportunity for exercise. It also introduces them to an important part of their culture. As we have argued in this chapter, playing sports in the right environment can promote character development.

We acknowledge that the principle of equal playing time applies principally to sports through the eighth grade. Distributing playing time becomes more complicated in high school and college. At higher levels, however, we still have an obligation to assure that all adolescents who want to play sports have the opportunity to do so. We have focused far too many resources on elite and varsity sports and not enough on "recreational leagues" open to all. We see no moral problem in sorting children and adolescents into different levels of competition as long as the opportunities for play are equal for all. Unfortunately, too many children are sitting on the bench, cut, or discouraged from playing sports at an early age.

Our research shows that the vast majority of coaches believe that playing time should be distributed equally through the eighth grade. Unfortunately, however, prior to adopting the Play Like a Champion program most Catholic-sponsored youth sports programs have not had strong playing-time rules. Opposition to equal playing time, albeit in the minority, is fierce. Although most national coach education programs recommend equal playing time, none insist upon it. We decided that we could not be true to our mission if we could not stand firm on such a basic issue. Equal playing time is the first principle of justice in youth sports because children have a right to play. No child should be denied an opportunity to play because of a lack of ability or effort.

As we noted, equal playing time is a matter of justice, not charity. There is nothing particularly kind or generous about giving children what is their due. Programs that call themselves Christian have a special obligation to be just. Jesus went out of his way to welcome children into his company and to urge his followers to do the same. Some coaches and athletic administrators try to justify unequal playing time as educational. For example, we often hear that children need to learn that they live in a competitive world and that inequality is a fact of life. Getting cut from a team or sitting on a bench toughen children up and teach them life lessons about the importance of hard work and accepting disappointment. Although we agree that children need to learn about the importance of hard work and how to cope with their limitations, we fail to see the relevance of this as an argument for denying children an irreplaceable opportunity to play. Children face enough disappointment and hurt in their lives without having adults create an environment that adds to their burdens. Play time is meant to be a relief from the cares of the world. This is true for adults as well as children.

But some coaches object that it is not fair for children who come late to practice or just don't work hard in practice to be given the same playing time as those who show up on time every day and give their all. These coaches are saying that playing time is to be earned—not necessarily by being the best but by putting forth the best effort. The converse of this is also true. Sitting on the bench is an appropriate punishment for a lack of preparation. At first glance, using playing time as a reward and punishment seems both fair and a good teaching method. No one can dispute that children need to learn the importance of practicing and always trying their hardest. But parents or guardians are responsible for getting their middle and elementary school children to practices and games on time. Effort is different. Effort appears to be a virtue-like quality that children acquire. In other words, effort is something that children learn. Is it fair for a coach or teacher to punish a child for lacking a competence that she or he has yet to master? Many children who fool around in practice or fail to listen to the coach may simply be acting as children or may suffer from a learning disability or attention deficit disorder, which affects an estimated 3 to 5 percent of all children. It is the coach's responsibility to help children to learn how to focus and to try their hardest. Simply demanding effort and then using playing time as a sanction are not responsible teaching methods. Children need to discover through their experience the value of effort. They can get that experience in game situations as well as practice. The coach's role is to help to shape children's experience so that they are encouraged to try their hardest.

As we noted earlier, from a moral point of view, children have a right to play. That right is not contingent upon ability or effort. Why guarantee equal playing time at the youth sport level? There is substantial evidence that the youth sport experience done well offers children a number of very important benefits. Sports offer much needed physical exercise, especially at a time when child obesity is at an all-time high, having more than doubled since 1980 to 18.0 percent in 2012.[21] Obese children are likely to become obese adults, who are at risk for a number of serious health problems, including heart disease and cancer. Quality sports programs also provide significant social, moral, and spiritual benefits, which is the point of this volume. On top of it all, sports are sheer fun, and what adult has a right to deprive children of fun?

Some athletic administrators and coaches complain that although they personally agree with the principle of equal playing time, they face impossible opposition from their athletic associations. Our research indicates that this perception is completely unfounded. Prior to our workshop, only 18 percent of the coach-participants indicate that they are opposed to or unsure about giving equal playing time. After our workshop, that percentage is down to 6 percent. The percentage of coaches strongly agreeing with giving equal playing time goes up from 48 percent before the workshop to 66 percent afterward. One of the main purposes of our workshop is to dispel what social psychologists call "pluralistic ignorance." This is a situation in which the majority of those in a group privately agree with a value but mistakenly assume that most others disagree with them. The only way to dispel pluralistic ignorance is to discuss one's private beliefs with others. This is the point of undertaking coach education through interactive workshops.

Preparing coaches to become moral educators requires at the very minimum that coaches enter into a process of open dialogue on concrete value issues of real import. Playing time has been the single most controversial and vexing issue in youth sports. Coaches need to be able to talk through their differences with a common concern for fairness. Coach education must begin with the coach but not end with the coach. Coaches need to learn how to participate in moral discussions in order to be able to lead moral discussions among their athletes. The model we use for coach education must mirror the model we teach coaches to apply to children.

THE MORAL DISCUSSION MODEL

Conventional approaches to character education assume that coaches are moral authorities who instruct children in the virtues. The developmental approach that we take treats coaches as moral seekers who pursue justice in dialogue with others. Although we hold strong moral positions ourselves, we try in our workshops to create an environment in which we welcome all points of view. Welcoming all opinions does not mean that we believe that all have equal value. Discussion serves to unmask weakness and raise new ideas for consideration. As coaches come to appreciate how discussions can foster their own moral growth, they become more committed to leading discussions with their teams. In this way, we address the problem that surfaced in the Stone Study when social studies teachers lost motivation for using the moral discussion approach once the research project had ended.

Becoming an effective moral discussion leader takes considerable practice. We use our basic coach workshop to help coaches understand why moral discussion is a better way to promote moral development than didactic moral teaching. In our follow-up workshops, we help coaches to develop their skills in asking probing questions and getting all members of the team involved. In introducing strategies of moral education to coaches, we give them an overview of the stages of moral judgment.[22] This serves two purposes. First, it makes clear that moral development entails more than obedience, conformity, and social acceptance. At the highest stages, moral development involves universal principles of respect for persons and justice. Second, the stages demonstrate that an overemphasis on conformity and punishment and rewards confirms children in immature moral stages rather than challenging them to moral growth.

We next give coaches a moral problem to resolve. This is one we have used with both coaches and athletes at the high school level:

Sue, a transfer student, is outplaying Mary (a two-year starter) in practice. Coach announces that Mary will be starting the first game. Sue is outraged, calls Mary a terrible player, accuses the coach of playing favorites, and threatens to quit. The players want Sue off the team. What should the coach do and why?

Coaches typically pick up on two problems. First, Sue has challenged her coach's authority. The coach is faced with a choice of expelling Sue from the team or finding some way for her to redeem herself. Second, the players on the team are trying to force the coach's hand in calling for Sue's ouster. Some coaches resent being pressured in this way. What values other than the coach's authority are at stake here? The coach clearly has an obligation to be fair in deciding on starters. The coach also seems to have an obligation to communicate why she or he has decided on a particular lineup. Sue's expectations seem understandable. But coaches may have lots of reasons for starting a veteran over a rookie player. In chapter 9, Sheehan notes that, from a spiritual point of view, this dilemma involves the value of forgiveness. In our experience, coaches and players never mention forgiveness as a value, even when we ask them whether the fact that Sue was on a Catholic-sponsored team should make a difference.

Why forgive in this situation? Coaches and players alike readily take note of the fact that Sue is new to the team and that the coach's method of communication was insensitive. With some probing, they begin to see that the problem extends beyond Sue or the coach. The team itself appears to have let Sue down by sticking up for Mary, a popular teammate, and not reaching out to Sue, the transfer. In seeing the value of forgiving Sue, coaches and players see the need for the coach and team to ask forgiveness from Sue. Forgiveness is important on both the moral and spiritual levels. It is a gift of God, which enables us to put our personal hurts and insecurities behind us to focus on what the other needs. It is also a moral requirement, a way of respecting the dignity of the other person and taking moral responsibility for our own moral shortcomings.

As coaches work through this problem themselves, they see the value of having their players work through similar situations. They also come to see that the only way a coach can adequately respond to such a situation and keep it from recurring is to work with players to build a sense of team. "Ownership" of the problem and the solution must rest with the team as a whole, players as well as coaches.

Note that the kind of moral education that we are advocating is democratic at its roots. We are asking coaches to help players to become good team members or good citizens of the team by taking on legislative responsibility. The idea that moral education ought to be democratic may seem threatening at first because sports have become so autocratic. Hopefully, coach-ministers will be child-centered and humble enough to surrender their personal needs for power and status in order to meet the developmental needs of their players.

Youth sport is a fundamentally moral as well as spiritual activity. In fact, within the Christian tradition, all that is spiritual is moral and vice versa. Coaches have a responsibility to respect children's right to play sports as well as to assure that children's sports experience nurtures their souls. We cannot assume that sports automatically foster moral development. The Play Like a Champion approach provides a model to help coaches to be effective educators.

NOTES

1. David Shields, Brenda Bredemeier, Nicole LaVoi, and Clark Power, "The Sport Behavior of Youth, Parents, and Coaches: The Good, the Bad, and the Ugly," *Journal of Research on Character Education* 3 (2005): 43–59.

2. Dorotheus of Gaza (1997), *Instructions 4*, quoted in Taize, *A Letter from Calcutta*, p. 4, available at http://www.taize.fr/en_article5234.html.

3. Maria Kavussanu, "Morality in Sport," in *Social Psychology in Sport*, ed. S. Jowett and D. E. Lavallee, 265–78 (Champaign IL: Human Kinetics, 2007); David Shields, Brenda Bredemeier, and Clark Power, "Character Development and Children's Sport," in *Children and Youth Sport: A Biopsychosocial Perspective*, 2nd ed., ed. F. Smoll and R. Smith, 537–59 (Indianapolis: Brown & Benchmark, 2001).

4. Shields et al., "The Sport Behavior of Youth, Parents, and Coaches."

5. Ibid.

6. James Fowler, *Stages of Faith* (New York: Harper & Row, 1981); Lawrence Kohlberg, *Essays on Moral Development*, vol. 1, *The Philosophy of Moral Development*, and vol. 2, *The Psychology of Moral Development* (New York: Harper and Row, 1981 and 1984); and Jean Piaget, *The Moral Judgment of the Child*, trans. Marjorie Gabain (London: Free Press, 1965).

7. Jim Thompson, *Positive Coaching: Building Character and Self-Esteem through Sports* (Portola Valley, CA: Warde Publishers, 1995), 113–20.

8. Shields et al., "The Sport Behavior of Youth, Parents, and Coaches."

9. Kohlberg, *Essays on Moral Development*, vol. 1, and Clark Power, Ann Higgins, and Lawrence Kohlberg, *Lawrence Kohlberg's Approach to Moral Education* (New York: Columbia University Press, 1989).

10. William Damon, *The Moral Child* (New York: The Free Press, 1990).

11. Piaget, *The Moral Judgment of the Child.*

12. Carol Gilligan, *In a Different Voice: Psychological Theory and Women's Development* (Cambridge, MA: Harvard University Press, 1982).

13. Nel Noddings, *Caring: A Feminine Approach to Ethics and Moral Education* (Berkeley: University of California Press, 1984).

14. Gilligan, *In a Different Voice.*

15. Nancy A. Clopton and Gwendolyn T. Sorell, "Gender Differences in Moral Reasoning: Stable or Situational," *Psychology of Women Quarterly* 17 (1993): 85–101; Lawrence J. Walker, "Sex Differences in the Development of Moral Reasoning: A Critical Review," *Child Development* 55 (1984): 677–91.

16. Power, Higgins, and Kohlberg, *Lawrence Kohlberg's Approach.*

17. Fowler, *Stages of Faith.*

18. Anne Colby, Lawrence Kohlberg, Theodore Fenton, Betsy Speicher-Dubin, and Mark Lieberman, "Secondary School Moral Discussion Programs Led by Social Studies Teachers," *Journal of Moral Education* 6 (1977): 90–111.

19. Robert Selman, *The Promotion of Social Awareness: Powerful Lessons from the Partnership of Developmental Theory and Classroom Practice* (New York: Russell Sage, 2007).

20. Colby et al., "Secondary School Moral Discussion."

21. Data taken from web site of the Centers for Disease Control and Prevention; see http://www.cdc.gov/healthyyouth/obesity/facts.htm.

22. Anne Colby, Lawrence Kohlberg, Betsy Speicher, Alexandra Hewer, John Gibbs, and Clark Power, *The Measurement of Moral Judgment*, vol. 1, *Theoretical Foundations and Research Validation* (New York: Cambridge University Press, 1987).

CHAPTER 6

Reclaiming Competition in Youth Sports

DAVID LIGHT SHIELDS AND

BRENDA LIGHT BREDEMEIER

Sports are often lauded for their potential to promote teamwork, dedication, commitment, optimism, perseverance, tough-mindedness, and numerous other positive qualities. For example, Pope John Paul II saw a connection between sports and Christian faith. Noting that sports call for such values as loyalty, fair play, generosity, solidarity, and respect, he asked rhetorically, "Are not these athletic values the deepest aspirations and requirements of the Christian message?"[1]

But sports can also be vicious and ugly. They can bring out our worst tendencies. In sport contests, we often think and act egocentrically. Sometimes, we cheat. We may even become violently aggressive and seek to elevate ourselves by dominating others.

Sports are a form of contest. They embody and celebrate competition. For those who want to promote character, this is an essential feature of the sport experience that must be faced squarely. If we are to embrace sports as a venue for positive youth development, then we need to come to terms with the meaning, nature, and consequences of competition.

In this chapter, we hope to show that the very term "competition" contains within itself both a dangerous and a redemptive memory. It is a dangerous memory because it is subversive of much of our current way of organizing and practicing sports. But it is also a redemptive memory because it can open us to a new, life-giving paradigm. When sports reclaim this memory of what competition is all about, they can provide experiential touchstones for a rich and vital character-affirming practice imbued with such values as love, freedom, justice, and compassion.

Before we try to reclaim competition, however, we need to first be honest about the extent of the problems associated with it. In this chapter, we can offer only a tiny sampling. We begin with Jake.

CONFRONTING THE PROBLEM

Jake sat down gloomily on the bench. Sure, he had made a mistake. But when his coach ripped him up one side and down the other in front of the entire squad, Jake's spirit began to shrivel. His love of the game melted under the heat of his embarrassment and anger.

Coach Ryan saw it differently. From his perspective, he was just toughening Jake up and helping him to focus. He saw Jake's error— starting to run up-field before he had full control of the passed ball— as a careless mental mistake. And it had cost Maryville High a critical first down in the homecoming game.

Coach Ryan isn't a tenured faculty member. As he sees it, his job requires producing winning teams. This does not prevent him from caring about his players, of course. He's a tough yet compassionate man who wants his athletes to succeed in all aspects of life. But his no nonsense, command-and-control coaching style has deep roots in both job insecurity and an unquestioned belief that the driving goal of competition is to win.

Coach Ryan is not alone. Nor is Jake the only victim. Consider the following situations drawn from our field notes (names changed):

- Whenever a player makes an obvious mistake, Coach Cox yells, "Oh come on. Stop playing like a girl." Coach Cox works with a six and under T-ball team.
- Mr. Jordan, a middle-school soccer coach, fires up his squad by telling his players to imagine that their opponents are guilty of raping their sister or girlfriend.
- Coach Thomas loves to preach good sport behavior, except, of course, when he is screaming at the officials.
- Coach Jenkins instructs her players on how to "hold" opposing players without getting caught by the officials.

Not all problems in sport competition are as glaring as these, of course. But across the country, sport programs are often, to use a metaphor, carriers of a dangerous virus. Frequently, it remains dormant and goes undetected. Occasionally, however, it erupts into cheating or violence or disrespectful behavior.

Take one random week in February 2009. Following a basketball game at a Brodheadsville, Pennsylvania, school, a melee broke out that sent two security guards to the hospital and led to riot charges against several students. The competition "virus" erupted again two days later in Denver, Colorado, when students at Mullen High School chanted racial slurs against the visiting Overland High basketball team. That same week, a team of sixteen- and seventeen-year-old rural Saskatchewan hockey players completed their season in first place; still, they were called "pussies" by opponents. Why? Because they finished their year without a single major infraction.

Are these just isolated incidents? That's the refrain that sport enthusiasts repeat endlessly. But the research suggests otherwise. For example, in one major survey of youth sport coaches, parents, and participants it was found that 9 percent of the youth self-reported cheating in their most recent sport season, 13 percent acknowledged trying to hurt an opponent, and 31 percent said that they had argued with an official. In the same survey, 13 percent of parents said that they had angrily criticized their own child following a sport event.[2]

The data from coaches also revealed significant problems: 7 percent acknowledged having taught their young athletes how to break a rule without being detected; 42 percent admitted having angrily

yelled at an official; 36 percent said that they had angrily yelled at one
of their players; and 8 percent acknowledged that they had made fun
of someone on the team. These disturbing statistics, moreover, are
likely to significantly underreport the problems, based as they are on
self-report data.

IS COMPETITION THE CULPRIT?

Pope John Paul II's optimism regarding sport competition stands in
stark contrast to the opinions of most social scientists. Social scientists
have long been interested in competition, and there is now a complex
and multidisciplinary literature on the topic.[3] While economists generally laud market competition, contrasting it to the deleterious effects of monopoly, psychologists and sociologists have found that
placing people in competition often results in bringing out dysfunc-
tional and hostile tendencies.

In his provocative and influential book *No Contest: The Case
against Competition*, Alfie Kohn summarized a century of research
on competition and concluded that competition is problematic from
at least three perspectives. First, it is bad from a *practical* standpoint
because it really doesn't, contrary to popular belief, lead to improved
performance or productivity. Whether we are considering the *quantity* of work, or the *quality* of what is produced, competition is less
beneficial than either cooperative or independent work arrangements.

More than that, competition is often harmful from a *psychological* standpoint. Competition typically leads to heightened anxiety,
chronic stress, lowered self-esteem, dependence on external evaluation, and reliance on performance-based standards of personal worth.
For some individuals, devastating feelings of humiliation and shame
persist for decades following a salient competitive failing. Platitudes
about "learning to deal with failure" miss the mark by a wide margin.

Finally, based on the research, Kohn contends that competition is
simply bad from a *moral* standpoint. Because of its win-lose structure,
competition invariably sets up antagonisms between people and, over
time, trains us to think that our own interests and well-being can be

served only at the expense of others. In short, competition links one person's happiness with another's sorrow. By repeatedly pairing my thrill of victory with your agony of defeat, competition leads us to take delight in the pain of others. Competition, by design, pits us against each other. Unfortunately, that stance of antagonism can become habitual, contouring our understanding of human relationships in profound yet subtle ways.

This isn't just the argument of some marginal social critic. Kohn's book is well documented and is based on decades of solid and reputable research. It is worth noting that the book was selected by the American Psychological Association to receive a prestigious book award, signaling that organization's appreciation of its key tenets. Despite our own enthusiasm for sports, we acknowledge that there is a great deal of truth in Kohn's position.

RECOVERING A DANGEROUS MEMORY

But here's the catch. Kohn, in our view, is not really talking about competition at all! Again, we need to come to terms with the meaning of the word "competition." The research that Kohn summarizes makes sense, but only in relation to a mistaken understanding of competition.

Part of the problem is that we have very inadequate language—a too limited vocabulary—when it comes to competition. Kohn's analysis is possible, if unfortunate, because the one word "competition" has been used to refer to two quite different, quite distinguishable, social practices. Both take place within a contest, but they are radically different ways of thinking about the contest. And what is true of one is not true of the other.

We need a new word, not to replace the word "competition," but to name what is really its polar opposite. Though it is a bit clumsy, we suggest the term "decompetition." We will return to it in a moment.

So what is true competition? The dangerous memory comes from the word's roots. The term "competition" comes from the Latin *-petere*, meaning "to strive" or "to seek," combined with the prefix *com-*, meaning "with." Thus, the original meaning of "competition" is "to strive or seek with." Notice that it is not "to strive *against*," but "to strive *with*."

What do people strive for in competition? What do they seek together? When it is true to its etymology, competition is an enjoyable quest for excellence. When we strive with our opponents in a contest, we bring out the best in each other through presenting a worthy challenge. Competition involves a contest of skills that reflects a seeking of excellence together.

Let us be clear. "Striving with" does not mean that contestants do not want to win the contest. True competitors are truly competitive. But in genuine competition, opponents appreciate that the fundamental purpose of the contest is to enable a mutual striving toward excellence.

Shortly after her retirement, Chris Evert, one of the best tennis players in history, was asked to name a match that she remembered fondly. She named a match in which she contested against Martina Navratilova. What is fascinating is that despite having the best win-loss record of any professional tennis player, the match she named was one that she lost. Why would she select such a match? The reason was this: it was because the two of them had pushed each other to the very boundaries of human performance. The fact that she happened to lose was far less important than the exhilarating experience of pushing up to the very limits of human possibility.

Problems arise, however, because this process of competition—of striving with another, of seeking excellence together—is really a fairly fragile process. It is a process that requires balancing seriousness with play, intrinsic motivations with extrinsic motivations, product orientation with process orientation. When the balance required for true competition is upset, competition can all too easily decompose or degenerate into decompetition. Competitors become decompetitors.

The prefix "de-" means "reverse of" or "opposite of." So decompetition is contesting that has devolved into something that is really the opposite of genuine competition. It is "striving against," not "striving with." It is important to recognize that decompetition is not just competition gone sour. It is a separate process with its own distinct dynamics, goals, values, and meanings. Unfortunately, our culture not only fails to make this crucial distinction, it has largely replaced competition with decompetition, all without us recognizing the change. To recognize and counter the change, we first must be able to name it.

If sports are to become vehicles that enhance character, if they are to serve excellence, ethics, and enjoyment, then we need to recover, restore, preserve, and celebrate true competition. Nowhere is this more important than at the youth sport level where children are first learning about the process of competition. We need to teach our young sport participants that competition is really a challenging and delicate process that must be actively striven for, rather than assume competition will occur automatically whenever a contest takes place.

To help us conceptualize the challenge ahead, and to assist us in tapping the dangerous and redemptive memory lodged within the word competition, it may be helpful to amplify some of the critical distinctions between genuine competition and decompetition. Table 6.1 summarizes some of these key distinctions. In the text that follows, we elaborate on them.

THE ROOT METAPHOR

Cognitive scientists have revealed that humans make sense of their experience largely through metaphorical interpretation.[4] We make sense of the abstract through use of the concrete. Without realizing it, we interpret abstract concepts and experiences through cognitive mappings drawn from concrete concepts and experiences. When, for example, we are experiencing a positive mood, we talk about being "up" rather than "down." Spatial relations are used metaphorically to map the abstract concept of mood.

What is a contest? Why do we have them? What is their purpose and meaning? In reality, contests are not self-interpreting. The purpose of a contest is not determined by its outward features or structure. Rather, contests have meaning only as we project meaning onto them. And we do that through the metaphors that we apply to them. This is the foundational idea of what we call contesting theory.[5]

Table 6.1. Competition and decompetition: A summary

	Competition	Decompetition
Deep Metaphor	Partnership	War/Battle
View of Opponent	Enabler/Partner	Enemy/Obstacle
Motivation	Love of the game (Intrinsic motivation)	Use of the game (Extrinsic motivation)
Goals	· Learning/Mastery · Pursuit of personal best	· Domination/Conquest · Pursuit of superiority
Focus	Process (Contesting)	Outcome (Winning)
Focus of Sportspersonship	Fair, respectful, safe play	Literal rule obedience (unless excused by informal norms)
View of Rules	Imperfect guides to fairness and welfare	Partially tolerated restraints
View of Officials	Contest facilitators	Opponents
Emotional Tone	· Positive emotions predominate · Play and seriousness in balance	· Negative emotions predominate · Seriousness crowds out play
Whose interests are served?	· Mutual interest · The "common good"	· Self-interest · The good of the victor
Ideal Contest	· Balanced opposition · Tension, drama, story	· Dominated contest · Certainty

Since contests derive much of their meaning from the metaphors that we bring to them, it is important to recognize and name the foundational metaphors of competition and decompetition. It is these root metaphors that animate and guide the experience of the contestants and move them to take certain actions, assume certain attitudes, and adopt certain values.[6]

Decompetition originates when the contest is interpreted through a root metaphor of a *battle* or *war*. Drawing from the war metaphor, the main goal of the decompetitor is to emerge from the battle victorious. In contrast, *partnership* is the foundational metaphor for true competition. By this metaphor, each competitor is viewed as an enabler (in the positive sense) for the other. There is a synergy that results from the mutual challenge that each competitor provides to the other. This synergy enables each competitor to reach new heights of excellence and mastery that could not be achieved in isolation. It is this underlying and animating metaphor of partnership that enables competition to be a striving "with" the opponent.

The deep metaphors of war or partnership, as we suggested above, operate largely out of awareness. Consider the war metaphor. True, some athletes and coaches explicitly think of the sport contest as a battle. Even more frequently, however, the war metaphor is a deep part of their cognitive structuring of the experience, rather than a conscious mental framework. Like a virus, it has effects even though it is often hidden below surface awareness and appearance.

The key point is that metaphors have implications. In the following sections, we elaborate on how these two root metaphors of battle and partnership differentially shape significant dimensions of the contestants' experience.

Opponents

Which root metaphor we consciously or unconsciously adopt when we enter a contest will lead us to desire different things for our opponents. Within the metaphor of partnership, I recognize that achieving my own best performance is contingent on the availability of a worthy challenge. It is my opponents who, through the challenge that they provide, enable my own best performance. Therefore, I hope that my opponents perform at their best; I hope that my opponents do well. I do not hope that they win, of course, but I do hope they play to their potential. The battle metaphor, on the other hand, has different implications. Rather than hope that my opponents perform well, I hope that they trip up. Drawing from the battle metaphor, my opponent is thought of as an enemy. At best, the opponent is simply depersonalized; at worst, vilified.

Motivation

Why do we compete? Though it is a bit of a simplification, motivations can be divided into two broad categories, intrinsic and extrinsic.[7] True competitors are motivated by a *love of the game* and by a desire to experience the intrinsic values inherent within the game. While intrinsic and extrinsic motivations are often experienced simultaneously, the true competitor draws primarily from the intrinsic motives. Competitors recognize that pitting one's skills against a well-matched opponent leads to an exhilaration and arousal that can tap deep reservoirs of physical, mental, and spiritual resources that are simply hard to summon in other ways. By spiritual resources, we simply mean responsiveness to dynamics that seem to pull us beyond ourselves, connecting us with experiences of wonder, purpose, and meaning.

In true competition, people can learn to take delight in exerting maximal effort in pursuit of a worthy objective. We compete because there is something inherently good, intrinsically valuable, about maximizing our human potential in pursuit of a goal consonant with our values.

Where there is decompetition, the primary motivation is no longer love of the game; rather, it is *use* of the game. The decompetitor is motivated by what he or she can get out of the game, whether in terms of material reward, adoration and praise, or simply feelings of superiority. Building on the underlying war metaphor, decompetitors seek to pillage the game, extracting bounty in the form of transient self-esteem, a college scholarship, peer adoration, or self-expression. In short, the true competitor is motivated primarily by the pursuit of values intrinsic to the game, while the decompetitor is motivated primarily by the pursuit of values extrinsic to the game.

Goals

Motivations and goals are closely related. But framing the distinction in terms of goals helps to deepen our understanding of the different dynamics of competition and decompetition. The goals of the competitor are multidimensional. They include the development and display of mastery and excellence, together with the experience of that host of emotions that come with strenuous play—emotions such as joy, exhilaration, excitement, and hope. These are the kinds of experiences and values that are intrinsic to sports and flow directly from a love of the game.

In contrast, decompetition is rather flat and unidimensional. It lacks texture and depth. The game is reduced to a single aim, and the decompetitor has but one ambition. The desired goal of the decompetitor is winning through domination and the reaping of whatever rewards are associated with victory. Rather than seeking to develop mastery, the decompetitor is seeking to display superiority. The hoped for emotional element is simply the thrill that comes with conquest and acquisition. The desired emotions are precisely those that are inherently experienced at the expense of others.

Focus: Process and Outcome?

One of the most critical distinctions between competition and decompetition stems from their different approaches to the relationship between the process and outcome of the contest. Is winning what matters most, or striving to win? This, of course, is an old and much debated issue. It pits one cliché against another. It pits, "It's not whether you win or lose," against, "Winning isn't everything, it's the only thing." Even though the debate is old, framing it in terms of competition and decompetition may shed new light.

Within true competition, winning and losing are required because these outcomes enable the *partnering for excellence*. Winning is significant because it enables striving to win. Yes, competitors want to win. But the desire to win is itself understood in a process mode. By this we mean that the desire to win is recognized as a driving force that brings the competitors together allowing for the experience of competitive partnership. That is, wanting to win is seen for what it can contribute to human flourishing. It is experienced as a spur, as something that can facilitate the seeking of excellence of performance and excellence of character. The primary focus is still on the process. The true competitor does not confuse the desire to win with the totality of what the game has to offer.

Within decompetition, the outcome becomes separated from the process and draws all significance to itself. In decompetition, the outcome cannibalizes the process. It becomes all that really matters. Winning is everything, just as in war. The values intrinsic to the process are casualties of the battle; they are collateral damage.

It is important to emphasize that both competitors and decompetitors can enter the game with the same intensity, focus, determination, and drive. Both want to win. But having said that, the role of winning is still distinct for the two. For competitors, winning and losing are acceptable because they enable a worthwhile process to take place. For decompetitors, the process is acceptable, the playing of the game is tolerable, because it allows for the reward of winning and the spoils that too often go with it.

Sportspersonship

It will come as no surprise that the competitor and decompetitor also have different views of sportsmanship, or *sportspersonship* to be more inclusive. Despite the popularity of the concept, it is a rather ambiguous word that means a variety of things to different people. Competitors tend to adopt a *moral view* of sportspersonship.[8]

Competitors are guided in their sport actions by the ideals of fairness, respect, and noninjurious play. Upholding the spirit of true competition, even when not required by the rules, is the core of sportspersonship. Thus, the competitor is willing to forego an advantage, even when allowed, if the advantage is viewed as unfair. Similarly, the competitor will seek to play safely, even if the rules do not cover every potential danger. In short, the competitor recognizes that competition rests on a precarious balance requiring attentiveness to the moral spirit of the game.

In contrast, decompetitors tend to adopt a *conventional* view of sportspersonship. Sportspersonship is viewed as behavior that conforms to the demands of politeness, civility, and rule obedience. The decompetitor may gladly shake hands with opponents after a game or perhaps even give a hand to help up a fallen opponent. The decompetitor may abide by the conventions of decorum present in his or her sport, and doing so is viewed as the essence of maintaining good sportspersonship. But the decompetitor does not acknowledge an important role for ethical judgment beyond the realm of convention.

Rules

For competitors, one cannot win without winning fairly. Since opponents are recognized as partners, it is taken for granted that they should have equal opportunity to succeed. But simply following the rules may not be enough. True competitors tend to view rules as essential but imperfect expressions of the ethical norms that undergird a fair and safe contest. They recognize the original intent of the rules was to create a contest such that the outcome would reflect mastery of game relevant skills and strategies, combined with a certain element of luck. Competitors focus on the spirit of the rules, rather than their letter. If a situation arises in which fairness or safety requires going beyond following the letter of the rule, the requirements of fairness and welfare take priority. In other words, when moral norms conflict with strategic game interests, the moral norms are upheld regardless of whether the rules require them to be or not.

It is a quite different case within decompetition. For decompetitors, rules are partially tolerated restraints, and circumvention of rules is to be expected when detection is unlikely. For the decompetitor, the scoreboard is the final arbiter of what counts as "winning," and whether or not one followed the rules to get there is largely irrelevant. Thus, rather than rules providing the *minimal floor* for good sport behavior, they provide its *maximal ceiling*. Rule adherence is probably the very most we can expect of the decompetitor, just as obeying the Geneva Conventions may be the most we can expect of combatants. Even rule obedience cannot be expected if the detection of violations is unlikely or there are informal norms allowing for rule deviation.

Officials

For competitors, officials are viewed as personal agents who share an important role in the process of competition by seeking to ensure equality of opportunity and treatment, and minimization of risk.

Within decompetition, officials are tolerated, because even the decompetitor recognizes that the adversary—the opponent—needs to be restrained. While the officials are there to enable or facilitate the game for the competitor, in an odd sort of way the officials become part of the opposition for the decompetitor; outwitting the officials is just one more game strategy.

Emotional Tone

In a partnership, positive emotions predominate. This is true even when the partnership involves contesting. As a result, true competitors maintain a balance of seriousness and play. The game is taken seriously, but it is also enjoyed in a spirit of spontaneity and play. In contrast, in decompetition, the contest is taken too seriously. There is little that is playful in a battle. In decompetition the play dimension is largely removed and negative emotions may spin out of control.

Whose Interests Are Served?

The competitor tends to view the contest as something from which everyone can benefit. Even in a losing effort, a competitor can gain. They can learn from their mistakes; they can strengthen their resolve; they can benefit from the character challenges that the contest presented. They can still enjoy the experience, the process of contesting, despite being disappointed in the outcome. By contrast, the decompetitor sees the contest as something that serves the interests of the victors alone. There is little to be gained in a losing effort. At most, losing is beneficial because it may facilitate future winning. There is little in the underlying battle metaphor that allows for a focus on the common good of all who participate.

The Ideal Contest

As we have seen, competition and decompetition entail fundamentally different views of the process-outcome relation. Let us now focus just on the process and ask whether the competitor and decompetitor have different views of the ideal nature of the game experience. Indeed they do.

For competitors, the ideal game is saturated with drama and uncertainty. There is mystery and tension involved, but it is not the tension of antagonists so much as the tension of the unknown. How will things turn out in the end? The ideal contest involves story and plot and turns of event. Playing a good game is like watching a good stage play or reading an engaging book. If the concluding scene or ending chapter are apparent too quickly, then the plot is too thin and uninteresting. So it is with the good game.

On the other hand, certainty is desired by those engaged in decompetition. Putting the game away early is ideal and running up the score is acceptable, because these actions guarantee victory, which is the primary value motivating decompetition. Since displaying superiority is the key goal, the more quickly and decisively one can win, the better. In fact, drama and uncertainty undermine the goals of the decompetitor. The closer the game, the less clearly one has demonstrated superiority, even if one eventually emerges victorious.

Promotive Interdependence

One final point needs to be made about the relationship among the various elements that comprise the two contrasting perspectives. The key point is this: each element within a given perspective reinforces and tends to call forward each of the other elements within that perspective. For example, if opponents are viewed as enemies, then that view of opponents will support and tend to elicit the adoption of domination as the desired goal. The adoption of domination as the desired goal, in turn, will support the focus on outcome over process, and so on. Psychologically, we call this a relation of *promotive interdependence*.[9] Each element within the structure, once embraced, supports the adoption of each of the other elements that comprise that structure. Adoption of one element of decompetition encourages the adoption of the entire decompetitive orientation.

Despite the relation of promotive interdependence among the elements of competition or decompetition, it is also important to qualify that point with a second, equally true observation. In the real world, neither perspective exists in an entirely pure form. To greater and lesser degrees, we are all saints and sinners, competitors and decompetitors. Our motives are always mixed, our goals always blended, our focus always blurred. The competition and decompetition models reflect what sociologists call *ideal types*. They are conceptual models that can help us distinguish two distinct types of social interaction, but they are abstract notions that are pure only in thought, not in reality. Still, we believe that people have strong tendencies to live within one metaphor more than the other.

THE ETHICAL EDGE

Within any contest, there are two alternative processes that can occur: competition and decompetition. One of the great myths propelling people toward decompetition is the belief that it is instrumentally advantageous.[10] If winning is highly desired, then, so the argument goes, maybe we need to excuse or overlook the ethical limitations of decompetition. Maybe it is an ethical compromise that needs to be taken to get to the victory stand. Even if it were true, this argument would need to be refuted. But it is based on a false assumption.

It is helpful to keep in mind that *competition is itself an ethic*.[11] For example, the true competitor:

- Respects all participants and the sport itself
- Supports the common good of the sport community
- Holds fast to principles of fairness and care
- Finds enjoyment that is not at the expense of others
- Embodies an "ethic of excellence" and gives his or her best regardless of circumstance

The fact that true competition is itself an ethic leads to an interesting paradox. It is true that *competitors must be willing to risk losing to sustain their ethical integrity*. Especially in the short term, cheating and other decompetitive tactics sometimes do provide a leg up. And yet the performance advantages are actually lined up on the side of the true competitor.[12] Upholding the ethical norms and standards of true competition, even when others are not, typically gives the competitor the best chance of winning. All other things being equal, the competitor is more likely to win than the decompetitor, especially in repeated encounters over time.

Commitment to ethical principles does not detract from athletic performance. Instead, it propels it toward its peak. It provides what we call an *ethical edge*. Some of the key performance advantages of true competition are identified in table 6.2. For example, there is substantial literature backing the performance advantages of intrinsic over extrinsic motivation.[13] While we provide these illustrative comments, a detailed and documented case for the "ethical edge" is beyond the scope of the present chapter. Interested readers are referred to our more elaborated treatment of true competition.[14]

Despite the many advantages of fair and ethical competition, there will be temptations to deviate. In the short term, it often seems easier to get the win through "minor" ethical compromises. The short-lived, transient benefits of decompetition, however, pale in comparison to the lasting performance benefits of true competition.

Over the long run, the "ethical edge" provides a performance advantage. Still, it is important to remember that *a person of character does the right thing for the right reason.* To act ethically, doing what is right must itself be the primary motivation. Commitment to true competition is sustained only when the competitor believes deeply in its core values and is willing to sacrifice to sustain them if necessary. If a contestant's motive for acting with "integrity" is primarily to gain advantage, then the person is likely to excuse short-term compromises and undercut the ethical edge. Paradoxically, the ethical edge kicks in only when ethics trumps all other considerations.

COMPETITION AND CHARACTER

The central point of this chapter is that if youth sports are to contribute to positive youth development, if they are to build character, then

Table 6.2. Performance advantages of true competition

	Mental Map of True Competition	Performance Advantages
Deep Metaphor	Partnership	
View of Opponent	Partner/Enabler	Less likely to be distracted by negative views of opponents
Motivation	· Love of the game · Intrinsic motivation	Intrinsic motivation is more stable, enduring, and energizing than extrinsic motivation.
Goals	· Learning and mastery · Pursuit of personal best	· The focus on learning encourages persistent effort. · Since "success" is self-referenced, the pursuit of success pushes beyond what is minimally required for victory.
Focus	Focus is on process (Contesting)	· Allows the athlete to stay focused on controllable aspects of performance (e.g., effort)
Focus of Sportspersonship	Fair, respectful, safe play	Unlikely to elicit "revenge" tactics on the part of opponents
View of Rules	Imperfect guides to fairness and welfare	· Less mental energy is wasted on looking for rule loopholes. · Fewer penalties are likely to be received.
View of Officials	Contest facilitators	· Less likely to become distracted by poor calls; it is easier to "keep your head in the game."
Emotional Tone	· Positive emotions predominate · Play and seriousness in balance	Positive emotions are easier to control and less distracting than negative emotions.
Whose interests are served?	· Mutual interest · The "common good"	Recognizing that everyone benefits, there is no fear of loss or fear of alienating opponents through giving one's best effort.
Ideal Contest	·Balanced opposition ·Tension, drama, story	Close games are not interpreted as challenges to competency, and so are less threatening and stressful.

sport leaders will need to find means of creating and sustaining true competition. While competition fits the value-affirming practice that Pope John Paul II articulated, decompetition does not.

We all know that there are major problems in youth sports today. Yet the problems that plague youth sports have less to do with kids than adults. And they stem from adults precisely because we, more than our children, have embraced a model of sports based on the presuppositions of decompetition.

It is important to remember that true competition requires a balancing of play and seriousness, that it is devoted to developing excellence—excellence of character as well as excellence of physical performance. It is rooted in deep appreciation and respect for opponents, which means that sport should serve the interests of all children and not just the more gifted.[15]

These characteristics fit in quite naturally with what tends to be the orientation of most children. Children play sports to have fun, spend time with friends, and develop skills.[16] The vast majority of children would rather play on a losing team than warm the bench of a winning one. Kids like well-matched games, and when they are in control of the sport experience, they will juggle players until the sides are roughly equal.

Adult-organized youth sports, by contrast, have become increasingly professionalized. Youth leagues have adopted the tournament structures, travel routines, practice schedules, selection mechanisms, and reward systems of commercial sport. They have been governed by a set of practices that are largely designed to identify and groom the best and neglect the rest. Children are encouraged to specialize in one sport at a young age, and the more talented are encouraged to compete for spots on select travel teams.

We need to remove from youth sports efforts to classify, rank, divide, select, and prioritize children. Youth sports should not be run like a caste system with special privileges and benefits (as well as demands and pressures) going to those labeled as gifted or talented, and second class treatment or outright neglect given the rest. Especially at the elementary level, children should be given equal playing time and they should gain experience in multiple sports and at multiple positions within a sport.

If kids are to develop an appreciation for true competition rather than be socialized into the prevalent system of decompetition, we need to contemplate how we structure and organize our youth sport programs. Youth sports allow kids to have fun, develop a love of sports, get exercise, and develop some skills. And youth sports should help children learn to handle the stresses of competition in a manner infused with grace and love.

YOUTH SPORTS AND SPIRITUALITY

At several points, we have implied that sports—and perhaps youth sports in particular—can provide a setting for the nourishment of the spirit, as well as the body and mind. In its broadest rendering, we see spirituality as the cultivation of a sense of wonder, purpose, and meaning. It is both deeply personal and self-transcending.

From this view of spirituality, we can see that the distinction between competition and decompetition might be useful to a broad range of faith-based communities. At the very root of the distinction between competition and decompetition are cognitive metaphors that not only structure our experience of contests but also reflect deep convictions about the fundamental nature of reality and human relationships. Ultimately, the metaphors arise from and give expression to spirituality.

The partnership metaphor springs from a basic conviction that human connection is more purposeful and meaningful than human division; that love is real and a reliable foundation for action; that justice and compassion are warranted; that beneath our conflicts and struggles is a deeper harmony; that we are bound together, despite our division into teams and groups, by common purpose to explore the wonders of existence and human potential. The spirituality of the war metaphor, by contrast, is the spirituality of division, of "us" against "them," of power and privilege as the ultimate foundations of ethics and action.

Fortunately, the spirituality nurtured by genuine competition, rather than decompetition, is a spirituality consonant with the views of most faith traditions. Sport itself can be a means and a metaphor for understanding and nurturing spirituality. Recovering true competition is only one element of supporting the soul of youth sports, but it is a vital one.

NOTES

1. John Paul II, "Message to Participants in the Twelfth Youth Games Held in Rome, Urges Them to Integrate Physical Gifts with Spiritual Ones," *L'Osservatore Romano*, November 3, 1980, 10.

2. David Shields, Brenda Bredemeier, Nicole LaVoi, and Clark Power, "The Sport Behavior of Youth, Parents, and Coaches: The Good, the Bad, and the Ugly," *Journal of Research in Character Education* 3 (2005): 43–59.

3. For summaries, see D. W. Johnson and R. T. Johnson, "New Developments in Social Interdependence Theory," *Genetic, Social and General Psychology Monographs* 131, no. 4 (2005): 285–358; D. W. Johnson and R. T. Johnson, "Social Interdependence, Moral Character and Moral Education," in *Handbook of Moral and Character Education*, ed. L. P. Nucci and D. Narvaez, 204–29 (New York: Routledge, 2008); Alfie Kohn, *No Contest: The Case against Competition*, rev. ed. (Boston: Houghton Mifflin, 1992); and Pauline Rosenau, *The Competition Paradigm: America's Romance with Conflict, Contest, and Commerce* (Lanham, MD: Rowman & Littlefield, 2003).

4. See Gilles Fauconnier and Mark Turner, *The Way We Think: Conceptual Blending and the Mind's Hidden Complexities* (New York: Basic Books, 2002); Jerome Feldman, *From Molecule to Metaphor: A Neural Theory of Language* (Cambridge, MA: MIT Press, 2006); George Lakoff and Mark Johnson, *Metaphors We Live By* (Chicago: University of Chicago Press, 1980); and George Lakoff and Mark Johnson, *Philosophy in the Flesh* (New York: Basic Books, 1999).

5. David Shields and Brenda Bredemeier, "Contesting Theory: Development of a Measure" (paper presented at the annual meeting of the Association of Moral Education, San Antonio, Texas, October 2012).

6. David Shields and Brenda Bredemeier, "Contest, Competition, and Metaphor," *Journal of the Philosophy of Sport* 38 (2011): 27–38.

7. Edward Deci and Richard Ryan, *Handbook of Self-Determination Research* (Rochester, NY: University of Rochester Press, 2002).

8. David Shields and Brenda Bredemeier, "Why Sportsmanship Programs Fail, and What We Can Do about It," *Journal of Physical Education, Recreation and Dance* 82, no. 7 (2011): 24–29.

9. David Johnson and Roger Johnson, *Cooperation and Competition: Theory and Research* (Edina, MN: Interaction Books, 1989).

10. Shields and Bredemeier, "Why Sportsmanship Programs Fail."

11. David Shields and Brenda Bredemeier, "Ethics to Excellence: Using Mental Maps to Reclaim Competition," *Journal of Coaching Education* 3, no. 2 (2010): 10–20.

12. Ibid.

13. Deci and Ryan, *Handbook of Self-Determination Research.*

14. David Shields and Brenda Bredemeier, *True Competition: A Guide to Pursuing Excellence in Sport and Society* (Champaign, IL: Human Kinetics, 2009).

15. Shields and Bredemeier, "Why Sportsmanship Programs Fail."

16. Vern Seefeldt, Martha Ewing, and Stephen Walk, *Overview of Youth Sports Programs in the United States* (Washington DC: Carnegie Council on Adolescent Development, 1992).

CHAPTER 7

Youth Sport and Spirituality

PATRICK KELLY, SJ

FOUNDATIONS FOR A SPIRITUALITY OF YOUTH SPORT

The historical and theological overview in chapter 2 provides scholars of spirituality with the foundations for a spirituality of youth sport in our contemporary context. As was discussed in that chapter, Christian theologians and spiritual writers have traditionally emphasized the goodness of the material world and the unity of the human person. These emphases were the basis for the integration of the body in religious practices, which was evident in the sacraments and the use of images in worship as well as numerous other ways. With respect to our own topic, an emphasis on the unity of the person means that the bodily experiences of young people in sport will necessarily impact them at the level of mind and spirit. This is what Pope John Paul II was alluding to when he referred to sports as a "form of gymnastics of the body and spirit."[1] As he put it:

Athletic activity, in fact, highlights not only the person's valuable physical abilities, but also his intellectual and spiritual capacities. It is not just physical strength and muscular efficiency,
but it also has a soul and must show its complete face.[2]

Another foundation for a spirituality of youth sports has to do
with the way Christians have understood the relationship between
faith and culture. St. Paul was a foundational figure in this regard. As
the apostle to the Gentiles, he spent most of his post-conversion life
making the gospel message known to the Greek-speaking world. And
his approach involved referencing aspects of the Greek cultural heritage, including sports. He wrote to the citizens of Corinth, "Do you
not know that in a race the runners all compete, but only one receives
the prize? Run in such a way that you may win it" (1 Cor 9:24). As
was discussed in chapter 2, Paul's writings influenced subsequent
theologians and spiritual writers who regularly used athletic metaphors to describe the dynamics of the Christian life. This original
opening up to the Greeks also set a precedent for Christians in the
medieval period, who tended to be accepting of customs, such as games
and sports, of the diverse cultural groups who were converting to
Christianity. These games and sports were practiced on Sundays and
feast days and were depicted in prayer books and on stained glass windows and woodcuts of that period. The humanists during the Renaissance and the early Jesuits also took as their model the schools of
ancient Greece, which led them to include play and sport in the schools
they were running for lay students.

In more recent times, Pope John Paul II commented on the passage above from St. Paul during a 1984 homily to 80,000 young athletes from around the world gathered at the Olympic Stadium in
Rome. He pointed out that St. Paul, in his attempt to make the gospel
known to the Greeks, drew from the concepts, images, terminologies,
and modes of expression, not only of the Jewish heritage, but also of
Hellenic culture. "And he did not hesitate to include sport among the
human values which he used as points of support and reference for
dialogue with the people of his time." According to the pope, St. Paul
recognized the fundamental validity of sport and its role in the formation of the person and of civilizations themselves.

In this way, St. Paul, continuing the teaching of Jesus, established the Christian attitude towards [sports] as towards the other expressions of natural human faculties such as science, learning, work, art, love and social and political commitment. Not an attitude of rejection or flight, but one of respect, esteem, even though correcting and elevating them: in a word, an attitude of *redemption*.[3]

A third foundation for a spirituality of youth sports has to do with the traditional emphasis of theologians and educators on the human and spiritual significance of play. Influenced by Aristotle's notion that moderation was central to a life of virtue, Thomas Aquinas, the humanists, and early Jesuits emphasized that a person should not be studying or working (or even engaging in religious exercises) all the time. They insisted that play and recreation were also important in a moderate, and therefore virtuous, life. Indeed, for Thomas Aquinas, *it was possible to sin by having too little play in one's life*. For Thomas, as we saw, play was very similar to contemplation in that both activities were enjoyable and done for their own sake; indeed, he even describes contemplation itself as a kind of play.

Unfortunately, important elements of these foundations were undermined as we entered the modern period. The emphasis on the unity of the human person was undermined by the dualism of body and mind/soul that we have inherited from the philosopher René Descartes. Descartes described body and soul as polar opposites. For him, the body was material, extended in space, and unconscious, while the soul was immaterial, unextended, and conscious. The problem was that Descartes and the philosophers who followed him were not able to explain how body and soul, understood in this way, interacted with one another. This made it very difficult for them to explain how bodily activities or experiences influence consciousness (to say nothing of "spirit"). Obviously, this understanding of the human person undercut the foundation upon which a theology or spirituality of sport could have been developed in the modern period.

Attitudes toward work and play also changed considerably as we entered the modern world. Work became more highly valued and even associated with "godliness," while play was consequently regarded with a new level of suspicion. Indeed, it was often associated with sin. This mentality was articulated in the United States in the nineteenth century by the editors of the Congregationalist magazine *The New Englander*:

> Let our readers, one and all, remember that we were sent into this world, not for sport and amusement, but for *labor*; not to enjoy and please ourselves, but to serve and glorify God, and be useful to our fellow men. This is the great object and end of life. In pursuing this end, God has indeed permitted us all needful diversion and recreation. . . . But the great end of life after all is *work*.[4]

The effects of this heritage are still felt in the United States, in the work orientation of our culture, which tends to take over all aspects of life. Indeed, even in youth sports in our context the play element is sometimes very hard to find. The *New York Times* recently ran a front-page story about youth sport, in which the author described hearing parents and others telling "tales of overburdened children playing sports out of season, of demands to specialize in a single sport as early as grade school, of competitive pressures that lead to national championships for 9-year-olds."[5] Bruce Ward, the director of physical education and athletics in San Diego's public schools, commented in the article, "The shame of it is you see how hardened these 14-year-olds are by the time they get to high school. They're talented, terrific players, but I don't see the joy. They look tired. They've played so much year-round, they are like little professionals."[6]

When work and productivity in youth sport are overemphasized, the young person can be adversely affected. Today young people who participate in sport suffer from overuse injuries at a dramatically increased rate compared to thirty years ago. In a newspaper interview in 2005, Dr. Lyle Micheli, director of the sports medicine division of Boston Children's Hospital, said that in the 1980s only ten percent of the young patients he treated came to him for injuries caused by overuse. But by the early 2000s such overuse injuries represented seventy percent of the cases he saw.[7] Some prominent orthopedists have even begun to speak of an "epidemic" with respect to youth sports injuries.

The dramatic rise in overuse injuries has occurred in large part because parents and coaches encourage children to specialize in one sport at younger ages than in the past. Children's bodies, however, are not yet mature enough to handle the kind of year-round training that goes with specialization in one sport. Parents and coaches encourage early specialization in the hope that the young person will gain an advantage over others when competing for college athletic scholarships or (if everyone's dreams come true) for positions on elite-level or professional sport teams. It is easy to see that youth sport is becoming instrumentalized, regarded as a means to the ends of money and status.

Of course, in our own context elite-level and professional sports *have* become connected to a great deal of wealth and status, especially since the mid-twentieth century. This association is in large part due to the effects of television coverage of sports that began at that time and that have since increased exponentially with the advent of cable television stations that broadcast only sports programming. While these developments have been very good for the business side of sports, they have also introduced distractions for the players themselves. According to former Los Angeles Lakers coach Phil Jackson, when NBA players become seduced by the wealth and fame associated with professional basketball, they end up with swollen egos. This makes it very difficult for them to be good team players or to experience the joy that motivated them to begin playing basketball in the first place. He writes:

> The battle for players' minds begins at an early age. Most talented players start getting special treatment in junior high school, and by the time they reach the pros, they've had eight or more years of being coddled. They have NBA general managers, sporting goods manufacturers, and assorted hucksters dangling money in front of them and an entourage of agents, lawyers, friends, and family members vying for their favor. Then there's the media, which can be the most alluring temptress of all. With so many people telling them how great they are, it's difficult, and, in some cases, impossible, for coaches to get players to check their inflated egos at the gym door.[8]

FLOW, SPORT, AND THE SPIRITUAL LIFE

It is important in the cultural context of the United States, where the work ethic has been so strongly emphasized and there is a tendency for sport to be regarded instrumentally, to recover the play element in youth sport. Unfortunately, just as play has been regarded with suspicion in U.S. culture, it has been neglected by psychologists as well. When it has been studied, the focus has almost exclusively been on how play helps an organism learn how to navigate its environment or how it increases competence or strengthening of the ego in children. That is, the focus has been on play as a means to some other end. According to Mihaly Csikszentmihalyi:

> These perspectives leave out one of the main aspects of play, which is the simple fact that it is enjoyable in itself. Regardless of whether it decreases anxiety or increases competence, play is fun. The question of why play is enjoyable has rarely been asked directly.[9]

Csikszentmihalyi wanted to explore why play is enjoyable in his first book, *Beyond Boredom and Anxiety: The Experience of Play in Work and Games*. He became interested in this question while writing his doctoral dissertation about the dynamics of the creative process in artists. For his research, he was spending time with artists who had immersed themselves in painting over many long years and yet had little expectation that their paintings would bring them much money or recognition. He was intrigued by the fact that they were completely absorbed in what they were doing and derived great satisfaction from discussing the subtleties associated with painting in spite of the fact that they were not likely to become rich or famous as a result. Mainstream psychological approaches, such as behaviorism or depth psychology, did not have a way to adequately account for what he was observing.

To better understand enjoyment, Csikszentmihalyi and his researchers studied people who were involved in autotelic activities. The word autotelic comes from the two Greek words, *auto* = self and *telos*

= goal, indicating that an activity has its own internal goal or purpose. From a psychological perspective, people participate in such activities for their own sake. One composer Csikszentmihalyi interviewed expressed this autotelic mentality well:

> One doesn't do it for the money. . . . This is what I tell my students. Don't expect to make money, don't expect fame or a pat on the back, don't expect a damn thing. Do it because you love it.[10]

Csikszentmihalyi and his team conducted pilot interviews with sixty respondents involved in various autotelic activities, including college hockey, college soccer, and handball players. They also included spelunkers, explorers, mountain climbers, and long-distance swimmers. From these interviews they developed a questionnaire and a more structured interview format. With these instruments, they approached rock climbers, chess players, female dancers, and basketball players from two Boston-area championship high school teams. To understand what some of the common features of enjoyable activities in both games and work might be, they also included in the study professional composers of modern music, teachers, and surgeons. During his research, Csikszentmihalyi discovered a "common experiential state" that people described during their participation in the activities listed above and during other activities. He referred to this as "flow" because this was a word that the respondents themselves sometimes used when asked about their experience.

Based on his research, Csikszentmihalyi made a distinction between pleasure and enjoyment. A person can experience pleasure while sitting on a couch eating a bowl of ice cream or doing other activities that don't require much attention or personal investment. Enjoyment, on the other hand, is experienced when a person gives all of his attention to an activity and goes beyond what is expected in some area of endeavor. "Playing a close game of tennis that stretches one's ability is enjoyable," he writes, "as is reading a book that reveals things in a new light, as is having a conversation that leads us to express ideas we didn't know we had."[11] After such activities, people find themselves saying, "That was fun," or, "That was enjoyable."

CHARACTERISTICS OF FLOW ACTIVITIES

Flow is most often experienced when a person is engaged in a challenging activity that requires skills. However, there needs to be something of a balance between the level of a challenge and the person's own skill level (or at least his perception of his skill level). If the activity is too challenging given a person's skill level, then he is likely to feel overwhelmed and anxious. On the other hand, if the activity is not challenging enough, the person will likely feel bored and uninterested. Flow is experienced when the challenge is at the growing edge of a person's skill level. This schema helps us to understand why youth sports contests between evenly matched teams can be so exhilarating, even if the skill level is not particularly high when compared with other age groups.

Another characteristic of flow activities is that goals are clear and feedback is immediate. The person knows what he is expected to do and, because he is getting immediate feedback, he knows if he is achieving what he set out to do. One of the reasons games and sports are such natural settings for flow to occur is because they have such clear goals and provide immediate feedback. A basketball player knows that the goal is to put the ball in the basket, for example. If he is practicing his free throws, he can keep track of how many he is making out of twenty on successive days and in this way chart his improvement or regression. The goal for a basketball team is to put the ball in the basket more often than their opponents and this means they have the more complex tasks of working together to stop the opponents (without fouling or goaltending) and working with one another, by setting picks, running plays, and passing the ball so that they can be in a position to take good shots.

ELEMENTS OF THE FLOW EXPERIENCE

During flow, a person centers his attention on a limited stimulus field. He experiences a "one-pointedness of mind." According to former San

Francisco 49er quarterback John Brodie, an athlete needs to have such a one-pointedness of mind in order to play well:

A player's effectiveness is directly related to his ability to be right there, doing that thing, in the moment. . . . He can't be worrying about the past or the future or the crowd or some extraneous event. He must be able to respond in the here and now.[12]

A high school basketball player describes the centering of attention this way:

The court—that's all that matters. . . . You can think about a problem all day but as soon as you get in the game, the hell with it! . . . Kids my age, they think a lot . . . but when you are playing basketball, that's all there is on your mind—just basketball. . . . Everything seems to follow right along.[13]

Another way to describe this phenomenon is to say that there is a "merging of action and awareness." What the person is doing and what he is thinking about are one and the same thing. His body and mind are united; his action and awareness are one. Many readers will recognize the similarities between "merging of action and awareness" and the Buddhist notion of "mindfulness."

Another feature of flow experiences is egolessness or loss of self-consciousness. For Csikszentmihalyi, this does not literally entail a loss of the self, but a loss of consciousness *of* the self. Because the activity requires all of the person's attention, there isn't any attention left over to be conscious of the self, which would typically appear in questions to oneself such as, "How am I doing?" "Should I be doing it this way?" or "What do they think of me?" An eighth-grade girl dribbling the basketball up the court in the final possession of a game when the score is tied must give all of her attention to what she is doing. She has to keep the ball away from the defender, know which of her teammates has a hot hand, what kind of defense is being played, what play her coach has called, and how much time is left on the clock if she is going to be able to participate in a successful play. She doesn't have any attention left over to be thinking about how popular she will be with her classmates if she makes a great play or what her father will say if she makes a mistake. That is, she can't be explicitly thinking of *herself* in this sense.[14]

And yet when the activity is over and the person reflects on herself anew, the self she is reflecting on has changed and grown. Csikszentmihalyi explains this dynamic:

> In flow a person is challenged to do her best, and must constantly improve her skills. At the time, she doesn't have the opportunity to reflect on what this means in terms of the self—if she did allow herself to become self-conscious, the experience could not have been very deep. But afterward, when the activity is over and self-consciousness has a chance to resume, the self that the person reflects upon is not the same self that existed before the flow experience: it is now enriched by new skills and fresh achievements.[15]

He points out that loss of self-consciousness and self-transcendence are integrally related:

> When not preoccupied with ourselves, we actually have a chance to expand the concept of who we are. Loss of self-consciousness can lead to self-transcendence, to a feeling that the boundaries of our being have been pushed forward.[16]

Another characteristic of the flow experience is a deeper sense of unity with one's surroundings, which can be experienced with respect to the natural world, physical objects in the environment, or other people, for example. One rock climber pointed out that while climbing he "felt part of the greater whole—oneness," and another said, "Up there you see man's true place in nature, you feel one with nature."[17] In team sports, players and coaches often mention the close bond that develops between the players. This bond develops because team sports require players to work closely together to accomplish the goals of the sport. But the bond or sense of closeness will only happen if the players can reach a point where they are no longer thinking in a self-centered way. The struggle every group leader faces, according to Phil Jackson, is "how to get members of the team who are driven by the quest for individual glory to give themselves over wholeheartedly to the group effort. In other words, how to teach them selflessness."[18]

The triangle offense that Jackson used with his NBA teams (developed by Tex Winter, his assistant) depends on the ability of the players to leave aside their self-centeredness and work together to create something that is more than simply a combination of the individual talents of each of the players. But, according to Jackson, not everyone can reach this point. "Some players' self-centered conditioning is so deeply rooted that they can't make that leap. But for those who can, a subtle shift in consciousness occurs. The beauty of the system is that it allows players to experience another, more powerful form of motivation than ego-gratification." This is not easy to do in today's NBA:

Most rookies arrive in the NBA thinking that what will make them happy is having unlimited freedom to strut their egos on national TV. But that approach to the game is an inherently empty experience. What makes basketball so exhilarating is the joy of losing yourself completely in the dance, even if it's for just one beautiful transcendent moment. That's what the system teaches players. There's a lot of freedom built into the process, but it's the freedom . . . of shaping a role for yourself and using all of your creative resources to work in unison with others.[19]

Flow experiences typically require a considerable amount of discipline and concentration and a significant expenditure of effort. After prolonged periods of concentration and effort, however, there develops an ease or an *effortlessness* to one's action and even the perception that one is being carried along by a current. For example, when a young person is learning how to shoot a layup with her off-hand, she initially has to think a great deal about which foot to jump off of, when to jump, the motion of her shooting hand, and so on. She has to practice the shot regularly. And she will make countless mistakes, miss shots, and probably have several run-ins with the garage door along the way. However, after she practices the layup many times, over an extended period, she will eventually be able to gracefully and seemingly effortlessly shoot the off-hand layup. It will almost seem like second nature, as though she has been doing it her whole life.

During flow, time is also experienced differently from time as measured by the clock, where there is no way to differentiate one minute or hour from any other. If a young person is experiencing flow while playing soccer at the school yard, several hours might pass by in what seems like ten minutes. He or she might even forget to come home for lunch. On the other hand, sometimes during a flow experience time seems to slow down and something that took only a few minutes seems to have lasted much longer.

For Csikszentmihalyi, a person can only enter into flow experiences if he or she has a reasonably stable or secure sense of self. "Being human we all want, first of all," he writes, "to survive, to be comfortable, to be accepted, loved and respected."[20] A young person who grows up in a home where there is neglect or abuse will find it very difficult to have the kind of flow experiences that enrich life and contribute to his or her growth.

> It stands to reason . . . that a child who has been abused, or who has been often threatened with the withdrawal of parental love—and unfortunately we are becoming increasingly aware of what a disturbing proportion of children in our culture are so mistreated—will be so worried about keeping his sense of self from coming apart as to have little energy left to pursue intrinsic rewards.[21]

Other scholars have written about similar themes. In her article "Meanings of the Body," Lynne Belaief writes about the importance of an experience of "ontological security," which "includes not only a firm sense of one's own existence but of the *rightness* of that existence."[22] For Belaief, when ontologically secure, we can enter into experiences for their own sake—we can play. And when we are playing, she points out, we are not following external orders, "but our own freedom."[23]

FLOW, SPORT, AND CHRISTIAN SPIRITUALITY

Several themes in Christian spirituality correlate with and can complement the insights of Csikszentmihalyi and practitioners such as Phil Jackson with regard to sport. One of the first that comes to mind is the recognition that we get off track when we become too attached to money and status. Throughout the gospels, Jesus warns of the dangers of attachment to money, and he repeatedly reminds his followers not to be concerned with their own status. Ignatius of Loyola writes in his *Spiritual Exercises* that it is characteristic of the "enemy of our human nature" to tempt people in the following way:

> People find themselves tempted to covet whatever seems to make them rich, and next because they possess some thing or things they find themselves pursuing and basking in the honor and esteem of this world. Then getting such deference raises up the false sense of personal identity in which a blinding pride has its roots.[24]

We have seen in this and other chapters of this volume how, when the motivation of parents and coaches is only on participation in youth sport as a way to make money and become famous, enjoyment tends to disappear. This approach is also related to a recent dramatic increase in overuse injuries. According to Phil Jackson, when professional athletes become attached to money and fame they forget why they play the game in the first place (for love of the game) and they are not able to be good team players, which undermines team performance.

When people are experiencing flow while playing sports, however, their participation is associated with personal development and self-transcendence. How can we understand the experiences of flow that people have in sports from a Christian perspective? The rest of this chapter addresses this question by bringing the insights from research on the flow experience into dialogue with themes in Catholic theology and spirituality.

THE SPIRITUAL DIMENSION OF YOUTH SPORT

One of the most important things that young people can experience from participating in sport is the enjoyment that is associated with doing something for its own sake. This kind of experience keeps one very close to the wonder and delight that accompany simple existence itself, which is good because it comes from God. At such moments, young people are able to live in the present without excessive worry and anxiety and have an experience of being a part of something larger than themselves, as they participate in the kinds of activities that lead to their growth and development.

Csikszentmihalyi has pointed out that when a young person knows that she is loved and accepted, she is in an optimal position to be able to engage in activities for their own sake. Belaief writes about the importance of having a sense of "ontological security" in order to be able to play.

The importance of knowing that one is loved and this leading to fullness of life is also a central theme in Christian spirituality. For the apostle Paul, love was far more important than anything else in the Christian life. And according to the author of the First Letter of John, "God is love" (1 Jn 4:16). Jesus tells his followers, "As the Father loves me, so I also love you. Remain in my love" (Jn 15:9), and he exhorts them to love one another. He tells them these things, he says, "so that my joy might be in you, and your joy might be complete" (Jn 15:11). Some contemporary theologians point out that a person who has experienced God's love and remains in this love has a sense of "ontological security" and hence is able to play. As the Jesuit Hugo Rahner puts it: "The person who has faith and truly loves God is also the one who can truly play, for only he who is secure in God can be truly light of heart."[25]

When a young person is participating in a sport he enjoys, he learns how to quiet his mind from distractions and pay attention to the task at hand. This happens at all levels of sport. Consider the experience of a professional golfer who is approaching the eighteenth hole, with one putt left to make in order to win the big prize money, as well as endorsement contracts and the fame that will come with his victory. He cannot be distracted by these external goods, or he will become nervous and tighten up—or in some other way lose his rhythm and miss the putt. To make the putt, he must play well technically while also maintaining his poise and concentration. If he is able to do this, it is an achievement in the realm of consciousness, in the sense that he did not let the external goods loom so large in his mind that they threw him off stride.[26]

When young people are involved in sports that are not clearly objectionable from an ethical point of view (boxing and some other sports would need to be discussed in this regard), the experience of concentrating on the task at hand can teach them that external goods are not the most important things in life; that, in fact, they are often a distraction from what is most important. They can learn that the quality of experience in life is what is important, regardless of whether they become wealthy or famous. Young people can learn this by immersing themselves in their sport, especially if it is under the tutelage of a coach who has an appreciation for the internal goods of the sport and is able to convey all that is involved in the pursuit of excellence in that particular endeavor.

As we discussed in chapter 2, for the apostle Paul one similarity between participation in sports and the Christian life was that both the athlete and the Christian deny themselves. The young person who is participating in sports, learns, for example, to moderate her diet in such a way that it contributes to the health of her body. She also learns that she can't do all of the pleasurable things she wants to do if she wants to become accomplished at her sport. If she wants to improve her ability to dribble a basketball with her off-hand, she needs to spend time practicing this skill. Or if she wants to be able to run faster, she needs to spend time and energy running and training. She can't simply sit around with her friends and eat pizza or ice cream. She also may have to give up doing other things she enjoys from time to time, like going to a party or seeing a movie. By engaging in self-denial in this way the young person is experiencing something that is, as John Paul II has said elsewhere, "very close to the cardinal virtue of temperance, a well understood and persevering asceticism, which always gives priority to spiritual values."[27]

Young people can also learn about the importance of the virtue of humility as they are willing to work on the areas of their game where their skills are not very well developed. As a teacher and a coach, I have noticed that the students and athletes who make the most progress are those who are able to take constructive criticism and spend time working on the areas of their studies or their sport where their skill levels are currently not very high. The ability to recognize one's areas of weakness requires a good deal of humility. The young person who learns the value of humility in the context of playing sports will also be able to recognize the importance of this virtue in other areas of life.

Our growth in the Christian life, after all, requires a willingness to look at the areas in which we struggle and ask for help in them. I think this was why Jesus emphasized the danger of being self-righteous, that is, of thinking we have it all together—whether because we follow all the rules or even because we behave in a virtuous way at times. This kind of stance could be such a problem precisely because we would no longer feel the need to make progress in the areas where we struggle, and so we would stop growing.

The experience that athletes have during flow of unity with their surroundings is also of profound importance from a Catholic perspective. As noted in chapter 2, Catholic theologians have traditionally emphasized the goodness of the created world. When participating in sports in the mountains or in other beautiful natural settings, the person is able to experience the awesomeness and majesty of the created world and this can raise his or her mind and spirit to God the creator. Some of the rock climbers interviewed by Csikszentmihalyi described their experiences in just this way. One rock climber commented: "I would begin to look at it in religious terms. Certain natural settings represent some intensity or eternity. You can lose yourself in that. It's linked to the idea of creation, intense wonder, and realization."[28]

John Paul II, a mountain climber himself in his youth, emphasized similar themes. In a talk to Italian Olympic medal winners in 1984, the pope pointed out that their experiences as athletes offers them, "among other things, also the opportunity to improve your own personal spiritual state."

> Called as you are frequently to engage in your competitions in the midst of nature, amid the marvels of the mountains, seas, fields and slopes, you are in the best position to perceive the value of simple and immediate things, the call to goodness, the dissatisfaction with one's insufficiency, and to meditate on the authentic values that are at the basis of human life.[29]

The experience that athletes sometimes have of a closer bond with other people also resonates with central themes in the Catholic tradition. In the Catholic view the person is social by nature. We are meant to live in society and to share the material and cultural goods of this life. Authority is necessary for societies to function, and so it is understood as a *bonum* as well. Those activities that strengthen the bonds among people and foster a sense of community are understood as human goods and are encouraged.

In Catholic spirituality as well, community has always been of fundamental importance. This can be seen in a dramatic way in the monastic traditions associated with St. Benedict and in other religious communities. But community is also part of a Catholic sensibility in a broader sense. From the Catholic perspective, salvation is something that happens with the help of others, whether it is the intercession of the saints, or the simple and less dramatic assistance of other members of our own community. Each of the sacraments, in one way or another, embodies this communal emphasis.

But such understandings of the human person or of the Christian life will only persist if they give meaning to young people's lives as they live them on a daily basis. One of the ways young people can begin to learn about community is by playing on a team. As we saw in the last section, through such experiences young people can learn important lessons about how to move beyond a self-centered approach to life and to understand themselves as part of a larger whole. In Catholic parishes and schools, young people should be encouraged to understand this experience of community in terms of their love for one another.

FROM FLOW IN SPORTS TO FLOW IN THE CHRISTIAN LIFE IN GENERAL

The experiences of flow that young people have while playing sports can also be significant for their lives after their playing days are over. For one thing, they can serve as something of an introduction to contemplation. This is possible because the elements of the flow experience are also present in contemplation. Perhaps in this sense we could call contemplation a *super-flow* experience. In chapter 2 it was noted that Thomas Aquinas thought play and contemplation are similar because both activities are enjoyable and done for their own sake.

In a commentary on a text from Ecclesiasticus, Thomas goes even further and refers to contemplation itself as a kind of play. The text Thomas is commenting on from Ecclesiasticus reads, "Run ahead into your house and gather yourself there and play there and pursue your thoughts." According to Thomas, the author uses the phrase "gather yourself there," to emphasize that "it is . . . necessary that we ourselves should be fully present there, concentrating in such a way that our aim is not diverted to other matters." He notes further, "And when our interior house is entirely emptied like this and we are fully present there in our intention, the text tells us what we should do: 'And play there.'"[30]

The close relationship between play and contemplation suggests that the young person who is learning how to play may, simultaneously, be learning something about the dynamics of the contemplative life. In this sense, one's participation in games and sports can have a much more profound and lasting influence on one's life than any amount of money or fame could ever have.

When considering the long-term impact of flow experiences in youth sports, it is also instructive to consider the similarities between flow experiences and Ignatius of Loyola's *spiritual consolation*. Ignatius, the founder of the Jesuits, had transformed religious life in the sixteenth century by emphasizing the importance of the ministries his men were doing in the world (that is, outside of the monastery). He encouraged the early Jesuits to "seek and find God in all things" and to be "contemplatives in action." But how does one "seek and find

God" in the midst of an active life in the world? For Ignatius, in the case of a person who was trying to grow in the Christian life, one of the most important things to pay attention to was what he called spiritual consolation.

Because grace perfects nature, it is not surprising that the experience of spiritual consolation is analogous to the flow experience. For example, for Ignatius, such consolation is associated with "genuine happiness and spiritual joy." It is also associated with effortlessness. Ignatius describes the experience of consolation as "gentle and easy, like a drop of water falling into a sponge" or as if one were "coming into one's own house through an open door." It feels as though obstacles are being removed so the person can move forward in doing good. But this effortlessness usually comes after much disciplined attention and practice. For Ignatius, this would involve reading the gospels, reflecting on one's life, and engaging in other "spiritual exercises." These "exercises" are meant, in part, to help the person gain some freedom from ego-centered motivations and attachments to money and fame. Finally, consolation is related to the growth and development of the person, helping him or her to move from good to better in the Christian life.

According to Ignatius, one's major decisions should be made related to and building on experiences of spiritual consolation. Indeed, for him, "consolation shows and opens up the way we ought to go."[31] From a theological perspective, we can say that during consolation the presence of the Holy Spirit is experienced in a way that is recognizable. While it is possible that a young person will experience spiritual consolation while participating in sports, we can say at the very least that the experiences of flow they have are *similar* to experiences of consolation. If young people have experienced joy, egolessness, union with others, a sense of ease or effortlessness (preceded by discipline), and self-transcendence in their participation in sports, they will be better able to recognize spiritual consolation when they experience it later in their lives. These earlier experiences of joy, egolessness, union, effortlessness, and self-transcendence can provide them with a reference point as they pay attention to what they are experiencing while discerning what God is calling them to study in college or to do with respect to work. In this sense, the experiences of flow in youth sport can continue to have significance in their lives as adult followers of Christ.

Of course, the experiences associated with spiritual consolation as they are described by Ignatius have a broader reach than the flow experiences as these have been described up until now in the research. The genuine happiness and spiritual joy associated with consolation can be experienced in the forgiveness of sins, for example. The peace associated with consolation can be experienced in the midst of sorrow or suffering because of an awareness of union with Christ. But this does not make the experiences of flow a young person has while playing sport and in other activities unimportant for the spiritual life. Such experiences are enjoyable and rewarding in themselves and are also "signals of transcendence." They point out to us what we are made for and help us to understand how, as Thomas said, "grace perfects nature."[32]

NOTES

1. John Paul II, "Pope to Milan Football Team," *L'Osservatore Romano*, May 28, 1979, 4.

2. John Paul II, "During the Time of the Jubilee: The Face and Soul of Sport," October 28, 2000, available at http://w2.vatican.va/content/john-paul-ii/en/speeches/2000/oct-dec/documents/hf_jp-ii_spe_20001028_jubilsport.html.

3. John Paul II, "The Most Authentic Dimension of Sport," *L'Osservatore Romano*, April 24, 1984, 3.

4. Quoted in William Hogan, "Sin and Sport," in *Motivations in Play, Games and Sports*, ed. Ralph Slovenko and James Knight, 121–47 (Springfield, IL: Charles C. Thomas, 1967), 124–25, emphasis in original.

5. Bill Pennington, "As Team Sports Conflict, Some Parents Rebel," *New York Times*, November 12, 2003, sec. A, p. 1, and sec. C, p. 16.

6. Ibid.

7. Bill Pennington, "Doctors See a Big Rise in Overuse Injuries for Young Athletes," *New York Times*, February 22, 2005, available at http://www.nytimes.com.

8. Phil Jackson and Hugh Delehanty, *Sacred Hoops: Spiritual Lessons of a Hardwood Warrior* (New York: Hyperion, 1995), 90.

9. Mihaly Csikszentmihalyi, "Play and Intrinsic Rewards," *The Journal of Humanistic Psychology* 15, no. 3 (Summer 1975): 41–63, at 42.

10. Ibid., 54–55.

11. Mihaly Csikszentmihalyi, *Flow: The Psychology of Optimal Experience* (New York: Harper and Row, 1990), 46.

12. Quoted in Michael Murphy and Rhea White, *In the Zone: Transcendent Experiences in Sport* (New York: Penguin Books, 1995), 22.

13. Quoted in Mihaly Csikszentmihalyi, "Play and Intrinsic Rewards," 47.

14. A person can be adversely affected even if he begins thinking about himself when an activity is going very well. The high school basketball player quoted earlier seems to grasp this point well. As he puts it, "When I get hot in a game . . . Like I said, you don't think about it at all. If you step back and think about why you are so hot all of a sudden you get creamed" (in Csikszentmihalyi, "Play and Intrinsic Rewards," 46). This element of the flow experience is very interesting, because it suggests that when a person is playing his best, he isn't really thinking about himself at all.

15. Csikszentmihalyi, *Flow*, 65–66.

16. Ibid., 64.

17. Mihaly Csikszentmihalyi, *Beyond Boredom and Anxiety: The Experience of Play in Work and Games* (San Francisco: Jossey Bass Publishers, 1975), 92 and 95.

18. Jackson and Delehanty, *Sacred Hoops*, 89.

19. Ibid., 91.

20. Mihaly Csikszentmihalyi, *The Evolving Self* (New York: HarperCollins, 1993), 219.

21. Csikszentmihalyi, *Flow*, 89–90.

22. Lynne Belaief, "Meanings of the Body," *The Journal of the Philosophy of Sport* 4 (1977): 50–67, at 59.

23. Ibid., 62.

24. David L. Fleming, SJ, *Draw Me Into Your Friendship, The Spiritual Exercises: A Literal Translation and Contemporary Reading* (St. Louis, MO: Institute of Jesuit Sources, 1996), 113. This quotation is taken from Fleming's contemporary reading of the literal text of Ignatius's *Exercises*.

25. Hugo Rahner, *Man at Play* (New York: Herder and Herder, 1967), 57–58.

26. I am describing the phenomenon of sports performance, and I am using a dramatic instance, where large amounts of money and fame are involved, to make a point. But such concentration would be needed at other levels of sport as well. If the junior high school basketball player thinks about how she will be well liked or popular by making a free throw, she might tighten up and miss the shot. In the case of this golfer, I am bracketing the larger, and important, questions about whether there *should be* the kind of money connected to sports that there is today. Surely, the presence of vast amounts of money at the highest levels of sport contributes to many of the excesses in modern sport. And, given the extent of the poverty in our world, the reality of such large amounts of money in sports needs to be discussed from an ethical perspective itself.

27. According to Pope John Paul II, participation in sports offers young people an opportunity to make progress in the virtues. In an address to the International Ski Federation in 1983, he said: "In this brief meeting, I am glad to emphasize—and this will not surprise you—that all sports are formative; that is, they can and must contribute to the integral development of the human person. More specifically, this sort of human enterprise can, for Christians, facilitate the growth of the cardinal virtues of fortitude, temperance, prudence and justice. Skiers, like all sportsmen, develop their physical fortitude, including their flexibility and agility. This is not the cardinal virtue of which I spoke—but rather, the technique thus acquired makes possible a strength of soul which transcends physical abilities. Similarly, I like to recall the message which the Apostle Paul addresses to the Christians of Corinth (cf. 1 Cor 9:24–27). The athlete denies himself constantly, in that his diet is controlled in order to avoid failures due to inadequate physical fitness. Here we are very close to the cardinal virtue of temperance, a well understood and persevering asceticism, which always gives priority to spiritual values. As for the prudence of the sportsman, it derives from his judgment and calculation, in short, his experience, which incites him to be always well prepared and well equipped. The cardinal virtue of prudence is even more valuable for Christians. It is prudence which spurs them to live in such a way as to be able to judge what is best for God and their fellow man. As for justice in sports competitions, you know as well as I what equality and impartiality it requires. It seems to me that sports can especially help Christians who practice them to work for the progress of these requirements to which modern society is so sensitive" (John Paul II, "Address to the International Ski Federation," *L'Osservatore Romano*, January 3–10, 1983).

28. Csikszentmihalyi, *Beyond Boredom*, 92.

29. John Paul II, "Sports Offers Opportunity for Spiritual Elevation," *L'Osservatore Romano*, December 10, 1984.

30. *Albert and Thomas: Selected Writings*, trans. and ed. Simon Tugwell (Mahwah, NJ: Paulist Press, 1988), 527.

31. *Ignatius of Loyola: Letters and Instructions*, ed. Martin Palmer, SJ (St. Louis, MO: Institute of Jesuit Sources, 2006), 21.

32. Thomas Aquinas, *Summa Theologica*, 3 vols., trans. Fathers of the English Dominican Province (New York: Benziger Bros.), 1:308.

CHAPTER 8

For the Love of the Game

Toward a Theology of Sports

RICHARD R. GAILLARDETZ

There is much discussion today by religious leaders and commentators regarding the growing "secularity" of our culture. Unfortunately, the very term "secular" has become a contested term. The Canadian Catholic philosopher Charles Taylor has provided some helpful guidance in sorting through the issues in his book *A Secular Age*.[1] Although the word "secular" is often used to speak of a general loss of religious belief or the demise of religious institutions, Taylor offers us a third sense of the word. To speak of our current age as "secular," at least in the West, is to describe a world in which religious belief has become simply one option among many. Many today insist that they can lead a full and meaningful life without any reference to religion or the divine. These persons are content to live within what he calls an "immanent frame," that is, a worldview that takes no account of the divine. Yet even within this immanent frame we can detect a lurking sense of transcendence present in ordinary human engagements. I will argue in this chapter that for many today, sport remains a sphere of human engagement in which the transcendent, or what Christians simply call grace, is still encountered. At first glance this stance might seem odd. After all, it is more common to find commentators employing religious frameworks to offer stringent ethical critiques of modern sport. We live in a hyper-competitive culture that characterizes members of our society as either "winners" or "losers." Modern athletics, one could argue, exacerbates an unhealthy sense of competition and encourages our youth, in particular, to believe their basic worth is found in their athletic ability. We have all read newspaper accounts of a misguided sense of athletic competition leading to horrific instances of poor sportsmanship by parents, coaches, and young athletes themselves. Moreover, it difficult to overlook the real dangers that hyper-violent sports like football, hockey, rugby, and boxing present to the long-term health of those who participate in such sports. Finally there can be no question but that modern sport, professional and amateur, has been tainted by steroids and doping scandals.

These ethical and cultural critiques raise legitimate concerns that will not be explored within this essay. In spite of the many excesses and cultural dysfunctions that are associated with modern sport, I will argue that there is an intrinsic religious and spiritual significance to the experience of being an athletic participant or sports fan. As such, the experience of sport merits further theological reflection. Such reflection, within the limits of a brief essay such as this, can only be suggestive, but perhaps these brief reflections can serve as a springboard for further reflection by religious educators, coaches, athletic directors, and athletes themselves. Let us consider, then, six overlapping theological optics for exploring the spiritual dimension of sport: (1) the delight of play, (2) the graced character of bodily existence, (3) the pursuit of excellence as an exercise in graced transcendence, (4) the paschal character of athletics and the embrace of failure, (5) teamwork, empathy, and solidarity, and (6) the spiritual significance of fandom.

THE DELIGHT OF PLAY

For a good part of early American history its citizens labored under the Puritan suspicion of play. The Puritans, as Patrick Kelly notes, regarded play with "suspicion and started to associate it routinely with sin."[2] They saw human labor and productivity as a sign of godliness. Within their framework play could only seem a dangerous distraction. Human play was frivolous and silly, and it seduced its participants into overlooking the eternal significance of human activity. Yet Kelly has documented the extent to which the Puritans represented the exception rather than the rule where Christian attitudes toward play are concerned. Even the sixteenth-century reformers like Luther and Calvin recognized the value of human recreation. There have certainly been voices in the Christian tradition that stressed a more severe asceticism that left little room for human play. Yet these voices must be countered by the actual experience of ordinary Christians. In medieval Christianity, Sundays and feast days were often the occasion for games and play.[3] Sometimes images of sport and athletes would even find their way into churches as with several remarkable stained glass windows found in Gloucester Cathedral in England.[4] Indeed, there is considerable evidence that in the ordinary lives of Christians there has often been a healthy embrace of sport in spite of the occasional jeremiads raised against it. Was this a case of ordinary people ignoring their religious calling in favor of the allure of the profane? Or was it instead a matter of ordinary Christians intuitively grasping a profound spiritual insight regarding the healing and transformative power of sport, an insight overlooked by their religious leaders?

We begin our investigation by returning to a topic covered in several essays in this volume, namely, the intimate connection between sport and play. There are disputes regarding what precisely delineates sport from other human activities. For the purpose of this essay, I will define sport simply as embodied, competitive play. It is important to get the noun and predicates right. Sport is competitive play, not playful competition. I agree with Vincent Capuano when he insists, "sport is a sub-species of play and not of competition."[5] Certainly competitive sport is more than mere play, but authentic sport will always have a sense of the playful.

There is an element of self-forgetfulness in genuine play. This is particularly evident when we watch children at play. They are marvelously unconcerned with how they look or what they are

accomplishing. The game is everything. One of the chief characteristics of authentic play is that one can easily lose track of time. This is
why authentic play may be even more important for adults than for
children; play becomes a spiritual antidote to our cultural tendency
toward self-absorption and the massaging of egos. The enthrallment
of play can induce a healing sense of joy and delight. In play a life that
can so often weigh us down with its oppressive burdens can, if only
for a time, appear transfigured as gift.

An ancient tradition in Christianity dares to see God's work
of creation as a form of divine play. The Dominican theologian St.
Thomas Aquinas, one of the most influential thinkers in Western
Christianity, wrote of God's playfulness in the act of creation.[6] God
did not create the world because God *needed* to accomplish anything.
Rather God created the world out of the abundance of divine love and
goodness. There was no "point" to God's creative activity, no external
goal to which God was aligned. Creation, we might say, was just a
matter of God being God! Consequently, the goodness of creation,
although wounded by sin and the tragic reality of evil, is delightful
to God.

Thomas also reflects on the value of human play. Drawing on
Aristotle, he describes play as the exercise of the virtue of *eutrapelia*.[7]
Thomas characterizes *eutrapelia* as a virtue oriented toward relaxation and refreshment from purposive labor. Like all virtues, genuine
play avoids the extremes of excessive play or play at inappropriate
times, on the one hand, and an undue somberness of spirit, on the
other. Although Thomas does not explicitly make this connection,
surely we can assert that if God's creative action is a form of divine
play, then when humans are at play, when they experience genuine
joy and delight, losing themselves in the love of the game, they share
in God's own delight. Humans at play commune with the divine. As
Hugo Rahner puts it, "it is only after we have spoken with all reverence of *Deus ludens* [the playing God, or God at play] that we can
speak of *homo ludens*."[8] This calls to mind a marvelous scene from
the film *Chariots of Fire,* in which Eric Liddell, a Scottish runner and
devout Christian, justifies to his sister his decision to forego Christian
mission work in order to compete in the Olympics. He explains to his

sister, "God made me fast. And when I run I can feel his pleasure." In our capacity to lose ourselves in the sheer joy of sport, whether we recognize it or not, we come in contact with the source of all joy and delight, our creator God. James Bacik writes:

Play, when joyful and involving, is an affirmation of the triumph of creative forces over destructive ones. Our spontaneous involvement in play can speak to us of the integrated life of the Spirit.[9]

This connection between divine play and human play helps explain, I believe, why Thomas could offer a startling comparison between play and prayerful contemplation. Both are pleasurable, fundamentally non-purposive activities to be enjoyed for their own sake.[10] Romano Guardini, one of the giants in the Catholic liturgical renewal movement in the middle of the twentieth century, expanded on Thomas's audacious connection. In an essay he wrote before World War II, Guardini suggested that Christians consider the liturgy, Christian worship, as a form of "play."[11] Guardini's point was that Christian worship should have that sense of play, of "wasting time" before God. Guardini's connection between play and liturgy can move in both directions. It is not just that the liturgy is to be likened to human play, but that genuine play can be likened to liturgy; authentic play, like Christian liturgy, can draw us into communion with God.

CELEBRATING THE BODY

There are distinct strands of the Christian tradition that have been suspicious of the spiritual value of sport, usually because of some ambivalence regarding the goodness of the body. Indeed many contemporary scholars have focused on certain anti-body Christian texts to justify claims about Christian ambivalence toward sport.[12] Christian writers like Tertullian and Augustine, in at least some of their writings, appeared to place the spiritual realm above the bodily realm. They did so in ways that could call into question the pleasures of bodily existence, whether they took the form of good food, good sex, or good play. These writers were so preoccupied with the capacity of our bodily needs and desires to be distorted by sin that they often forgot that these needs and desires were themselves God's gift to us worthy of redemption.

In spite of some excessive tendencies, Christianity has generally opposed those ancient sectarian movements like Gnosticism or Manichaeism that repudiated the bodily realm and saw salvation as an escape from the material order.[13] Gnosticism located the divine in an entirely separate spiritual realm; creation was the result of a cosmic mistake by a lesser divinity. Human salvation came from the secret knowledge of this cosmic situation and a determination to leave the material world behind. Gnostic Christians presented Christ as the savior who could help fallen humanity escape this fallen material world. As such, they could not accept the Christian conviction that Jesus was an embodied human. Some Gnostic texts would hint at this by offering stories of Jesus walking on a beach without leaving footprints or the observation that Jesus never blinked!

Although there were Christian sects that surrendered to this Gnostic cosmology, it was widely repudiated by ancient Christian thinkers, such as Irenaeus of Lyons. Irenaeus and others were committed to the Christian truth that creation and redemption were integral features of the divine plan and that Christ came not to help us escape our humanity but rather to heal it. The Second Vatican Council wrote:

> In reality it is only in the mystery of the Word made flesh that the mystery of humanity truly becomes clear. . . . Christ the new Adam, in the very revelation of the mystery of the Father and of his love, fully reveals humanity to itself and brings to light its very high calling.[14]

The biggest check against the Gnostic suspicion of the body for early Christians was their belief in the incarnation, that bedrock teaching that God has assumed the full human condition in Jesus of Nazareth, including human bodily existence. The doctrine of the incarnation reminds us that our bodies are fundamentally good and that the grace and beauty of bodily form and movement can be another expression of the divine. Consequently, there is nothing wrong in exploring our untapped bodily capacities.

An authentic theology of sport grounded in the Christian belief in the incarnation must certainly avoid the Gnostic hatred of the body. At the same time, Christianity must take care to avoid what Dietmar Mieth refers to as the "Dionysian tendency": the cult of the body.[15] We can find this attitude in aspects of classical Greek culture that idolized the human form and focused exclusively on the perfection of the human body. Christianity would repudiate this tendency as well. St. Clement of Alexandria called for the mean between these two extremes: "physical activity, yes, the cult of the body, no."[16]

We still encounter both extremes today. The Gnostic tendency endures in the lingering condescension toward athletic activity manifested by some religious figures, intellectuals, and aesthetes who have no hesitation in finding the divine in a Wagnerian opera or a Caravaggio painting, but find it incomprehensible that some might find the divine in athletics. The Dionysian tendency is particularly pronounced in the objectification and idealization of the athletic body, an especially real concern for female athletes for whom celebrity requires not only great athleticism but the eroticizing of the female athletic form. It is present in a contemporary cult of the body evident in cosmetic surgery, the clothing industry, the marketing strategies of health clubs, and the allure of doping and performance enhancing drugs. A healthy spirituality of sports celebrates the grace and the beauty of the human form in action while insisting that the perfection of our body cannot serve as an end.

A healthy appreciation for the goodness of the body opens up reflection on how the athlete's experience of embodiment can become the occasion for the encounter with the divine. Many athletes will describe a heightened bodily awareness in sport that, precisely in its bodiliness, enables an experience of transcendence. In chapter 7 in this volume, Patrick Kelly discusses the work of psychologist Mihaly Csikszentmihalyi.[17] Csikszentmihalyi draws attention to the capacity of sport to bring not so much pleasure as enjoyment. This occurs when the athlete enters into an activity requiring real skill that stretches the participant. Csikszentmihalyi refers to this experience as "flow," an experience of the merging of being and doing.

Athletes will describe their experience of "flow" as an experience of mysterious harmony, a oneness with one's surroundings that is difficult to explain. For example, rowers will recount a profound sense of bodily harmony with the larger world. Whether rowing as part of an eight-person boat, a four, a pair, or even as a single, rowers recount the experience of finding a deep rhythm with their stroke, one enacted with a practiced precision. The rower slides her body, hands, and oar in unison toward the "catch" over her feet. At precisely that moment she smoothly drops the oar blade into the water then explodes with her legs, torso still inclined forward yet with a straight back. Then at the last moment, as the legs are fully extended, she leans her torso back as she pulls the oar to her chest, squeezing that last ounce of power. In the final act she drops her hands, lifting the oar from the water; her arms shoot forward and she repeats the stroke. It is a complicated movement requiring precision and rhythm. Yet once the rower has mastered the stroke and found her rhythm on the river, the experience can be sublime. There is a sense of effortlessness, as if the boat is transported not through but over the surface of the water, gliding on the very brink of flight. Now consider the experience when a boat of eight rowers enters into that same rhythm in perfect unison. An eight-person shell gliding silently, gracefully across the water in complete harmony is one of the most beautiful things to witness in all of sport. A high school rower once described to me how his coach would encourage the rowers, once they had achieved that marvelous harmony among the rowers, to close their eyes and feel the shell being propelled across the water as if by some hidden force. For him, it was one of the most profound spiritual experiences he had ever had. Runners describe something similar as they find "the zone" when one foot follows effortlessly upon the other, muscles working in perfect unison, as if their feet are no longer pounding the ground but hovering above it. It is the experience of the basketball player who finds himself in another kind of "zone." With each shot he launches he doesn't just hope that it will go in but, in a real sense, *knows* that it will go in. For athletes this sense of bodily harmony is a mysteriously spiritual one that, if one has but "eyes to see," is an encounter with the divine.

THE PURSUIT OF EXCELLENCE

This leads us to a third perspective on sport, the pursuit of excellence. Let us return to the origins of sport in Western civilization, ancient Greece.

Agon: The Spirit of Competition

In ancient Greek culture, sport was considered from two different perspectives. The first was termed *agon* and referred to the spirit of competition, and the second was *arête*, and was oriented toward the pursuit of excellence.[18] There is an inclination to oppose these two, but the agonistic character of sport is always, at its best, also a pursuit of excellence.

Why has the competitive aspect of sports become subject to such criticism? Much criticism is rooted less in competition itself than in the way in which competition has become debased in contemporary culture. This debasement is reflected nowhere more dramatically than in the proliferation of taunting gestures on the field of play, where triumph must be punctuated by the humiliation of one's opponent. I have in mind the increasingly common gestures that we see when a basketball player dunks over an opponent, a defensive end sacks a quarterback, or a cornerback dislodges the ball from a receiver and then stands over the player, defiantly shaking his head or performing a "Superman" (where the athlete symbolically rips open an invisible shirt to reveal his Superman-like identity). Such actions debase competition by suggesting that the success of one athlete must lead to the diminishment of the other. It doesn't have to be that way.

I remember seeing the hall of fame football player Earl Campbell, one time running back for the Texas Longhorns and the Houston Oilers, getting tackled by a linebacker and immediately popping up and patting the defender on the back as if to say, "Good play, we'll see what happens next time!" This is certainly a gesture of good sportsmanship, but it is more than that; it is also a recognition that in competition the real distinction is not between winners and losers but between those who risk competing and those who do not. At the heart of sportsmanship is the recognition that there is an important difference between genuine competition and "winning at all costs." An authentic experience of competition, the agonistic dimension of sport, leads directly to *arête*, the pursuit of excellence.

Arête: The Pursuit of Excellence

Excellence suggests the pursuit of perfection, the possibility of developing a skill in such a way as to exceed one's present capacity and fulfill untapped potential. To believe in the capacity for excellence is to believe that the human person is fundamentally open-ended. Through commitment and effort we can transcend the perceived limits of human ability. We can become more than we are. In a sense, to believe in the possibility of excellence is to believe that we participate in our own creation. Let me take a slight theological detour here to develop this point a bit.

The great spiritual writer Thomas Merton, in his *New Seeds of Contemplation*, once wrote:

> A tree gives glory to God by being a tree. For in being what God means it to be it is obeying Him. . . . But what about you? What about me? Unlike the animals and the trees, it is not enough for us to be what our nature intends. . . . Therefore the problem of sanctity and salvation is in fact the problem of finding out who I am and of discovering my true self. Trees and animals have no problem. God makes them what they are without consulting them, and they are perfectly satisfied. With us it is different. God leaves us free to be whatever we like. We can be ourselves or not, as we please. . . . Our vocation is not simply to be, but to work together with God in the creation of our own life, our own identity, our own destiny.[19]

Merton captures here the way in which God has created us as creatures who must grow into our destiny. We do this, of course, not on our own but by responding to and cooperating with God's grace. We are made for, if you will, graceful development. There is no good reason to exempt athletic achievement from the areas of life in which humans grow in their response to God's invitation.

The ability of the dedicated athlete to develop and pursue excellence through training and commitment is not unrelated to the larger call to growth as human persons. Let us return, yet again, to Thomas Aquinas who describes the virtue of *magnificence*.[20] Magnificence refers to the accomplishment of greatness. It is realized whenever a person makes the most of their God-given gifts. According to Thomas the opposite of magnificence is the vice of *parvificence*, often rendered in English as *meanness*. Meanness here does not convey the contemporary sense of the word, suggesting some malicious action, but rather it refers to one who makes too little use of their gifts and abilities.[21] Through the pursuit of excellence in any and every sphere of life, we strive to become the person God invites us to be. Andrew Cooper reflects on the connection between the pursuit of excellence and the appreciation of sports as a craft:

> By investing an activity with one's dedication, aspiration, discipline, skill, and knowledge, one's identity is linked to it. In some indefinable way, part of one's self is in the work. Through craftsmanship, a sport becomes an expression of the athlete's total self and the means by which the self recognizes its own excellence.[22]

The great athlete becomes for us a hero, the unseemly cousin of the saint or artist, not because of any moral, spiritual, or aesthetic greatness to be sure, but in the intensity of their determination to achieve excellence in their chosen path. David Tracy in his book *The Analogical Imagination* captured this commonality of the hero (athlete), the thinker, the artist, and the saint when he noted that what distinguishes them from us is the intensification of their journey in self-exploration and the discovery of their hidden potentialities.[23] Theirs is a courageous journey that many of us fear to make.

Consider the climactic scene from the movie *Tin Cup* (1996). The movie is about a journeyman golf pro named Roy McAvoy. Blessed with tremendous athletic ability, Roy has squandered much of it in favor of a life of drinking and carousing. However, he meets a woman that helps rekindle his competitive instincts, and he sets upon the arduous quest of qualifying for the U.S. Open. He succeeds and, after a disastrous first round, shoots a 62 to make the cut. On the final day Roy finds himself in a three-way tie for the lead as he approaches the final hole, a difficult par five. After his drive he has to decide whether to make a conservative play and lay up short of the water hazard situated right in front of the green. This safe play would likely assure him at least a tie. The other option, one that his caddie vociferously opposes, is to risk the tournament and "go for it" by attempting a demanding shot that must clear the hazard to reach the green. He attempts the difficult shot and promptly puts it in the water. Although he could have accepted the penalty and advanced the ball to a few yards in front of the hazard, Roy insists on dropping the ball at the same spot as his previous shot, convinced that he can make this shot. That ball too goes in the drink. Then, shocking both spectators and TV commentators, he repeats the same shot over and over again, each time landing in the water hazard and incurring an additional penalty. He finally succeeds in reaching the green but only after taking himself out of the competition. The movie effectively evokes a sense of incredulity that an athlete would deliberately "throw away" a chance to win the U.S. Open in order to make the perfect shot. In *Roy McAvoy, agon* meets *arête* and, against all reasonable expectation, the quixotic search for excellence trumps the drive to win.

Susan Saint Sing, an accomplished athlete and coach in multiple sports, offers further reflection on the athlete's quest for excellence.

I believe they do it, we do it, to see what we are made of—meaning to see if there is anything more, anything other than flesh and sweat and blood. We do it to see if there is a soul looking at us in the extreme fumes of exhaustion. As in a near-death experience, we go in a controlled fashion into these realms to see, to explore the depths of ourselves, begging of the Other.

Like a pilgrimage, a cleansing, a retreat, we emerge more
human, more alive, more aware.[24]

The athlete, like the artist and the saint, through his or her particular abilities, reveals to us something of our own capacity for transcendence, for greatness, in the particularities of our lives. By means
of this transcendence, in whatever form it may take—whether hitting
a golf ball 275 yards down the middle of the fairway or completing a
work project, surpassing our own expectations—we touch the graced
dimension of sports in company with Tiger Woods, Mia Hamm, Le-
Bron James, Serena Williams—a realm both sublime and universal.
    Our appreciation for the pursuit of excellence is particularly in
evidence in our attraction as fans to great sports heroes. Consider a
scene from the movie *Vision Quest* (1985). The film is about a young
high school wrestler who decides that he wants to take on a new challenge during his final year in school. He sets for himself the goal of
dropping two weight classes in order to wrestle a boy who was undefeated in his last three years of high school wrestling and considered
unbeatable. On the night of the championship match between Louden
and his feared adversary, the young wrestler was distracted and depressed about a failed romantic relationship. He goes to visit Elmo, an
old man who works with Louden at a hotel. Elmo and Louden had
worked together for some time and had developed a kind of father-son
relationship. Louden was shocked to see that Elmo was wearing a coat
and tie and had taken off work to go watch Louden wrestle that night.
Louden expresses his surprise that Elmo was willing to lose a night's
pay just to see a wrestling match.

Louden: It's not that big a deal Elmo, it's six lousy minutes on the
mat, if that.
Elmo: Ever hear of Pelé?
Louden: Yea, he's a soccer player.
Elmo: A very *famous* soccer player. I was in a room here [at the
hotel where they worked] one day. I'm watching a Mexican chan-
nel on TV. Now I don't know nothin' 'bout Pelé. I'm watchin'
what this guy can do with a ball and his feet. Next thing I know

he jumps up in the air an' flips into a somersault and, ah, kicks the ball in, upside down and backwards! The goalie never knew what the heck hit him! Pelé gets excited an' rips off his jersey an' starts running around the stadium waving it around over his head. Everybody's screaming in Spanish. I'm here sitting alone in my room. I start cryin'. Yea, that's right, I start crying, 'cause another human being, of the species I happen to belong to, can kick a ball, and lift himself and the rest of us sad-ass human beings up to a better place to be, if only for a minute. Let me tell ya, kid, it was pretty glorious.

It ain't the six minutes, it's what happens in that six minutes. Anyway that's why I'm gettin' dressed up and giving up a night's pay for this function.

Great athletes remind us that we need not accept our own mediocrity, that the extraordinary is attainable for all of us. This does not mean, of course, that we can all imitate Pelé. What it means is that, if we are willing to summon the resources, there is an extraordinary feat lying within each of us. Athletes inspire us because in their extraordinary achievements they disclose for us the untapped potentialities of "the species I happen to belong to." Put simply, great athletes differ from us in degree and not kind. Tempted though we are to make them into gods, our favorite athletes are humans like ourselves who display the greatness of our common humanity on the field of competition. What we share, and it is vital that we not lose sight of this, is not their athleticism, but their capacity for transcendence, their ability to achieve excellence.

All of us who dare to venture on the field of play share in the pursuit of excellence at our own level, and on occasion we are blessed to enter, if only for a brief moment, into that rarified realm where our heroes regularly abide. I am an avid though relatively unaccomplished golfer. Like many golfers my age, I derive tremendous satisfaction in that rare moment when I hit a great drive 250 yards down the fairway. However, for me, the most satisfying shots are not off the tee but around the green. They demand the combination of imagination, creativity, and finesse that represents athletic excellence at its most sublime. A number of years ago I was playing a round of golf with a friend when I had the occasion to flirt with excellence. I was playing a very difficult course and faced a particularly demanding shot. My ball was about 15 yards to the right of the green with a large bunker right in front of me. The ball was lying up high in the rough. The green was fast and heavily sloped toward a water hazard on the opposite side of the green. There was no easy option. I had to hit a golf shot that would allow me to clear the bunker and still keep the ball from rolling off the green into the hazard on the other side. A delicate flop shot was called for. A flop shot is a difficult finesse shot in which the golfer must open the face of a wedge and execute a full swing even though the golfer is but a few yards away from the green. Since the ball was lying up in the rough, there was a risk that I would cut under it and hit the ball in the trap, leaving myself an even more intimidating sand shot. Alternatively, if I hit it too hard or, God forbid, bladed the shot, the ball goes into the water hazard on the other side. I forced myself to clear my mind of all the ways in which this shot could go wrong and concentrated on the rhythm of the shot, forcing my body to take a fuller swing than my mind wanted to. I hit the ball perfectly, lofting it high in the air and landing it gently on the fringe of the green from which it rolled to a mere five feet from the cup. If I were to try that same shot twenty times, I would be hard-pressed to get it that close to the flag twice. But for that one shot, at that one moment in time, I achieved excellence. And as the saying goes in golf, it's that one shot that keeps you coming back! That brief flirtation with excellence is what drives many of us in sports.

IN PRAISE OF FAILURE

Many early Christian writers used the image of the athlete to describe the Christian life. St. Paul writes:

> Do you know that in a race the runners all compete but only one receives the prize? Run in such a way that you may win it. Athletes exercise self-control in all things; they do it to receive

a perishable wreath, but we an imperishable one. So I do not run aimlessly, nor do I box as if beating the air. (1 Cor 9:24–26, NRSV)

Dedicated athletes reveal the same sense of endurance, commitment, and self-control that ought to characterize the Christian disciple. Patrick Kelly observes, "early Christian writers compared the martyrs to athletes because they persevered in the face of trial and tribulation and kept their focus on their goal."[25]

Fidelity to the gospel requires Christians to embrace deprivation and failure as the paradoxical means by which conversion and growth in the Christian life can happen. This is the paschal shape of the Christian life. The term "paschal" recalls the Hebrew Passover (Pasch), in which God delivered the Israelites from slavery into freedom. Christians hold that in death Christ too "passed over" into the Father, effecting our own liberation from sin. But it is a mistake to think of the paschal mystery only in connection with the final events of Jesus's life. For what transpired in the last days of Jesus's life on earth was but a dramatic culmination of his entire life. The central challenge of Christian life is to internalize and make this spiritual rhythm of life-death-life our own. With Jesus we are to *live* out of the assurance that we are God's good creatures, *die* to any tendency to make ourselves the ultimate reality in the universe, and *live* anew in lives of loving attentiveness and service to others. In this vein Ronald Rolheiser distinguishes between two kinds of death:

First, regarding two kinds of death: there is *terminal* death and there is *paschal* death. Terminal death is a death that ends life and ends possibilities. Paschal death, like terminal death, is real. However, paschal death is a death that, while ending one kind of life, opens the person undergoing it to receive a deeper and richer form of life. The image of the grain of wheat falling into the ground and dying so as to produce new life is an image of paschal death.[26]

The question is whether only Christians enter into this paschal experience. Is it not possible that any human who willingly embraces the deathly dimension of life, who acknowledges the inevitability of failure without giving in to despair, bitterness, and blame, enters into the paschal mystery and is in someway trafficking in the divine?

Virtually all sport forces athletes to deal regularly with failure. The best basketball players will be fortunate to make half their shots. Tiger Woods has won a remarkable 26 percent of the professional tournaments he had entered as of 2014. The second best winning percentage is Jack Nicklaus's 12 percent. Yet the vast majority of golfers on the PGA tour will compete for an entire year without winning a single tournament. Some of them may not win a tournament in their entire career. Nowhere is failure more a profound part of sports than with baseball. Bacik reminds us that

> the best hitters make outs more than 60% of the time. Mickey Mantle struck out over three times as often as he hit a home run. . . . The best major league baseball teams know the agony of defeat over sixty times in a season. The winningest pitcher in major league history, Cy Young, lost over 300 games.[27]

Athletes are willing to risk competition in the face of the likelihood of failure. They have prepared for it through training, perfecting a specific set of skills. They hone a particular skill with full intention and discipline, failing with great regularity until finally they master the skill. When athletes look failure and defeat squarely in the eye and do not shirk from it, they experience the deathly dimension of sport and its invitation into paschal living. In *The Joy of Sports*, Michael Novak writes:

> For the underlying metaphysic of sports entails overcoming the fear of death. In every contest, one side is defeated. Defeat hurts. No use saying, "It's only a game." It doesn't feel like a game. The anguish and depression that seize one's psyche in defeat are far deeper than a mere comparative failure—deeper than recognition of the opponent's superiority. . . . A game tests, somehow, one's entire life. It tests one's standing with fortune and the gods. Defeat is too like death. Defeat hurts like death.[28]

The failures one experiences in sports can be daunting, but they can also offer vital human lessons, teaching us that it is only through the risk of failure that we can come to know the giftedness of life itself. The Australian golfer Greg Norman taught us something about the paschal character of authentic athletic competition.

In 1996 Greg Norman entered the final round of the Masters golf tournament, one of the four "major" golf tournaments on the U.S. professional golf tour, with a six-stroke lead. For three days he had put on an impressive exhibition of golf on one of the most famous and demanding golf courses in the world. Most fans and media viewed the final round as largely a foregone conclusion. No golfer had ever lost the Masters on the final round with a six-stroke lead, and Greg Norman was not just any golfer but one of the top players on the PGA tour at the time. Yet on that final day, the impossible happened. As Norman's lead began to evaporate, I remember feeling almost queasy. Watching Norman's final round was like watching someone slowly and methodically stripped naked and humiliated before your eyes. By the thirteenth hole, millions of sports fans began to consider the unthinkable, that Norman was going to do what no golfer in Masters history had ever done—lose a six-stroke lead in the final round. But it would not end mercifully on the thirteenth hole. There was no manager to throw in the towel; the network could not gracefully switch to another sports event. For the next ninety minutes we watched the clinical dissection of Greg Norman's psyche, staring at a close-up of him as he lined up a putt. We searched his face for some psychic fault line, wondering what mental sales pitch he was giving himself. I remember half-wishing the camera would pull away and leave Norman to himself.

He lost the tournament that day to Nick Faldo. The most remarkable aspect of the 1996 Masters, however, was what transpired immediately after the final hole was completed and in the days that followed. After his historic collapse, Norman did not hang his head. He did not imitate the likes of other athletes too numerous to mention who, in far less trying circumstances, behaved like the arrested adolescents they often were in response to inquiring sports journalists. Norman answered every question with dignity and calmly reminded a skeptical sports media that he would indeed get out of bed the next morning, take stock of his world, and be glad to be alive. Was he devastated by his loss? Yes. But, Norman reminded us, this was after all a golf tournament—no more, no less. A *New York Times* columnist interpreted Norman's response as evidence that he lacked the "fire in the belly" necessary to win the big one. How odd that we evaluate determination and drive by success when these ineffable qualities are tested far more severely by failure. In his graceful acceptance of failure Norman embodied the paschal rhythm of authentic human existence. He did not quit, he failed, and there is a huge difference between the two. Knowing that he did not quit, that he competed as best he could until the end, enabled Norman to accept failure as part of competition.

In a culture so often obsessed with ease, efficiency, and convenience, the committed athlete does two things. First, she reminds us that what is most profoundly human in us is our capacity to embrace the difficult, to face failure, to endure, to transcend our limits in pursuit of excellence. But at the same time, her determination to face that which is difficult, her drive for excellence, shines an uncomfortable light on the woundedness of our human condition. It reveals our own tendency to cower in the face of difficulty and accept a comfortable mediocrity. When each of us faces difficulty and failure, stares down our own creaturely limits and perseveres toward our desired goal in the midst of the particular circumstances of our lives, we share company with all great athletes.

TEAMWORK, EMPATHY, AND SOLIDARITY

The fifth theological perspective on modern athletics to merit our consideration is the athlete's experience of team participation. Christianity teaches that humans are intrinsically social creatures. The creation stories in Genesis 1–3 affirm that God has created human persons for relationship. Christians believe in a triune God who does not *have* relationships but *is* perfect relationality. Humans are created in the image and likeness of this God and fulfill their God-given calling when they enter into authentic, life-giving relationship with others. Consequently, from the perspective of the Christian faith, it is in human relationship with others that, in a basic sense, we work out our relationship with God. If that is the case, then any social context becomes the occasion for authentic communion with God through others. This suggests that the athlete's experience of team camaraderie is ripe with spiritual potential.

Perhaps the only other human bond of communion that can match that between teammates is that among soldiers. Many athletes will speak years later of the powerful bonds created among team members who spent hours each day in training, honing their skills and learning how to work cooperatively with one another as a seamless, efficient unit. We must not underestimate the strength of this bond. Consider how a fan will often react to a player on their favorite team who is in an extended performance slump, as often occurs in baseball. With each strikeout or weak ground ball the fan gets more and more incensed, cursing the player and the coach who refuses to bench him. Yet when a slumping player returns to the dugout after yet one more strikeout he is more often than not met with a consoling pat on the back from his teammates. All athletes have had the sobering experience of failure. They know, as few fans can, how fragile athletic success can be. The fragility of success and the inevitability of failure help create a remarkable solidarity among teammates. Sports can create an enormous capacity for empathy with one's teammates, and that empathy, in turn, generates a deep sense of team solidarity. Why is this empathy of spiritual significance? Because it is the human capacity to care for others, to move out of the cocoon of our own self-absorbed existence, that is the basis for human love. And Christians believe that every act of love is a communion with the divine. As we learn in 1 John 4: "if we love one another, God lives in us, and his love is perfected in us." There is no human movement toward the other in an act of love, caring, or compassion in which God is not implicated.

Sports teams can also be for athletes a school in moral formation. This theme has been played out so often in sports movies as to be a cliché. We know the plotline: the gifted but self-absorbed athlete must learn to subordinate personal achievement for the success of the team. But within this Hollywood cliché is an indisputable truth; team sports call athletes to look beyond individual achievement in favor of the welfare of the team. Team play is an exercise in solidarity with others. Moreover, this subordination of individual fame for the sake of the team is an athletic enactment of the paschal grammar that we mentioned above. Every athlete who "dies" to her own desire for personal celebrity for the good of the team enters into the distinctive paschal rhythm of authentic human existence.

THE SPIRITUAL EXPERIENCE OF SPORTS FANDOM

Finally I would like to consider briefly the significance not of athletic activity but of athletic fandom. One of the great things about sports is that it creates a bond not only among athletes but also between fans and athletes and even among the fans themselves. These affective bonds can be every bit as deep as those among athletic teammates. In his wonderful book, *Baseball as a Road to God,* John Sexton recalls his childhood experience with a friend of kneeling in prayer, clutching a crucifix in front of the radio as they listened to game seven of the 1955 World Series, pitting their beloved Brooklyn Dodgers against the hated New York Yankees. He writes:

> The essence of the agony and the ecstasy Dougie and I experienced during the final innings on October 4, 1955, is not in the confluence of baseball and religion on a surface level—listening to a broadcast while clutching a crucifix—but is in its depth, the feelings and sensitivities that were evoked by the experience.[29]

This sense of almost mystical depth is not always positive. I am a Texas Rangers fan, and I remember as if it were yesterday the sixth game of the 2011 World Series. The Rangers were up in the series 3–2. In that game the Rangers were not once but twice a single strike away from winning that game and, for the first time in their team history, the World Series. As fans, we could taste victory. It was the final reward by the baseball gods for following a team for almost forty years filled mostly with futility. And then, with one swing of David Freese's bat, it was gone. Of course it was only game six. There still was a

seventh game to be won, but I think most Rangers fans knew the series was over. To say that loss hurt simply doesn't do justice to the experience. For weeks, just the mention of that game would evoke an
invisible gut punch. Fans care about their teams . . . a lot. The great
sports writer Roger Angell understands this and celebrates it:

> It is foolish and childish, on the face of it, to affiliate ourselves
> with anything so insignificant and patently contrived and com-
> mercially exploitative as a professional sports team, and the
> amused superiority and icy scorn that the non-fan directs at the
> sports nut (I know this look—I know it by heart) is understand-
> able and almost unanswerable. Almost. What is left out of this
> calculation, it seems to me, is the business of caring—caring
> deeply and passionately, really *caring*—which is a capacity or
> an emotion that has almost gone out of our lives. And so it
> seems possible that we have come to a time when it no longer
> matters so much what the caring is about, how frail or foolish
> is the object of that concern, as long as the feeling itself can
> be saved. Naiveté—the infantile and ignoble joy that sends a
> grown man or woman to dancing and shouting with joy in the
> middle of the night over the haphazardous flight of a distant
> ball—seems a small price to pay for such a gift.[30]

CONCLUSION: THE COACH AND PARENT AS MYSTAGOGUE

In a volume on youth sports it seems worthwhile to conclude these
theological reflections by a consideration of the role of the coach in
youth athletics. Throughout this essay I have explored the intrinsic
spiritual significance of sports by which athletes and fans, through
sports, can be drawn into the realm of God's presence—in a word,
grace. With that in mind I propose that we think of the coach or
parent as a *mystagogue*. The term is borrowed from a related term
used in ancient Christianity, "mystagogy." This term had a different
meaning then, but for our purposes we can describe mystagogy as
a process by which we discover and deepen our immersion in the
graced-dimension of our lives. A mystagogue, then, is a person who

helps others to see that they are already living lives imbued by the Holy Mystery of God. The mystagogue helps others to deepen their sense of God's presence and calls them to embrace the paschal rhythm of authentic human life to which we are all called.

Coaches and parents become mystagogues when they help athletes to recognize the spiritual dimension of their participation in sports. When a coach encourages the athletes in her charge to truly *enjoy* the sport, to delight in their own athleticism and that of those around them, the coach is helping those athletes commune with their God who shares in their delight. When a parent or coach encourages an athlete to pursue excellence through discipline and training, they are helping that athlete to understand that they have been put on this earth to make good use of the gifts given to them; they are called to *magnificence*, to the full employment of their gifts, however generous or meager they may appear to be. Coaches and parents are mystagogues when they help athletes to understand that it is their calling from God not simply to coast through life but to persevere, to grow, to become the person God has called them to be. Finally, coaches and parents function as mystagogues when they help athletes to understand the inevitability of failure and the importance of facing failure with grace and a determination not to let failure be the final word of their lives but a necessary obstacle to be faced and overcome.

In this essay I have followed Thomas Aquinas in seeking the virtue that lies between two extremes: the first would simply dismiss sport as a meaningless distraction from the seriousness of life; the second would make sport the most important sphere of human existence. Sport is neither. However, for those "with eyes to see," and it is precisely the task of coaches and parents to help youth athletes "to see," sport can become one of the many human activities by which we encounter *Deus ludens*, God at play, and that is no small thing.

NOTES

1. Charles Taylor, *A Secular Age* (Cambridge, MA: Belknap Press, 2007).

2. Patrick Kelly, *Catholic Perspectives on Sports: From Medieval to Modern Times* (New York: Paulist, 2012), 16.

3. Ibid., 27–62.

4. For a discussion of these images see ibid., 27–36.

5. Vincent Capuano, "Introduction," in *The World of Sport Today: A Field of Christian Mission* (Vatican City: Libreria Editrice Vaticana, 2006), 94. This is a collection of papers offered at a Vatican symposium sponsored by the Pontifical Council on the Laity.

6. St. Thomas Aquinas, *Summa Contra Gentiles*, I, 91, 1. Thomas has in mind passages like Proverbs 8:30–32.

7. St. Thomas Aquinas, *Summa Theologiae*, II-II, Q. 168, a.2.

8. Hugo Rahner, *Man at Play* (New York: Herder and Herder, 1967), 12.

9. James J. Bacik, *Spirituality in Action* (Kansas City: Sheed & Ward, 1997), 109.

10. St. Thomas Aquinas, *Expositio super Boethium, "De Hebdomadibus,"* as quoted in Rahner, *Man at Play,* 2.

11. Roman Guardini, *The Spirit of the Liturgy* (New York: Crossroad, 1997), 70.

12. See especially Allen Guttmann, *The Erotic in Sports* (New York: Columbia University Press, 1996) and *From Ritual to Record: The Nature of Modern Sports* (New York: Columbia University Press, 1978).

13. Patrick Kelly expounds on this Christian resistance to Gnosticism and Manichaeism as a persuasive rebuttal to the claims of Guttmann and others in Kelly, *Catholic Perspectives on Sports,* 63–117.

14. "The Pastoral Constitution on the Church in the Modern World," # 22, translation taken from Austin Flannery, ed., *Vatican Council II: Constitutions, Decrees, Declarations* (Northport, NY: Costello, 1996).

15. Dietmar Mieth, "Towards an Ethic of Sport in Contemporary Culture," in *The World of Sport Today: A Field of Christian Mission,* 23–43, at 29–30.

16. St. Clement of Alexandria, *Paidagogos,* 3, 9–10, quoted in Mieth, "Towards an Ethic of Sport," 30.

17. See Mihaly Csikszentmihalyi, *Beyond Boredom and Anxiety: The Experience of Play in Work and Games* (San Francisco: Jossey Bass Publishers, 1975), and *Flow: The Psychology of Optimal Experience* (New York: Harper and Row, 1990).

18. For an extended consideration of these two dimensions see Hans Ulrich Gumbrecht, *In Praise of Athletic Beauty* (Cambridge, MA: Harvard University Press, 2006), 69–75.

19. Thomas Merton, *New Seeds of Contemplation* (New York: New Direction Books, 1961), 31–32.

20. St. Thomas Aquinas, *Summa Theologiae*, II-II, Q. 134.

21. St. Thomas Aquinas, *Summa Theologiae*, II-II, Q. 135.

22. Andrew Cooper, *Playing in the Zone: Exploring the Spiritual Dimension of Sports* (Boston: Shambhala, 1998), 134.

23. David Tracy, *The Analogical Imagination* (New York: Crossroad, 1981), 124.

24. Susan Saint Sing, *Spirituality of Sport: Balancing Body and Soul* (Cincinnati: St. Anthony Messenger Press, 2004), 24.

25. Kelly, *Catholic Perspectives on Sports*, 102.

26. Ronald Rolheiser, *The Holy Longing: The Search for a Christian Spirituality* (New York: Doubleday, 1999), 146.

27. Bacik, *Spirituality in Action*, 99.

28. Michael Novak, *The Joy of Sports*, rev. ed. (Lanham, MD: Madison Books, 1994), 47.

29. John Sexton, with Thomas Oliphant and Peter J. Schwartz, *Baseball as a Road to God: Seeing beyond the Game* (New York: Gotham Books, 2013), 11.

30. Roger Angell, *Five Seasons: A Baseball Companion* (New York: Popular Library, 1978), 89.

PART 2

Practices and Perspectives

CHAPTER 9

Playing Like a Champion Today II

*Youth Sport and Growth in Body,
Mind, and Spirit*

KRISTIN KOMYATTE SHEEHAN

*Sports in the community can be a great missionary tool, where the Church
is close to every person to help them become better and to meet Jesus Christ.*
—Pope Francis[1]

Much recent research reveals that young people are dropping out of sport at alarming rates due to the often toxic elements in the culture of youth sports. In response to the growing concerns around this and other issues in youth sport, the University of Notre Dame created the Play Like a Champion Today Sports as Ministry initiative in 2006. Play Like a Champion Today offers workshops around the country to help youth and high school sport coaches and parents understand how sports participation can be a positive experience and help young people develop in body, mind, and spirit. As Christians, we are not supposed to simply go along with whatever the value orientations of a given culture might be, after all. We are also called at times to challenge these value orientations. In this sense, we take as our inspiration Paul's Letter to the Romans, where he writes, "Do not conform yourselves to this age but be transformed by the renewal of your mind, that you may discern what is the will of God, what is good and pleasing and perfect" (Rom 12:2).

Most people understand that sports can help young people to grow physically, but the Play Like a Champion Today workshops seek to help coaches and parents understand how they can enable young athletes to grow emotionally, morally, and spiritually through sport. While such growth can happen in sport, it does not happen automatically. Coaches and parents must recognize this holistic growth potential and approach sports in a manner that fosters it. The Notre Dame approach is centered on the familiar mantra, Play Like a Champion Today. Perhaps one of the best known slogans in the collegiate sporting world, this slogan is posted on a sign in the Notre Dame football locker room. As the players exit the locker room on their way into competition, they hit the sign, indicating their commitment to play like true champions individually and as a team. Let's look at each dimension of this mantra to highlight its spiritual undertones.

PLAY

"I was with him forming all things: and was delighted every day, playing before him at all times" (Prv 8:30). This verse from Proverbs depicts ancient Wisdom playing before God in a co-creative role. At the most basic level, sports are games that are meant to be played. Why do we play? We play because it is fun, it is enjoyable. Yet, saying sports are for fun isn't quite enough. As Christians we believe that we do not live for bread alone, but for what nourishes our spirit. We play to unleash dormant potential within ourselves and those with whom we are playing. When we play or coach sports, or when we observe sports as spectators, we are provided with the distinct opportunity to express our freedom, to display our creativity, and to discover beauty.

Bart Giamatti, the former commissioner of Major League Baseball, offers a vision of sport in his book *Take Time for Paradise*. Giamatti asserts that we learn more about the values of a society when we watch how it plays, how it takes its leisure, than by examining how it goes about its work. Giamatti writes that sports are "a shared moment of leisure. Sports represent a shared vision of how we continue, as individual, team, or community, to experience a happiness or absence of care so intense, so rare, and so fleeting that we associate their experience with otherwise described as religious."[2] Sports for our young people and their coaches and spectators must be recognized as a true opportunity for *play*, a time to *re-create* themselves as individuals and communally. When all the fun of sport is stripped from the experience, we diminish its full potential. The best evidence that youth sport is losing the play element is the current drop-out rate. Seventy percent of young people will drop out of sport by the time they are thirteen years old.[3] The number one reason given by young people for dropping out is that sport is not fun anymore. In this context, we need to ask ourselves what we are doing (or not doing) as coaches and parents to keep our kids engaged, active, and loving the game. At a very fundamental level, we must conceive of sports as play, recreation, fun. In this proper perspective, we will not only nurture strong competitors, but also help to create whole persons, who are nourished in body, mind, and spirit through their participation. As Pope Francis rightfully says, "It is important *that sports remain a game*! Only by remaining a game will it do good for the body and spirit."[4]

LIKE A CHAMPION

Everyone knows what it means to play like or be a champion. Right? For many, the word "champion" immediately calls to mind the team that won the league title or the player who scored the most points. However, Play Like a Champion Today workshops help coaches understand the broader meaning of champion. If we think sports are all about winning, then we must rethink our approach from a spiritual perspective. The way sport contests are designed, in every case, there is a team that wins and a team that loses. Those of us who choose to play and watch sports have chosen an activity in which we can't all be winners. True competitors always play to win, but recognize and accept that they won't always win. The Latin phrase *ludere causa ludendi* reminds us to "play for the sake of playing." So, playing like a champion doesn't primarily refer to the scoreboard—it refers to the heart and to character. Legendary basketball coach John Wooden said, "When you ask, did I win? Did I lose? Those are the wrong questions. The correct question is: Did I make my best effort? That's what matters. The rest of it just gets in the way."[5]

Playing like a champion means putting forth your best effort in all circumstances, playing within the rules of the game and playing in harmony with your teammates. Playing like a champion means accepting victory with humility and understanding defeat as an opportunity to learn and get better in the next competition. If we aren't willing to help young people play like champions in a Christian community, then why should we play at all? When coaches and parents emphasize the true meaning of the word champion, they enable athletes to develop not just physically, but as whole persons. Once coaches and parents create the sport environment that places emphasis upon the tremendous potential of the entire process of sport, rather than the outcome of an individual game or season, it is probable that young athletes will have the freedom to soar to their highest potential, and to experience the transcendence that is possible in sport.

TODAY

The "Today" of Play Like a Champion Today is the crucial element that binds the full mantra together spiritually. The ancient Greeks had two words for time, *chronos* and *kairos*. Whereas *chronos* refers to sequential time, *kairos* signifies a period of time in which something special happens. Whereas *chronos* is quantitative, *kairos* is qualitative in nature. From a Christian perspective, *kairos* provides an opportunity for us to experience God's presence. When we apply this to sport, it helps us to recognize that no matter what happened in practice last week, no matter what the league standings, each practice, each game has significance unto itself. Each athletic experience presents an opportunity for an athlete to go beyond him- or herself, to experience self-transcendence. We as adults should nurture the opportunity for "Today" moments to happen for athletes.

I invite you to think of your "Today" moment, as an athlete, a coach, or a sport parent. Perhaps it was jogging on a wooded path on a crisp winter morning with snow gently coating bare branches, or building a sand castle with your daughter on a golden beach as the sun glistened on the water. Perhaps it was witnessing the girl on your cross country team make it through her first race without stopping to walk, or rejoicing as the boy on the soccer team who had never scored a goal put the ball past the goalie. Maybe it was watching the basketball player reach out to console his teammate after he missed the final free throw that would have won the game. We all can have "Today" moments if we place ourselves in the environment that nurtures these experiences. It is adults' joint responsibility to create the right environment in their attitude toward sport, in their behavior throughout sport events, and in their treatment of the young people who are playing.

How can we as coaches and parents foster young people's awareness of the spiritual dimension of the sport experience? When we think of the word "coach," we likely think of a teacher, a role model, even a mentor. These are proper and real conceptions of a coach, but there is also a spiritual vision of a coach as a minister. In our Play Like A Champion Today workshops, we ask coaches to identify the qualities and traits of a coach. They name such qualities as motivator, committed, patient, empathic, positive in attitude, role model, leader, teacher, generous with time and talent, respectful, tolerant, and oriented to service. Once coaches vocalize the qualities of a coach, we ask them whether these qualities intersect with the traits of a minister, and if so, how? Through the discussion, coaches realize that the qualities of a coach indeed are the qualities of a minister as well. Typically the only thing that a coach does that they do not identify as overlapping with what a minister does is understanding the Xs and Os of a particular sport. Frequently in our workshops, a coach mentions prayer as something a minister does, but not a coach. In every case, another coach pipes up that she or he prays with her or his team prior to games and practices. Many other coaches nod in agreement, confirming this important role of a coach. The overall consensus among coaches is that prayer in sport is not only a possibility but an essential component to coaching within a Christian community.

The Holy Spirit has gifted the church for centuries with a wide variety of ministries. Especially since Vatican II, lay ministers have played an increasingly important role in the church. Coach-ministers provide a service to the young people they coach and to their families, to the community they coach in, and to the church. The Latin term for ministry, *ministerium*, simply means service. All Christians are called to ministry by the nature of their baptism. Coaching is a special calling and is a form of ministry. Saint Teresa of Avila once commented that we as Christians are Christ's hands and feet on earth; it is our words and our actions that preach the gospel and further Christ's legacy. By serving children and encouraging their development, the work that coaches do is ministry. Yet being a coach-minister means much more than simply beginning practices with an "Our Father." The gift coaches give in their time and talent develops the people of God and can renew the body of Christ. Coach-ministers are the spiritual leaders of their team. The choice lies with the coach whether she or he will embrace the role of minister and how she or he will lead the team spiritually.

In his book *Ministry*, Richard McBrien gives a working definition of ministry that can help coaches further understand their role as coach-minister.[6] He outlines four levels of ministry, the first of which is General/Universal ministry. This is any service rendered to an individual person or group of people in need of that service, rooted in our common humanity. The next level is General/Specific ministry, which is a service rendered to others based on a specific competence, such as nursing, legal expertise, or coaching. These two levels of ministry have nothing to do intrinsically with religion and could include coaching in any sport league, at any level. The third level is Christian/Universal ministry, which is a general service provided to others in Christ and because of Christ. The call to ministry in this third sense is rooted in our baptism and confirmation. Finally, the fourth level of ministry is Christian/Specific, which is a specific service rendered to others in Christ and because of Christ in the name of the church and for the sake of helping the church fulfill its mission. I would assert that this level is what all coaches in faith-based leagues should strive to reach in their role as coach-minister. Coaches who see themselves in this level of ministry are called by God to do good for others (not simply for one's own child), by rendering unselfish service (not to feed one's own ego by having the "best" team), empowered by the Holy Spirit (not by the false god of winning), all for the purpose of bringing about the kingdom of God (not to collect trophies in a case). This kingdom is characterized by holiness and grace, justice and peace, love and hope.

According to McBrien, ministers are charged with a mission that takes place through word, witness, worship, and service.[7] Let us look at each of these terms with respect to youth coaches.

Coaches are ministers of the word. This does not necessarily mean quoting from the Bible during practice, but it does mean lovingly teaching each young person on a team the skills of the particular sport as well as life skills. It means communicating respectfully with each person on the team, their parents, and the officials. A coach's words can lift up or tear down. As ministers of the word, coaches will want to make sure their words flow from their own encounter with the Word made flesh.

Coaches also minister through their witness. Coach-ministers provide more than a service, they are also a witness to the reality they communicate. Thus, coach-ministers cannot separate their role from their personhood. The qualities a coach embodies are directly witnessed by the athletes they coach and all those who are a part of the athletic experience. Coaches must be continually mindful of their behavior on and off the field. We need to take seriously Paul's advice to Timothy, "Let no one look down on you . . . but rather in speech, conduct, love, faith, and purity show yourself an example" (1 Tim 4:12).

Coach-ministers lead worship. This does not mean that coaches celebrate mass during practice, but coach ministers begin games and practices in prayer, thanking God for the opportunity to play. Prayer on a team is not a way of summoning a far-away God but instead calls attention to the presence of God among the players and in the sport environment. Prayer also helps to put the sport event in the proper perspective.

Finally, coach-ministers do not look at their role as a means to attain rank or status, but as a service to the young people on their team and in their league. Coach-ministers remember to provide their service to all the players on the team, not just the best players or the easiest ones to coach.

The Play Like a Champion Today national workshop data from over 40,000 coaches indicate that most coaches had not previously regarded themselves as ministers. The data also indicate, however, that most coaches after connecting the role of coach and minister welcome the designation of coach-minister and are willing to embrace certain responsibilities that follow from such a designation, such as fostering the spiritual development of the young people on their teams. When coaches conceptualize their role as ministers, their entire coaching style and philosophy will be influenced. How they treat all members of their team, opponents, and officials is impacted. How they develop each player's skills and sense of confidence is affected, and even how they make line-ups and decide on playing time is influenced.

One coach who attended a Play Like a Champion Today workshop in Indianapolis shared with us how he concretely carried out the role of coach-minister. He paired each of his players with another player on the team and asked them to pray for that team member throughout the season. He then explained the idea to the team parents. He asked the parents to encourage their child to pray for their spiritually adopted team member at evening prayers, at the dinner table, or whenever they typically pray. He reported to us that it was a powerful team building experience for his team and a faith developing opportunity for the players and their parents.

Another Play Like a Champion Today coach shared with us how she lives out her role as spiritual leader of her teams. She holds short team meetings after each practice and game. Instead of discussing just how the athletes performed physically during their play time, she explores spiritual values within sport. She proposes questions to her players, such as, "Should we pray for a victory in our game today?" and "What role does God play in sport?" Inviting the team to talk through these salient issues enables them to consider and understand the spiritual dimension within sport.

Once coaches understand their role as ministers and spiritual leaders of their teams, our workshops present a practical approach for coach-ministers and parents to help young people truly grow through sport. The acronym for this approach is GROW: Goals + Relationships + Ownership = Winning. The formula is drawn from self-determination theory, a psychological theory of motivation which asserts that persons are motivated to succeed (Win) when they feel competent (Goals), connected (Relationships), and have control over their environment (Ownership).[8] This method enables young people to become physically skilled athletes as well as athletes of character.

Setting and achieving goals is integral to achieving success in sports as well as in life. Looking at sports from a ministerial perspective, coaches and parents can help young people set physical and mental as well as moral (sportsmanship) goals. It is this third dimension of goals that is often neglected and it is where young people most often can experience spiritual growth. Emily[9] can set a physical goal of making 75 percent of her free throws over the course of the season. Her mental goal may be paying full attention to the game even when she is not playing on the court. These are necessary and noble goals, but coaches and parents must take the next step in helping Emily set moral goals in sport that can also be spiritual in nature. For Emily, this may be helping Hannah (who has a weaker shot) get stronger and more accurate in her shooting by pairing up with Hannah in practice or staying after practice to shoot further with her. This enables Emily to directly learn and practice the Christian virtue of charity in sport. Those of us who have given of ourselves to help others directly know that when we serve others, we grow in Christ ourselves. When we encourage young people to be "other-centered," we help them become more like Christ and we help kids gain a deeper understanding of what it means to serve as part of a Christian community. Our spirituality is deepened when we live out the creed of Blessed Basil Moreau, founder of the Congregation of Holy Cross, who exhorted us to "make God known, loved, and served."

My son played on a baseball team consisting of twelve-year-old boys of varying sizes, personalities, and abilities. One of the players, Tyler, was struggling. Every time he went up to bat, he struck out. It was obvious in Tyler's facial expressions and body language that he was growing more and more discouraged as the season progressed. He had lost his confidence and was in a true slump (something every athlete might be able to relate to). In response, Tyler's coach gave him extra batting practice and helped him visualize the ball hitting his bat prior to going up to the plate (physical and mental goals). Additionally, the team recognized Tyler's need and started cheering for him while he was at bat. "Tyler, Tyler, Tyler, Tyler," they would chant in unison. The effect of the team's rallying cry created the difference and Tyler broke his slump. After this breakthrough, Tyler's hitting began to flow easily. Through this experience, the team learned that the "community of believers" can create a difference, can even move mountains. This story illustrates how setting moral goals with child athletes as a coach or sport parent helps young people to grow as Christian persons. It also illustrates the importance of building relationships in sport, which is the second element in the GROW approach.

Being a coach-minister means helping young people focus on relationship building. As people of God, we each have a personal relationship with Christ, but we are also members of a community of believers. Our personal piety expands and is strengthened when lived in the context of community. When we understand our unique place as members of the larger community of believers and our responsibility within that community, we grow spiritually. As coach-ministers and parents we can help athletes advance in their spiritual development by helping them to build positive relationships on their sports teams. We can guide athletes to recognize that every player on the team is vitally important and that they are better as athletes and as people when the whole team functions together.

To illustrate this, I would like to share a story from Susan, one of our Play Like a Champion Today coaches in Tulsa, Oklahoma. Brice was an eighth-grade boy who did not quite fit in. Unfortunately, his coordination hadn't quite caught up to his physical growth. Brice's parents encouraged him to join his school's volleyball team. Although he was a bit clumsy and lacked confidence, his height enabled him to make a strong shot every so often. Susan, as a coach-minister cognizant of relationships on the team, recognized that the other play-ers often did not bump the ball to Brice. Instead of just demanding that the players work together on the court, Susan decided to focus on building relationships on the team. She hosted a team pizza party and encouraged the team to choose a nickname. As the athletes chose to call themselves the "rednecks," they naturally took the next step of giving each player his own nickname. Brice, or "Legs" as he was dubbed by the team, started to be joked with in the school halls, and in practice balls slowly start getting bumped to Brice. As the days and weeks went on, Susan continued to encourage a norm of friend-liness on her team. She made this a topic of discussion at team meet-ings, helping the players to discover why it is important to include everyone on the team, not just for the strength of the team, but as people of God. As the players began to understand the importance of community, balls started to be bumped to "Legs" on a more regular basis. Brice's parents contacted Susan to let her know that Brice was actually excited to go to school since he had connected with kids on the team. Susan as a coach-minister empowered the team to under-stand the Christian virtue of justice. These volleyball players all came to know they are fuller, more whole creations of God when none are excluded and all are a full part of the community of believers. Coach Susan and her athletes in their compassionate inclusion of Brice be-came like Christ to him. As Pope Francis explains, "Sport fosters con-tact and relationships with people who come from diverse cultures and walks of life. It accustoms us to live and welcome differences, to turn them into a precious opportunity for mutual enrichment and discovery. Above all, sport is a precious opportunity to recognize one another as brothers and sisters on the journey, to foster the culture of inclusion."[10]

Another example of building spirituality through sport relation-ships exists in Coach Bridget's cheerleading team. Lily was new to the school and the cheer team, having just moved into the town when her father was transferred by his company. Lily's physically small stature made her perfect for the position of "flyer" (the athlete that goes on top of the pyramids). Lily worked hard in practices to prove that she could perform very well in the flyer position. However, Molly was a senior member of the team who had always been the team's flyer. As the competition season drew near, Coach Bridget announced that Molly would be the only flyer in their routine. Lily was furious with that decision and yelled at Bridget in front of the team, saying that was not a fair decision and then storming out of the practice. At first, the team was shocked and rallied around the coach, expressing disbelief in Lily's insolence.

Then Molly offered an alternate view. She acknowledged that Lily was an excellent flyer. Sarah said that she had not done anything to help Lily feel included at the school or on the cheer team. Laurie reminded the team that they had all gone out for pizza after last week's practice and did not invite Lily. All the girls agreed they had not fully welcomed Lily to their community. At that point, Lily came back into the gym and apologized to Coach Bridget for her outburst. Bridget accepted Lily's apology and apologized as well for not explaining the reason behind her decision. One by one, the team members apologized to Lily for not helping her feel a real part of their team. This led to a discussion among the team members about how they might change their routine to incorporate two flyers. Both Molly and Lily ended up flying and the routine became more competitive. The Christian virtues of forgiveness and mercy were discovered that afternoon in the gym. As members of a community of believers, we all can make mistakes (even as adult coaches); yet, we have the tremendous opportunity to experience reconciliation, strengthening our bonds with one another, and encountering God's presence in our midst.

Lily's story is also an example of ownership in the GROW approach. Spiritual growth can occur when young athletes are allowed ownership over their own sport experience. And yet, this is probably the most neglected element of the GROW approach. Being fully Christian and a member of a larger community of believers is predicated upon the freedom to choose faith. Allowing young athletes to own their participation in sport confirms their active role in their sport and in their faith. The example of Lily and her teammates illustrates a common occurrence on a team—two athletes desiring a key position and the coach making a controversial playing time decision. The outcome of a team situation such as this could easily have caused irreparable harm to the team chemistry and ill feelings from many (coach, teammates, parents). This team, however, freely chose how they would react to their team dilemma and worked out their situation in such a way that it helped them to mature as young women and as Christians.

It is a common tendency to treat young athletes like puppets, to script every play and every move or to dictate how athletes will act on the field and as teammates. We raise our children teaching them the tenets of faithful living, but eventually, they must choose to put those values and faith into practice. As much as we adults might wish to script the lives of our children or the young people we are close to, we intrinsically know there comes a point when young people must make their own choices. Every day, kids are faced with decisions, some simple and some complicated. By giving athletes ownership in sport, we can build their confidence and ability to make good and noble choices in life. It takes faith on the part of coaches and parents to allow athletes ownership over their play. It takes courage as a coach-minister to commit to letting the kids play the game for its own sake. They will make mistakes—many mistakes—in fact the mistakes might sometimes result in lost games. Coach-ministers will permit this to occur, clearly understanding that young people can grow from their mistakes. Growth occurs, not in the outcome of the players' decisions, but in the process of enabling athletes to make their own choices. This way of treating young people is analogous to how the Divine Creator treats each of us. We are created with unique talents and abilities and allowed freedom to choose how we will use these gifts. Our Creator has not only given us the gift of freedom, but requires us to make our own choices. Coaches and parents can strategically allow and enable young athletes to own their play and reclaim sport for all that it can be. This enables young people to choose higher values within sport on their own and to grow through the process.

At a Play Like a Champion Today conference, Mike, one of our coach trainers, shared the story of his sixth-grade girls' basketball team. Mike's team was playing against a team that included Allison, a player with an obvious special need. Allison physically struggled through the game, did not score, but received a fair share of playing time and had a smile on her face the whole game. In the post-game debrief, Mike's players mentioned that they thought it was wonderful that the team included this player. The next time Mike's team met up with Allison's was at the end of the season tournament. The girls as a team went to Mike before the game and told him they had decided that they would like to see Allison score a basket. So, when Allison went into the game, Mike's team would employ creative strategies to allow her to get the ball and shoot. One athlete "missed" the pass intended for her to allow Allison to get the ball. Allison's shot went up, but was wide. Another of Mike's players "allowed" the ball to be stolen from her. Allison shot again, but was short. At this point, none of Mike's players went to the hoop for the rebound. Every one of them stayed back, enabling the other team to recover their own rebound. At that instant, the other team realized what Mike's team was doing. After that every pass was fed to Allison until one made its way through the net. "SWISH!" The entire gym erupted in applause not only for Allison but in response to witnessing this special moment. All in the gym grew that afternoon: Mike's team when they made the choice to be loving and reach out to someone in need; Mike and all the adults in attendance as they experienced gospel values in action; Allison and the other team as they found another group caring about them. As the spiritual leader of the team, Mike experienced a real victory that day. He enabled his players to make choices on the court, not just about which play to run but about being people who care about others and who give lovingly for the greater good. This example illustrates the value of giving ownership to athletes in sport. In their self-guided generosity, these girls directly participated in building up the Kingdom of God. Their action became prayer to and praise of our Creator.

Winning in the GROW approach is also integral to understanding the spiritual potential in sport. We win as athletes, coaches, and parents when we understand that the score on the scoreboard is not the most important thing in sport. Certainly, we relish winning contests and excelling in competition, but we truly win when we understand that personal and spiritual growth through sport are possible and that they can be fostered by coach-ministers and parents. We win when we understand that we have the distinct opportunity to help kids grow in Christ through our focused presence with them in youth sport and when we embrace this opportunity.

Sports arouse passion, make great physical demands, and require mental focus that brings forth inner resources. Sports can and do test the human body and mind while feeding the human spirit. In play we can experience an intense joy. We are aware that the moment won't last—but when we are in the moment, we feel that we have stepped out of the ordinary. Through sport, we can achieve such transcendent qualities as beauty, excellence, freedom, and communion. By stirring deep feeling and imagination within athletes, coaches, and spectators, sport can create an opportunity for self-transcendence. In Dante's *Divine Comedy*, the angels in the highest level of heaven are playing before God and that pleases God. This chapter has sought to help coaches and parents understand the spiritual potential in youth sport, and to show how to create an environment that will help each young person to grow not just physically, but spiritually through their participation in sport. Together, we can help every young athlete to truly play as the angels did in Dante's *Divine Comedy*, pleasing God and enabling God's presence to be felt in our world.[11]

NOTES

1. Kerri Lenartowick, "Pope Encourages Athletes to Play for the Church," *Catholic News Agency*, June 7, 2014, available at http://www.catholicnewsagency .com/news/pope-encourages-athletes-to-play-for-the-church.

2. Bartlett Giamatti, *Take Time for Paradise* (New York: Summit Books, 1989).

3. Carleton Kendrick, Ed.M., LCSW, "Why Most Kids Quit Sports," quoting Michael Pfahl, executive director of the National Youth Sports Coaches Association, available at http://life.familyeducation.com/sports/behavior/29512.html.

4. Pope Francis, address to members of the Sports Associations for the Seventieth Anniversary of the Foundation of the CSI (Italian Sports Center), St. Peter's Square, Rome, June 7, 2014.

5. John Wooden and Steve Jamison, *Wooden: A Lifetime of Observations and Reflections On and Off the Court* (Lincolnwood, IL: Contemporary Press, 1997), 56.

6. Richard Mcbrien, *Ministry: A Theological, Pastoral Handbook* (New York: HarperCollins, 1987).

7. Ibid., 16.

8. Edward Deci and Richard Ryan, *Intrinsic Motivation and Self-Determination in Human Behavior* (New York: Plenum Press, 1985).

9. While all stories related in this chapter are true, the names have been changed for reasons of confidentiality.

10. Pope Francis, address to the Italian Paralympic Committee, St. Peter's Square, Rome, October 4, 2014.

11. For further reading the author suggests the following materials: Andrew Cooper, *Playing in the Zone: Exploring the Spiritual Dimensions of Sports* (Boston: Shambhala Publications, 1998); Susan Saint Sing, *Spirituality of Sport: Balancing Body and Soul* (Cincinnati: St. Anthony Messenger Press, 2004); and "The Play Like a Champion Today Sports as Ministry Coaches Training Manual" (University of Notre Dame, 2006).

CHAPTER 10

Catholic Youth Organization Sports

A Mission-Oriented Focus

DOBIE MOSER

In spring of 2013 part-time soccer referee Ricardo Portillo died one week after a teenage soccer player made a fatally flawed decision and punched him in the face during a suburban soccer league game in Taylorsville, Utah. Portillo saw the goalkeeper pushing another player and issued a yellow card. At his sentencing, the teen said he "was frustrated at the ref and caused his death." I am still trying to wrap my mind around that. Portillo left three daughters behind. He had a passion and love for soccer and had officiated youth contests for years. His oldest daughter, Johana, said that she and her sisters had pleaded with their father to stop refereeing because of risks from angry players and parents. "We are all there to have fun," she said after the tragic event. "Not to go and kill each other."

It is hard to know all the factors that led to Ricardo Portillo's death. But one factor is clear in this and the many other recent shameful episodes in youth sport: winning has become too important. Unfortunately, in the United States today, winning often *is* everything in youth sport. This is true in spite of threadbare slogans that the game is "about what's best for the kids" and that "sports builds character." More often sports reveal character, and too often the picture revealed is ugly. Everyone who watches television is aware that boorish behavior happens frequently at the professional and collegiate levels. Unfortunately, such behavior is often acceptable as long as the team or athlete is winning. The Tiger Woods "winning takes care of everything" ad expresses all too clearly the attitude that all is well when an athlete is winning and making money for advertisers, television, team owners, leagues, and so on. Unfortunately, such a mentality often "trickles down" to youth sports leagues.

Two competing visions are battling to become the *dominant vision* in youth sports in the United States today. One vision is sports as work and business; that is, to play a sport is to climb onto a ladder where success means each rung leads to greater benefits for fewer persons with the perks and demands increasing with every step up. The sports as ladder to success vision includes significant financial investment, travel leagues, national tournaments, private coaches, families who place sports at the center, early specialization in one sport and year round training, adults setting increasingly demanding goals for children and driving them to achieve those goals, and the necessity of winning individual and team records. The problem is that, according to research performed by the NCAA, only 1:13,000 high school seniors who play a varsity sport will ever receive a dime for playing that sport.[1] The primary question driving this vision is: What is best for the best of the best (my child and a few select athletes), and how can that be achieved for these individuals above all else?

An alternative vision held for youth sports is sports as *play* that contributes to the overall formation of young people. This vision includes fun with teammates and friends, skill development for short- and long-term benefits, sports as a way to learn life lessons, the health benefits of exercise, youth naming their own goals and developing strategies to pursue them, youth assigning their own meaning to their sports experience, and a clear recognition that young people have many interests worthy of their time and attention. The primary question driving this vision is: What would make the youth sports experience most beneficial for the overall formation of every young person and his or her teammates?

The first approach is individualistic and zero-sum. A very few win and most everyone else loses. The second approach is interpersonal and communal, and the benefits of this approach redound to everyone.

It is wishful thinking at best and delusional at worst to think that the harmful parts of youth sports culture in the United States cannot or have not already entered into our Catholic parishes and schools. Only when we evaluate sports programs in Catholic settings through the lens of mission can we take strategic steps that are both preventive and that help to build a sports culture that reflects and animates our gospel mission and values.

This is why Catholic Youth Organization (CYO) sports programs need to be intentional, forthright, and strategic regarding their sports vision and where it is rooted. The Diocese of Cleveland CYO program, like many CYO programs throughout the country, attempts to be clear and unequivocal about our vision: Sports are about the overall formation of young people with the goal of their becoming healthy adult Christian citizens.

This approach is rooted in the teaching of John Paul II, who emphasized that "the dignity of the human person is the goal and criterion of all sporting activity."[2] He pointed out that the person does not exist to serve sport, but rather sport should serve the person. Indeed, for him the key principle of a sound philosophy of sport is "the *dignity, freedom* and *integral development* of the person."

WHAT SPORTS BEHAVIORS UPHOLD OR VIOLATE OUR GOSPEL MISSION AND VALUES?

For years the Catholic Youth Organization at the national level has been asking our coaches to identify the best behaviors of CYO coaches that help to achieve gospel mission and values, as well as behaviors we should never see because they violate gospel mission and values. Coaches have identified the following behaviors. These concrete behaviors are manifestations of the two different visions outlined earlier.

The first behaviors are associated with sport as play, with an emphasis on the overall formation of every young person on the team. Coaching behaviors that help to achieve our gospel mission and values include:

- Have fun with the kids and help them to enjoy the experience
- Help team members want to come back and play again next year
- Teach specific skills and repeat fundamentals often
- Treat wins and losses as part of the game but not the whole purpose for playing
- Give every person on the team a chance to play and contribute to the team
- Encourage every child to give his or her best effort in practices and games
- Prepare for practices with a practice plan
- Have fun coaching
- Don't focus on officials—focus on your players and how you can help them play well
- Praise young people often—try to catch them doing something good
- Treat every child on the team with equal value, even though their skill levels and temperament require treating them differently
- Help team members improve their physical conditioning and health
- Respect your opponents and the officials
- Help teammates and opponents up when they fall
- Listen to team members and help them to learn to think on the field/court
- Remember the age and stage of development of team members and treat them accordingly
- Challenge every team member to grow and improve in their personal and team skills
- Be prepared at games and help players prepare for games
- Stay focused on what's best for the kids instead of focusing on yourself
- Pray with kids before and after practices and games

The following behaviors that coaches have identified tend to be exhibited when a coach approaches sports with the sport as work mentality. In such cases, youth sports are taken too seriously, as a means for upward mobility, money, and fame. And winning *is* the only thing. This can lead to treating members of the team or opponents in a way that does not acknowledge their dignity as human beings created in the image and likeness of God. Coaching behaviors that have no place in CYO sports include:

- Focusing on winning so much that the sport and game is no longer fun
- Pressuring team members to cheat or do "whatever it takes" to win a game
- Teaching players to play dirty and risk injury to any player on either team
- Yelling or swearing at officials, coaches, or players on either team
- Running up the score when a contest is clearly decided
- Yelling at kids and publicly humiliating them when they make a mistake
- Playing favorites on the team, especially with regard to their own child
- Intimidating team members or opponents
- Setting a bad example for team members and fans
- Playing the blame game, which removes responsibility from the coach and players
- Being a poor role model who violates good sportsmanship and CYO values
- Smack talking and talking trash with opponents or officials
- Using pre- or post-game prayers and handshakes to intimidate or be poor sports
- Breaking or throwing sports equipment
- Fixing team rosters to stack teams while leaving other teams with unskilled players
- Constantly picking on team member weaknesses and breaking their confidence
- Celebrating achievements in ways that humiliate opponents
- Allowing team members to ridicule a team member or opponent

ROLES IN CYO SPORTS

Young people are able to thrive in Catholic sports settings when there is an intentional effort to be aware of and attentive to the diverse roles we have. Doing so allows the different parties to operate in their roles in a manner that supports the Catholic mission of CYO sports. Here are the primary roles in CYO sports.

Players play. It is their game to learn, play, win, and lose while living out Catholic values. There will be an intentional effort made to remind coaches and parents to be aware of the risks when adults attempt to live through their child's athletic experience as if it were their own.

CYO sports are youth ministry. CYO sports are part of the Catholic Church's larger effort to reach out to and build the faith of young people through youth ministry.

CYO coaches are youth ministry leaders. The CYO coach is serving as a parish minister, similar to other ministry roles in the parish (lector, eucharistic minister, service project leader, etc.). Therefore the coach will receive the training and formation that will enable him or her to serve most effectively in his or her role as a CYO coach.

Coaches teach. Coaches instruct, guide, and teach sports skills and strategies as well as Catholic values in age appropriate ways.

CYO teams are Christian communities. The team members learn and experience Christian faith by praying together, by learning to reflect and assign meanings to their experiences in light of gospel values, and through loving relationships that help them to discover and know God more fully.

CYO parents are partners. CYO programs will make an intentional effort to engage parents to bring their gifts and talents to help the CYO program further achieve its stated mission and values. It is the role of parents to provide encouragement, love, and emotional support regardless of winning or losing. They are to model Christian behavior and values in support of the program mission and values.

Officials officiate. Officials are trained to provide a safe environment for all participants and to assure that contests are played according to the rules.

CYO is about competing the right way—win or lose. Our stated values in CYO will determine how we run our program, how we coach our teams, how we interact with teammates, opponents, and officials, and how we compete in athletic contests.

BUILDING BLOCKS

For young people to thrive in CYO sports programs there are important building blocks that need to be present:

1. Mandatory coaches' training and formation: This component is so critical that if a coach is not trained then he or she should not be permitted to coach young people. The training is about the person of the coach and his or her Christian formation. As was mentioned above, coaches are first and foremost teachers. One of the most important things the coaches will learn in their training is age appropriate pedagogy for their sport.
2. Program evaluation: Every sports season should be evaluated by all of the key parties involved: youth participants, coaches, parents, and sports administration. The evaluation needs to be rooted in the stated mission and values of the program. The evaluation information is used to build on the program strengths and to address program issues that are recurring. Parents sometimes have concerns about how their child is being treated and how the program is being run. Yet they often fear that speaking up may bring about negative consequences or retaliation against their child. Systematic, ongoing program evaluation allays this fear and provides them (and all others involved) with a context to provide feedback in a timely and forthright manner.
3. Working with parents as partners: Parents love their children and have a range of reasons for having their child on sports teams in Catholic settings. And it has been pointed out that sometimes parents can be the source of the greatest headaches for the coach. One of the reasons for this is that parents are increasingly viewing sport as a means to upward mobility for their child, specifically as a way to get a college scholarship or even, for the chosen

few, a professional contract. Therefore we have found it helpful to have parents explicitly reflect on and discuss questions, such as:

a. What are my expectations for my child and for every child on the team?
b. What does success look like?
c. What can I do as a parent to help my child's team to represent the best of CYO mission and values?
d. What particular strengths, talents, and resources am I willing to contribute as a parent, and how might I use them to help my child's team come closer to representing our Catholic mission and values?
e. When did I exhibit positive parenting skills today and when did I not do so? What will I do next time?

For sports in Catholic settings to focus first and foremost on our mission and values does not preclude high athletic achievement or competing at high levels. A mission focused Catholic sports program demonstrates our conviction that *how* athletic achievements occur has everything to do with their value and significance. When our Catholic sports programs effectively integrate our mission and values we can serve as a hopeful alternative to the sports as work and business model that is fraught with so many problems.

WHEN GOSPEL MISSION AND VALUES DRIVE THE CYO OR CATHOLIC SCHOOL PROGRAM

When the sports program for young people is inspired by the stated Catholic mission and values, it makes a difference in a number of concrete ways. Here are two important examples.

• No cutting of players guarantees access for every child to participate on a team and in game situations. In most CYO programs this also includes the opportunity for all children in the Catholic parish to participate in a Catholic sports program. Therefore being on the team is not limited only to young people who attend the parish school. This simple step helps to break down internal barriers within a parish by providing opportunities for young people from our parochial schools and public schools to play together on their parish team.

- Guaranteed playing time for every child in every sport becomes part of the sports structure, especially through eighth grade. While this looks different in each sport and will vary according to the ages of the participants, this approach highlights that participation and childhood development are more important than winning records. An additional benefit of this approach is that coaches are more mindful about giving practice time and skill development attention to *all* team members, since all team members will have a direct opportunity to influence the outcome of an athletic contest.

Ricardo Portillo's Mass of Christian burial took place at Our Lady of Lourdes Catholic Church in Magna, Utah, on May 8, 2013. May he rest in peace. May his legacy help all persons involved in youth sports to stop, reflect, and take ongoing and determined actions to make sports safe and life giving for all children, parents, coaches, and officials. May his love for the young people he cared for and the game that was his passion compel youth sports leaders to reject the winning-is-everything approach, which can lead to such terrible violence, and instead help and encourage young people to discover and celebrate the *play* in sports.

NOTES

1. "The Play Like a Champion Today Sports as Ministry Coaches Training Manual" (University of Notre Dame, 2006), appendix B, 67.

2. See http://thesportjournal.org/article/blessed-john-paul-ii-speaks-to -athletes, which provides numerous addresses by Pope John Paul II to athletic teams, coaches, and families regarding the dignity of the human person and the importance of sport and play in developing the person and community.

CHAPTER 11

WE

A Model for Coaching and
Christian Living

JIM YERKOVICH

WHY WE?

We have a real problem and a real opportunity in Catholic schools today. The problem is that we have not done a good enough job of thinking about the relationship between the Catholic identity and mission of our schools and our sport practices. And so, while mission statements and sports practices exist side by side in our schools, legitimate questions have been raised about the relationship between the two. The opportunity we have now is to reflect on these questions—a process that I believe can enrich both our Catholic identity and our sport practices.

There is a real thirst among administrators, campus ministers, educators, and coaches for models and ways of approaching sports practices that will allow them to embody the values of Catholic education. I have seen this thirst over the past few decades as I have met with school leaders in many different parts of the country. Some bishops in the United States have also recognized the importance of taking youth sport seriously. Archbishop John Quinn of San Francisco, for example, commented that youth ministry is the church's mission of reaching into the daily lives of young people and showing them the presence of God. He pointed out that to ignore athletics in the daily lives of young people is to overlook a prime opportunity to meet youth "where they are."

If we don't give this topic consideration in our schools, we will end up going along with the drift of the wider society with respect to sport, which is not always in the best direction. This is what has been happening to some extent in Catholic schools in recent decades, and it is probably this that lies behind the need that many people feel for a change. Unfortunately, the drift of the wider society during these years has been more and more in the direction of a "scoreboard world" in which the score at the end of the game is the only thing that matters.

The scoreboard world emerged as the "bottom line" approach of the business world encroached more and more on all other areas of life. Education, for example, is often viewed solely as preparation for a job and the money that it brings. In the service of this, having a high grade point average all too often becomes the exclusive objective for students and their parents. One of the places this "bottom line" mentality is most present, however, is in sports, expressed in a phrase like "winning is the only thing." This mentality is most pervasive at the highest levels of professional and collegiate sport. But it is also present at lower levels and in youth sports. One of the ways this is transmitted is when well-intentioned coaches use the same bottom line approach they use at work while coaching youth teams. Unfortunately, this approach does both sports and the young people who play them a disservice. In a scoreboard world, it is important for a coach to think about how he or she can be countercultural.

If you ever doubt the significance of your role as a coach, just consider, as Fr. John Cusick invited coaches to do at a conference entitled "Coaching as Calling" in Chicago in 1998, that apart from Father or Sister, "Coach" is the only person in the school who is called by their title. He pointed out that students don't say "Teacher" or "Principal." But the coach they call "Coach." Fr. Cusick reflected on what it was like after his ordination to suddenly have people calling him "Father." He felt good about the fact that people were giving him this sign of respect, after all those years of preparation, but also felt the sense of responsibility that went along with this title and role. Likewise, when our students call us "Coach" this is a sign of respect, but there is also a great responsibility to be a positive influence in their lives.

In a climate such as the one we live in today, it is important for a coach to ask himself why he wants to coach young people in the first place. It could be that a person becomes a coach because he wants to have a winning record and attain some level of stature in society. But this approach does not work very well. For one thing, it can't sustain a coach for very long. After some losing seasons he is likely to leave coaching. A person with such a motivation could also end up using his players for his own ends and this is ultimately not satisfying to anyone (not to mention the fact that it does not work—a coach cannot be successful unless he or she is trusted by players).

A more adequate motivation for becoming a coach would be related to the positive experiences a coach has had while playing a sport. I believe that this experiential dimension is the more important dimension of coaching. If a coach is operating out of this motivation, this will influence both how he approaches each day of practice and how he interacts with his players. Because it has to do with the quality of human experience, this approach also shifts from an exclusive focus on winning to how the coach can affect the lives of young people in a way that can have long-term benefits.

We are all familiar with St. Paul's exhortation to the Corinthian people, when he said, "Every athlete in training submits to strict discipline, in order to be crowned with a wreath that will not last; we do it for one that lasts forever" (1 Cor 9:25). This is what we as Catholic educators need to be shooting for as well. We cannot be aiming only for a perishable wreath for our student-athletes; this is not enough. And because of this, we cannot afford to let things drift along in whatever direction they are going in in the wider society.

Unfortunately, there are not a lot of models for correlating spiritual values with youth sports. And yet, it is crucial that we have such models. In this chapter, I will share with you the WE model we use at Judge Memorial High School. This model has been very effective in helping our players see how basketball can teach important life lessons. My hope is that readers will be able to either use this model or will be stimulated by reading this chapter to come up with their own.

WHAT WE?

There are different ways to describe what it is we do with our teams at Judge Memorial Catholic High School. I heard a priest on a retreat talk about "smuggling" in values through school activities. This is one way of describing it. Another way of describing it is in terms of explicit and implicit curriculum. There is an explicit curriculum in a school that is dealt with at faculty meetings. This addresses such things as the content of courses, the progression of studies, and the means for evaluating student progress. There is also an implicit curriculum that is usually not talked about as much but that has as much or more influence on the lives of young people. This has to do with things such as the way people relate to one another in the school; this is reflected in those things that happen in the hallway, in the cafeteria, or on the athletic field that make a person feel different for better or worse.

In sports, too, there tends to be an explicit and an implicit curriculum. The explicit curriculum includes a schedule, the goals of a team, and how they will attain those goals through training and practices and strategies for different games. But there is also a curriculum that usually remains implicit, which has to do with how the coaches or players relate to each other and what the experience of playing on a team is like. I believe these are actually some of the more important aspects of high school sports. It is this we try to get at with our WE philosophy.

At Judge, we approach the game of basketball as a model for life. Basketball, like any team sport, flourishes on team play. If you play this game as a team, great things happen. And the players understand that. If they are selfless and give of themselves to the team, they get better and the team gets better. Father Michael Himes of Boston

College has described Christian education as an education wherein the person learns to give of himself or herself. In this sense, Christian education is learning to be community. This happens in the athletic context all the time.

While the players can understand these ideas from their own experience of playing the game, it is also very helpful to provide them with examples. For example, we point out that the best teams in college basketball are those that fit together and have chemistry. These teams almost never have the leading scorers in the nation. Michigan State, the 2000 NCAA basketball champions, for example, did not have a player who averaged more than sixteen points a game. However, they beautifully wove all the players into the mix, each one accepting his role and contributing his specific talents to the team. Another good example of this was seen in the 2002 World Championship games, where the Argentina basketball team defeated the United States. The Argentinians had much less individual talent than the U.S. team, but they played together as a team better than the U.S. and ended up winning the game. I tend to use examples from basketball with my team, but probably one of the best examples of team play is found in the U.S. women's soccer team that won the World Cup in 1999. The best players on the team, like captain Mia Hamm, were committed to the success of the team first and always highlighted the accomplishments and talents of their teammates. Another tool for a coach is to tell stories of the teams at his or her own school from previous years. These can be even more effective because the players are usually familiar with the former players the coach is mentioning. These types of examples bring the point very close to home.

We also ask our players to reflect on how we find happiness in life. In basketball, it is when we are together as a team and when we play together that the game is most satisfying. Just like in the game of basketball, so too in our lives don't we find our greatest happiness and fulfillment when we are living and working together? My thinking in these matters was heavily influenced by a class I took at the University of San Francisco from Father John Marion, SJ, who emphasized that we as human beings are "co-beings." According to Father Marion, this is the way we are created by God, to live in relationship with Him and one another. The experience of "co-being" starts in our families, where hopefully we know the experience of loving and being loved. Then, as we get a little older we start making friends outside of the home as we go to school and play with other children in the neighborhood. These are very important experiences in our life and can help us to have a positive sense of ourselves. Later, we might start dating. For high school students, dating relationships often take on great importance as anyone can see by observing what makes them ecstatic or depressed. Later, some people meet a life partner and try to create a loving environment for their own children to grow up in.

If these are the most important experiences we have in life, it is also true that the greatest hurts we experience have to do with whatever we experience as threatening the relationships in our lives. For adolescents, not feeling like they are part of the peer group is acutely painful, and they tend to be very sensitive to any signs of rejection. When we grow older we come to know that nothing can hurt us like a divorce or the death of a loved one. Experiences such as these feel like the absence of WE and are our greatest hurts.

Coaches themselves experience such hurts from time to time in their own lives. I think it is better to acknowledge this and be open with young people about it rather than pretending it isn't the case. My dad died during the season a few years ago, and that was an experience that I talked about with my players. My relationship with my dad was very important in my life. When he died, I experienced a real void. The players and coaches know that they are an important part of the WE of my life, but family relationships are even more fundamental. Talking about these types of experiences helps to remind us that our relationships are the most important aspect of our lives.

And yet, the values we are discussing are not usually highlighted in media coverage or popular conversation with regard to sports. The tendency of the media and of much typical conversation is to focus exclusively on who wins and who loses. Many of our young people begin to think that this is all that matters as well. They slowly start to think that happiness or fulfillment will be found in winning and the opposite in losing. This, of course, is not always true. While there is a great feeling that comes with winning, and no competitive person likes to lose, it is not always the case that winning leads to personal happiness. Anyone who has been part of a championship team knows this truth. I tell my players, "Sometimes you can win and not have won anything at all. And sometimes you can lose and not have lost anything at all." Even championships can have a hollow feeling if the values associated with their achievement are not such that build up the person and a sense of community.

When the focus is not on winning, it is often on individual players and the number of points they score. This focus begins to influence the way young people think about their sport as well, as they strive to be the individual star or to score the most points. Because of the messages they get from the surrounding culture, they think that this will make them happy. Satisfaction never comes from great individual performances or awards alone, however. With regard to this, I tell my players a story about Ollie Johnson, a teammate of mine at the University of San Francisco, who received the highest individual honor a player can receive at the NCAA tournament. Our team lost the regional final game to UCLA in 1964, and Ollie was the first person from a runner-up team in NCAA tournament history to win the Most Valuable Player award. He won the award after having scored thirty-seven points and grabbing twenty-seven rebounds in this game. After the game, when Ollie was walking out of the locker room he left the trophy underneath a chair. I said "Ollie, you left your trophy, here it is." He said, despondently, "Oh yeah," and took the trophy. Obviously, he was upset and the trophy didn't mean that much to him. He told me he was upset, in part because we lost the game, but mostly because it never felt like we came together as a team. I remember he said, "I just wish everything could have been different." I'll never forget those words.

And I knew what he meant. Our team situation wasn't very good at all. Even though we were the third-ranked team in the country, there was a lot of contention and strife on the team. There were players who felt the coaches were playing favorites, getting some players summer jobs that were more lucrative than others. There was racial tension on the team. And so Ollie was taking out of the locker room a trophy that signified him as one of the best players in the country and he was saying that he was not fulfilled. It is true, I thought to myself at the time, that you *can* win and not have won anything at all. Ollie won this individual award, but he was empty inside. This is because awards can't make up for the deeper desire we have for right relationship with others. This is expressed well in Jesse Owens's comment: "Friendships born on the fields of athletic strife are the real gold of competition. Awards become corroded; friends gather no dust."

If we are WE people, and we find happiness and fulfillment when we live and play together, it is also the case that there is a tendency in all of us to focus only on ourselves. There is an "I" mentality in each of us that is very persistent. It is important to be aware of this part of ourselves and to struggle against this every day. This can be done by focusing on how we do simple, everyday things. For example, it is important to pay attention to how we speak, even to the words we use. At Judge we try to have the coaches and players use "WE" language rather than "I" language, saying things like "WE played very well today," or "WE had a good practice," rather than, "I had twenty points," or "I had thirteen rebounds."

When players begin to think of themselves as members of a community, this can have a profound impact on their personal lives that lasts much longer than their playing days. Bill Bradley describes the strong bond that can develop between teammates when he writes:

> Your devotion to your teammates, the depth of your sense of belonging, is something like blood kinship. . . . Rarely can words fully express it. In the nonverbal world of basketball, it's like grace or beauty or ease in other areas of your life. It is the bond that selflessness forges.[1]

I know that this type of bond that is forged through selflessness has been experienced by many of our players because of the letters I receive from them after they leave Judge. It is clear that the WE aspect of the experience of playing basketball at Judge is something they remember, as they write such things as "WE came together in '93" or "Yours in WE." Even the more humorous letters that ask things like,

"How are things in WEsville?" show me that something of the experience of community has stayed with them. In their letters, the players hardly ever mention how many games we won or lost, but they write a good deal about having had a positive experience on the team. Jim wrote to me, for example, from college, saying, "It is amazing to think that the love for a game could bring such a diversified group of people together. I hope that future teams are able to come together as well as the team of '92–'93. . . . It is a feeling unlike any other and it is something everyone should get to experience."[2] Richard, one of the most gifted student-athletes we ever had at Judge, who went on to play basketball at Rice on a scholarship, wrote:

> Keep up the WE tradition. I can't tell you how much it has meant to me. As I look back, that is the overriding memory I have, of that special bond we all shared through the team. It was not only the greatest athletic experience I have had, but the greatest experience, period. And I'd just like to thank you for allowing me to be a part of it all.[3]

As I've said, these experiences can also have an impact on the players long after they are done playing. For Brian, learning how to be a part of a team has helped him in his marriage, as he expressed in a letter:

> Beyond the fact of work, my life and marriage are running smoothly. God is really blessing our relationship. Athletics has taught me a lot about the necessity of teamwork in more ways than one. It should be a fact of life. Your countless reminders of "WE" must have worked.[4]

In the end, it is love that is the key factor that makes WE come alive in a group of players and coaches. Some coaches would never use the word "love" when talking to their team. But there needs to be love on a team just as there needs to be love in all areas of life. In fact, in my mind, Jesus made the greatest WE statement of all time when he said that the two greatest commandments are that we should love God with our whole heart, soul, and strength and our neighbor as ourselves. Sport provides an important context for young people to be able to learn how to live these core teachings of Jesus.

In the context of a loving and supportive environment we discover our gifts and flourish as persons. The following quote from Louis Evely expresses this well:

> What is society, fraternity? It is an association where one is more than oneself, thanks to others, where one has need of others in order to be oneself. . . . Because there are others who expect something of you, who believe in you, who hope in you, you become bold enough to be as good, as tender, as humble, as simple, obliging and generous as their approval has encouraged you to be.[5]

It is possible that the players who wrote the letters referred to above would have had a meaningful experience at Judge if we did not have the WE model as the basis for our program. But I think what the WE model does is to make explicit what is most important. This makes it more likely that the players and coaches will have a memorable experience that can carry over into other areas of their lives.

WHENCE WE?

I knew when I was in high school that I wanted to be a high school teacher and coach because of the great impact my teachers and coaches had on my life and the positive experiences I had playing basketball, baseball, and football. I wanted to be the same kind of person for other young people that my teachers and coaches had been for me.

And yet, I know that the pressures associated with being a head coach can really begin to mount, especially for young coaches. While I had the good fortune to be successful as a young coach, I could feel myself becoming more and more concerned with winning, and in the process I was losing sight of some other values. Because of this I was becoming more frustrated and dissatisfied with my role as a coach; I wanted to be able to do more in this role.

I wasn't happy with the talk I would give to my team in the beginning of each year on the importance of teamwork. As I was approaching this talk in 1978, I knew I needed something to make it more meaningful. I didn't know what that would be at the time, but I was just hoping and praying that I would find something. On the Wednesday prior to the Saturday before this annual talk the word "WE" came to me. This came as something of a revelation to me personally, as it occurred to me that the concept of WE was what was central to the game of basketball and to the meaning of human life.

As I became convinced of the truth of this, I thought, "Why don't I call this our WE talk and try to make this our philosophy, the way that we are going to try to play basketball, to live and relate to one another?" I knew I would need to do some practical things to make WE a reality. The first thing I did was to call a sporting goods store and tell them that I needed twelve of the cheapest shirts they had. (I thought the players would use them to wash their cars with or kick around in, so I didn't want something real expensive.) Fortunately, they had some $3.50 T-shirts. I had them print on the shirts "Judge Memorial Basketball" with a basketball in the middle and the word "WE" in the middle of the basketball.

We gave out the shirts on Saturday and I gave the team a talk emphasizing, as I have said, that in basketball when players play together, the game is played better and it is a more satisfying experience. Similarly, when people can learn to live together and respect and love one another, life is lived better and it is more fulfilling. I told them that we have four and one-half months to be together, and that hopefully during this time we will become better people. "If you are not a better person, if I am not a better person after the season is over, then what are we doing this for?" I asked them.

I also gave the players a simple booklet that was comprised of various kinds of writings, such as poems (some written by students), excerpts from novels, newspaper articles, writings on religion, all of which emphasize the importance of community. One of the players' favorite writings was given to me by Doug Vierra, a member of the team that first year. It is by Philip Yancey and called "Benedict Arnold Seagull":

Geese don't get high-powered press coverage
like sea gulls.
They're seen as dull, ordinary birds
which only attract notice twice a year
during migration. . . .

Like the Blue Angels, they fly wingtip to wingtip. . . .
You can hear the beat of their wings
whistling through the air in unison. . . .

And that's the secret of their strength.
Together, cooperating as a flock,
geese can fly a 71-percent longer range.
The lead goose cuts a swath
through the air resistance, which creates
a helping uplift for the two birds behind him.
In turn, their beating makes it easier on the birds
behind them, much like the drag of a race car
sucked in behind the lead car. . . .
Each bird takes his turn at being the leader.
The tired ones fan out to the edges of the V
for a breather, and the rested ones surge toward
the point of the V to drive the flock onward

If a goose becomes too exhausted or ill
and has to drop out of the flock,
he is never abandoned.
A stronger member of the flock will follow
the failing, weak one to his resting place
and wait until he's well enough to fly again.[6]

The booklet also includes quotes like John Wooden's, "Happiness begins where selfishness ends," and "It is amazing how much can be accomplished when no one cares who gets the credit." One of my favorite quotes from Coach Wooden is: "The three things that mankind craves most—happiness, freedom, and peace of mind—cannot be attained without giving them to someone else. True happiness comes from making someone else happy."[7]

After my first WE talk in 1978, an interesting thing happened. We had just spent $1000 on new warm-ups and the players really liked them. At a Catholic school new warm-ups are an infrequent budget item. Three of the seniors came to me on the Monday following the talk and said, "Coach, do we have to wear our new warm-ups on Tuesday night?" I told them we had only worn them for two games and I wondered what the problem was. They said, "We want to wear our 'WE' shirts." They wore the "WE" T-shirts every game, all year long. And the brand new warm-ups went up on the shelf.

We have done other things over the years to keep us focused on what is most important. In addition to the shirt and the booklet we also give the players a jacket or a sweater that has the word "WE" on the front. One of our assistant coaches who is also the art teacher developed a WE logo for all of the items associated with our athletic program, such as the stationery, cards, advertisements, programs, and team bags. After the experience in 1978 with the warm-ups, we decided to have the WE logo on our uniforms and warm-ups as well!

I was amazed at how important the WE concept became for the players, as I didn't think I did a very good job presenting it. The game of basketball, it turns out, is a very powerful context within which to teach young people some of the most important lessons about life. After many years of coaching teams I am convinced that the WE concept has been so successful with our players and others for the simple reason that we are in fact WE people, made to live together in community. This is how we find fulfillment.

HOW WE?

In order for any model to work, it has to be fostered in concrete ways every day. As I wrote above, one of the ways we foster our WE approach is to pay attention to our language and the kinds of words we use. In general, we try to talk and act as "WE" and to limit the use of the word "I." But there are many other things we do. For example, as coaches we try to be positive with our players. When being positive, we try to help the players realize that basketball is most rewarding when they are playing together. This means doing those kinds of things that may not get them headlines but that are indispensable to playing the game well. There are many such aspects of the game. For example, the players need to be aware of one another's presence in order to have the right kind of "spacing" on the court. If players are too close together there is no room for them to drive to the basket. If players are too far apart, on the other hand, passes can be intercepted. Players also need to look for the open player and help their teammates get open to receive a pass.

Another way we encourage the WE approach can be seen in the way we coach defense. Defense is a part of the game that especially depends on team play. Players must realize as they guard the player they are assigned to that they are being supported by their four teammates as well. As coaches we try to encourage players to pay attention to these aspects of the game by giving positive feedback. We praise players for having spacing on the court, for an assist, or for helping out on defense as much or more than we do for the number of points they score.

Players contribute to the team in many different ways. This is why it is important to talk with each player at the beginning of the season about the role he or she will play. This is an area where I was very influenced by former UCLA coach John Wooden, who felt that the acceptance of one's role was one of the greatest lessons to be learned while playing on a team.

At Judge we had a player a few years ago named Vince who wasn't a very good player in terms of basketball skills. I sat down with him before the year and talked about his role. I told him that I saw him as someone who would contribute a great deal to the togetherness of the team because of his personality and leadership ability. I envisioned him sort of as the glue that held the team together. But I also knew, realistically, that he might not play very much. I wanted to make sure he felt comfortable with such a role. It turned out that he did.

He ended up playing less than we both thought he would. If you watched the videos of those twenty some games, however, you would see him up clapping and cheering for his teammates in every game. He was one of the most limited players I ever coached in terms of basketball ability, and yet he is one of the most important players I've ever had on a team.

Thankfully, Vince felt that being a member of the team was a positive experience and was able to recognize the significance of his own contribution. He wrote about this in an essay for his English class at the beginning of his senior year:

> For this essay I have decided to write about an experience that has had more influence and effect on me than any other that I can think of. Last year, my junior year, I made the varsity basketball team. I wasn't a starter, I didn't score many points, and I didn't even play much. But it was by far the greatest experience of my life.
>
> If you have never been on a team I can't expect you to understand. The family that is built is a very impressive thing, especially in basketball because there are so few (only twelve). Our team motto is 'WE'. Our coach, Jim Yerkovich, came up with it about fifteen years ago and it has been the Judge Basketball motto ever since.
>
> Making the Judge Memorial basketball team has had the most positive influence on my life. I have realized that the most important part of my life is the people involved in it. The best way to deal with people is to put them before me. As Gale Sayers wrote: "I'm Third. 1= God, 2= others, 3=me." I've also realized that "The Best Potential of Me is WE."[8]

When the teacher showed me Vince's essay I was very pleased, because it showed me that what we work hard for as a coaching staff was happening. Vince felt very much like he was a part of the team and that this was a positive experience for him even though he did not play in as many games as he would have liked.

Along these lines, it is important that the bench-starter relationships be cultivated. One thing I always watch during a game is the body language and demeanor of the players on the bench. This tells you a lot about a team. At Judge, we expect the players on the bench to be actively involved in the game, supporting the players who are on the floor. When players are taken off the court, we want them to reciprocate the support they received. This is not always an easy thing for players to do, but if the coaches emphasize the importance of this, good things can happen. One year, more than halfway through the season, I replaced a senior in the starting lineup with a sophomore. This made a tremendous positive difference for our team. The pressure defense of the sophomore player created havoc for other teams, which resulted in overall team success. I talked with the senior player about the change, and while he accepted it on the surface, it was still very difficult for him. In the state tournament semifinal game, the sophomore made a big play to get us into the championship game. The senior, who was sitting next to me, in a moment of exhilaration, jumped up, put his hand on my shoulder, and said, "Coach, isn't he something!" These are the kinds of experiences that happen on a team that usually go unnoticed, but I think they are some of the most important experiences in sports.

Parents of players are going to be focused on their own child; this is only natural. But parents also want to have a sense of perspective. They want to have an appreciation and understanding of the dynamics of a team sport, especially if they did not participate in one themselves when in high school. To foster this understanding we meet with the parents at the beginning of each season and talk to them about our approach. We give the parents a mini version of the WE booklet, to give them a sense of what it is we try to communicate to their sons.

When we talk with parents we encourage them to approach the team the same way the players do. We encourage them not to emphasize in their conversations individual success or the lack of it. We encourage them to look for the good in their son's teammates and to refrain from conversations that are critical of them. We tell them that while it is normal for them to focus on their own child, the best thing for him is that he learns how to be a part of the team. This is an important way that they can help him to grow as a person.

We also encourage the players to talk to their parents about the WE philosophy and what it means to them. It is most helpful if the players are able to get the parents to see that the relationships between the players are more important than anything else. If this can happen, then the parents begin to act in ways that are much less "I" oriented than they otherwise would have acted. They also begin to realize that the less "I" oriented they are, the happier they are.

One year I had a particularly challenging situation with one player and his family. The prior year Adrian had played on the junior varsity team and scored twenty points a game by taking about twenty-five shots per game. When he came up to the varsity team, because of the skills of the other players on the team I asked him to take less shots and to play a role that emphasized defense and rebounding more. He and his family really struggled with this role. The situation got so bad that this was the only time in my thirty-six years of coaching when I felt a player didn't want to be at practice and I didn't want the player there. Eventually I had to call him in and say, "Adrian, this is just not working. I don't think you like being here. I've asked you to play a different role, but it doesn't seem to be working out."

About ten minutes into our talk he said, "Coach, last night I ran away from home. I came back and I stayed on the porch until about one in the morning. My parents and I had a big argument about what was going on on the team and how many points I was scoring. I asked my parents never to come to another basketball game." In fact his parents did not come to the next four or five games.

We talked for two and one-half hours that day. After the talk he decided to give basketball one more try. My relationship with him changed for the better, and as he began to reconsider his role on the team our team's play dramatically improved. We were 2-4 at the time of our talk. After the talk, we won 17 of the next 18 games, and Adrian played an important role all year. The season culminated with our winning the state championship. Ironically, this player I asked not to shoot as much ended up making the game winning shot with little time left on the clock in the first game of the state tournament. If he had not made that shot, we would not have won the state tournament.

After winning the state championship that year we were invited for the first time to the prestigious Alhambra Catholic Invitational Tournament in Maryland. Many of the parents of the players came to the tournament that year as they have in subsequent years. Adrian's parents had started coming back to games again and they came to the tournament as well. When they saw their son was happier with the new approach and that things were going well with the team, they became one of the most supportive families with respect to our philosophy. They even had an artist carve a wooden "WE" for every player and every parent on the team.

As he walked up the aisle for graduation Adrian handed me a letter which read, in part:

> Just a note of thanks and appreciation for all your help and support during my years at Judge. This year was the greatest of my entire life. Winning the state championship and capping it off by taking fourth place in ACIT. The WE experience is one that will live on forever. I hope I can always stay WE as you have taught me well. Thanks for helping me grow and learn well that in the long run, WE is a more satisfying situation than I.[9]

Over the years, parents have become some of the biggest supporters of our approach. In 2002, our team once again traveled to the ACIT tournament in Maryland. At the banquet at the end of the season the parents gave me a beautiful collage of pictures from the trip with the word WE featured prominently in the center. This collage captures for me the WE experiences we all had on this trip. There are pictures of kids and parents eating together, visiting places such as the Aerospace museum, the U.S. Capitol, and the Lincoln Memorial, and praying together at the Shrine of the Immaculate Conception. Oh yes, there are also pictures of the team playing basketball. At the banquet, the parents also gave me a scrapbook of the whole season, with a section about each player. The scrapbook has the word WE artfully woven into a beautifully stitched cover.

WHITHER WE?

Because they have an experience of community while playing on the team, I believe that our players have an experience of educational and spiritual significance. As the U.S. Bishops wrote in their letter *To Teach as Jesus Did*:

Community is at the heart of Christian education not simply as a concept to be taught but as a reality to be lived. Through education, men and women must be moved to build community in all areas of life; they can do this best if they have learned the meaning of community by experiencing it. Formed by this experience, they are better able to build communities in their families, their places of work, their neighborhoods, their nation, their world.[10]

It is encouraging to me how adaptable the WE philosophy has been for others. My daughter, Mary Chris Leadbetter, who coaches the girls' basketball team at Judge, has developed a very effective pyramid of success with "fundamentals" at the base, qualities such as "teamwork" and "effort" in the middle, and "WE" at the top. The WE philosophy has also caught on in our wider school community at Judge in various ways. For example, the salutatorian made it the theme of his speech one year. It has also led other teachers to think about ways they could approach their own activity. The theater department put on a play with the title of "WE," for example. The dance teacher at Judge uses the WE philosophy to emphasize our need to care for one another and has creatively incorporated social justice themes into the school's dance routines. Because her students give public performances, the message about social justice reaches the wider community. The WE philosophy, along with other approaches, has resonated with the hopes of many Catholic educators and coaches in the United States. Aware of the need for further exploration of these types of issues, the National Catholic Education Association (NCEA) has formed an "Athletics and Activities as a Classroom for Values" program. Now there are NCEA publications as well as sessions at the NCEA national conferences devoted to athletics and other extracurricular activities.

But the WE model has also spread beyond the Catholic school context. John Wooden, the former UCLA coach, has commended the philosophy and exchanged writings with me. Other coaches such as University of Georgia coach Jim Harrick have had their teams wear WE shirts. I have conducted summer camps in Australia for youth, which have been received so well that I was also asked to work with the professional team there. Somewhat surprisingly, the WE model has even reached into the business world, which is the place where the scoreboard world mentality tends to dominate. A friend of mine from high school has had WE sweaters made for the vice presidents of the company where he is CEO.

The WE model provides our basketball coaches at Judge with one way of answering the question, "Why coach?" When basketball is approached with the WE emphasis the coach has a chance to teach students how to play a sport at the same time he or she is teaching them about life. This makes the experience itself more rewarding for both coaches and players. But also, when the game or season is over, the coach and the players have something that puts their experiences into perspective. This approach adds a depth to successes and helps to put losses into perspective. In this way a coach can earn the title "Coach," living out his or her calling to help young people grow and become better people, preparing them to be, as John Paul II says, "the protagonists of the future and the builders of a new civilization based on solidarity."[11]

NOTES

1. Thomas J. Whalen, *Dynasty's End: Bill Russell and the 1968–69 World Champion Boston Celtics* (Boston, MA: Northeastern University Press, 2004), from the foreword by Bill Bradley, p. xiv.

2. From personal correspondence in the possession of the author, from Jim Murray, received December 1993.

3. From personal correspondence in the possession of the author, from Richard Holmes, received October 1985.

4. From personal correspondence in the possession of the author, from Brian Bentrude, received November 1990.

5. Louis Evely, *We Are All Brothers* (New York: Herder and Herder, 1967), 76.

6. Adapted from text in Philip Yancey, "Soar Like the Birds—But Do It Right," *These Times* (March 1981): 30, available at http://documents.adventist archives.org/Periodicals/WM/WM19810301-V90-03.pdf.

7. Quoted in Neville L. Johnson, *The John Wooden Pyramid of Success*, 2nd ed. (Los Angeles: Cool Titles, 2004), 184.

8. Essay regarding WE program by Vince Chatterton, a student, written in September 1989.

9. From personal correspondence in the possession of the author. Because of the very personal and sensitive nature of this story, I am using a pseudonym for the student's name.

10. United States Conference of Catholic Bishops, *To Teach as Jesus Did: A Pastoral Message on Catholic Education* (Washington DC: United States Conference of Catholic Bishops, 1973).

11. "Sports Can Become Instrument of Reconciliation and Peace, to the Executives of Italian National Olympic Committee Rome, January 17, 1985," *L'Osservatore Romano*, weekly English ed. N.6, February 11, 1985, 8–9.

CHAPTER 12

Connection, Reflection, and Validation in Sport

SHERRI RETIF

Educators walk always on sacred ground—people's lives.
—Thomas Groome, *Educating for Life*

Coaches, as educators, have an opportunity to influence young people's lives and model positive behavior more than most adults. We do walk on sacred ground. The memories created in our daily conversations and by our actions can, and often do, have a lasting impact on our students' lives. I am fortunate to have been around the game of basketball all of my life and have coached high school players for the past twenty-five plus years. Coaching is not a linear journey; there are peaks and valleys and twists and turns. With motivated players, a talented coaching staff, and loving family, I have found meaning beyond the Xs and Os and wins and losses. For me, sports are a spiritual endeavor. As both a basketball coach and spiritual director, the integration of sport and spirituality has been a lifelong journey of relating practice and theory. My life experiences impact my beliefs and my beliefs impact my life experiences. In this matrix of everyday life, I am invited to meet God, self, and other, and weave my spiritual core with my day-to-day responsibilities.

In this chapter, I offer experiences that have shaped the meaning of our basketball program. While I have coached in large public and small private schools, half of my experience has been in a co-ed independent school with less than five hundred high school students. I speak from my perspective as both a coach and parent and realize that our interpretations can be as unique as our fingerprints. At the same time, I imagine my coaching methods will resonate with others' experiences. In sharing these insights, it is my desire to create awareness and conversations that will illuminate the positive aspects of youth and high school sports.

While there is a plethora of philosophies in today's highly competitive culture of sports, my belief is that sports are about relationships. Hopefully they are about positive relationships that support, inspire, and provide a holding place for our young people to compete and cooperate, lead and follow, and share their fears, joys, talents, triumphs, and defeats. Foundational to any successful program is a relational "ethics of care,"[1] a sincere concern for how students "think and feel." I am reminded of Xavier's women's basketball Assistant Coach Mike Neighbors, as he exploded onto the court running to the aid of his player who collapsed on the floor after missing two end-of-the-game, uncontested layups. His focus was solely on her emotional health and well-being, not the fact that Xavier University had just lost the opportunity to clinch their first-ever spot in the women's basketball Final Four. Coach Neighbor's natural instincts displayed a "player first" mentality.

I am convinced that sports are a venue of self-discovery, of mystery, a place where students negotiate and renegotiate their sense of purpose and agency, who they are, and why they are here on this earth. This place of discovery invites recognition of the tensions between the desires for human distinctiveness and inclusion, between personal freedom and care for others. It allows for the asking of questions such as: Why am I different from my teammates and opponents? What makes me unique and how do I embrace my individual blessings? How do I discover a sense of belonging to the larger community?

In witnessing students' experiences and listening to their stories over the years, I have noticed three recurring themes. Young people have a desire (1) to connect with others, (2) to make meaning of failures and successes, and (3) to receive affirmation and hope. Sure, high school sports are about mastering technique and training for success, but the depth of the experience demands that we respect and nurture the inner life of the student as well as the lifelong values of the game. As coaches, we can facilitate connection, reflection, and validation in our students' lives. I am in full agreement with Michael McNamee (chapter 4) that sports are a social site for young people to develop mature and reflexive attitudes in relation to their evolving value scheme. Attentiveness to our everyday actions and modeling right behavior can build bridges of trust that help foster the appropriate ethical development of young people. Our players are most served by developing a sense of community that values relationship and connects with their life experiences. It is important for coaches and players alike to bring a growth mindset to the game. According to Eric Erikson,[2] adolescence is a time of challenge to make sense of their lives and to find some kind of meaningful purpose. Pope John Paul II in his address to members of the Italian Sports Center emphasized that sports should respond to "the fundamental questions the new generations are asking about the meaning of life, its purpose and its goal."[3]

Foremost, I believe that nurturing the inner needs of the individual is not mutually exclusive from striving for excellence as a team. As coaches we encourage our athletes to balance their needs and the team's needs every time they step on the court, every time they put on a uniform. This is a balancing act, a "sacrificing" not in the sense of giving up personal goals or aspirations, but of making one's dreams and desires "sacred," holy or holistic—a part of the whole. The Latin root of the word sacrifice is *sacrificium; sacer*, sacred; + *facere*, to make. With this understanding, the focus for our players becomes collaboration of shared aspirations—not just cooperation for the sake of teamwork but a wholehearted collaborative participation and re-sponsibility where each member acknowledges one's unique talents and contributes to a shared vision, an alliance where we are safe in our vulnerabilities and not threatened by another's strengths. Within this sacred whole, teammates learn to celebrate one another. Such a mu-tually interdependent collaborative effort confirms self-worth, invites self-discovery, and initiates personal maturity.

Establishing collaborative efforts can be an arduous task. Each athlete, each team is different, and each environment creates different needs. No matter how much time and energy is put into building team cohesion, it is important to recognize that every player, coach, and parent has different expectations and belief systems, and therefore it is best to build the team structure from the inside out. Constructing team cohesion requires daily attention and guiding principles. I am reminded of a not-so-pleasant situation with a distraught parent who questioned his daughter's "role" on the team. In honoring his exper-tise with his child's needs, I approached our meeting with an empa-thetic ear. As our conversation deepened, it became apparent that I was viewed as an adversary, someone who did not have his daughter's best interest at heart. There was much work that needed to be done in this relationship. I had obviously been deficient in explicitly communicat-ing my overall objectives with this parent (and perhaps others). The conversation taught me the importance of communication, not only with players, but parents as well. For the following year's preseason parents' meetings, I prepared a letter explaining my objectives and guiding principles.[4] Written documentation allowed ownership of core values and easy reference for clarification of explicit objectives. I have included a copy of a preseason parents' letter, which is modified and refined each year, at the end of this chapter. The reader is welcome to use this letter for their own purposes.

In addition to being presented coaching objectives at the first practice, the students are reminded of basic expectations that lay the groundwork for trust and responsibility. Over the years, I have learned to keep player rules to a minimum. Too many rules suggest a top-down leadership pattern that is a distraction to shared vision and be-comes more restrictive than supportive. Our basic expectations are: be at practice; make value-based choices; be honest; and respect yourself, your teammates, and your coaches. Relationships grounded in integrity and mutual respect can usually overcome any adversity. Even though intentions are in the right place, it is reasonable to believe that there will always be misunderstandings and mistakes to work through. Such mistakes can be "portals of discovery," which provide opportunities for growth, as James Joyce suggests.

In his article "Changing Families, Changing Schools," Robert Evans offers wonderful insights on working with parents. While parents can understandably become anxious about their child's success, Evans cautions parents about hovering. He notes that children require the latitude to discover their strengths and maximize them, learn their limitations and compensate for—or accept—them. Giving our young people the right amount of latitude to learn from their experiences is one of the hardest tasks of caring for them. It is important for parents to have appreciation for their child's unique abilities and give them space to do their own problem-solving. As the adults, we should work to balance intervention so that it is neither too little too late, nor too much too soon.[5]

Realistically, there will be conflicts and misunderstandings working with parents and students when developing talent and building team cohesion. While all outcomes will not necessarily be favorable, approaching conflict as an opportunity helps prepare all involved for the challenges to come. As Fredrick Douglass once remarked, where there is no struggle, there is no progress.

Team building goes through four natural stages of development: forming, storming, norming, and performing.[6] The initial "forming" is the coming together where individual responsibilities are unclear. The second stage, or "storming," occurs as players struggle to find their niche and a sense of belonging. Often cliques and factions can develop at this period, but inclusive role modeling by student leaders and coaching staff can eliminate team divisions. The third stage occurs as the team develops its personality and working style. Relationships often become friendships of mutual respect. Players begin to honor viewpoints of others and appreciate skills of their teammates that they didn't know existed. By the fourth stage, the team has implemented a clearly defined shared vision with an understanding of roles and responsibilities. While disagreements or conflict will still occur, the best-case scenario is for the team to be self-correcting and self-monitoring. Of course, some teams will flourish in the fourth stage of team building, whereas others will stagnate if individual beliefs are continually prioritized over a defined shared vision. Understanding the natural progression of team development allows one to build structures to support the various stages of growth. Enhancing communication is a recommended first step to building team chemistry and healthy relationships within the program. A values-based team vision can be sculpted as players and coaches use two-way communication.

COMMUNICATION

Communication is the real work of leadership.
—Nitin Nohria, dean of Harvard Business School

Throughout the season we emphasize both written and verbal communication between the players and coaches. A fall questionnaire invites players to share their summer experiences and commitments both as students and athletes. Here students are asked to reflect on their potential strengths and contributions to the team for the upcoming season. They also list areas of their game they hope to improve. The end of the questionnaire invites players to share a little about themselves; this is especially helpful in getting to know new members of the team as well as drawing out their strengths. Year to year these questionnaires initiate reflection and focus. They help establish the players' sense of contribution while marking their growth and maturity. Of course, some players will learn more from this exercise than others. Since this exercise is employed to enhance communication, it is important after collecting and reading the questionnaires to provide immediate feedback to the players' reflections. Our fall handout includes nine simple questions:

(1) Tell me about your summer basketball experience.
(2) What have you done to make yourself a better basketball player? (ex: camps, daily individual workouts, etc.)
    —on average, how many shots did you take in a 5-day week?
    —how much ball-handling did you do on your own?
(3) What have you done over the summer to make yourself a better student?
(4) What do you believe are the strengths of your game?
(5) List 3 aspects of your game that you would like to improve this year.
(6) What do you feel your responsibilities are to the team and your teammates in your role as a good teammate?
(7) Aside from your basketball talents, what do you believe are your strengths or best qualities that you bring to the team? (ex: sincerity, generosity, etc.)
(8) What is the best book you have read, and movie you have seen, recently?
(9) List your favorite musician, singer, song, musical genre, any or all of the above.

Question 6 provides an opportunity for the players to articulate what it means to be a good teammate, and at the same time it allows the coaches to develop a better understanding of the different personalities on the team. Such information provides the foundation necessary for creating a sense of belonging and enhances the role and responsibility of the athlete. Having players use their own words creates a real sense of ownership. Below I share the reflections of two players, reflections that are teeming with concepts such as accountability and right relationship.

What do you feel your responsibilities are to the team and your teammates in your role as a good teammate?

Since I'm a captain this year, I really want to work on being positive every single practice. I feel I'm a good leader, but sometimes I let things from my day come into the gym with me. I hope to leave those things behind this year and be an uplifting teammate both on and off the court. I believe in making the extra pass and that doing the little things, like boxing out every time, will make the team better as a whole. (Dana Lotito '11)

To be a good teammate, I feel like I need to know my role and embrace what I'm asked to do. Some games I may need to score more, while other games somebody else will do the scoring and I will be asked to play really tough defense. I think in order to be a good teammate, I have to think of what makes most sense for the team and put the needs of my team in front of just my personal needs. It also involves being happy and excited for everyone's successes. (Kiernan McCloskey '13)

In addition we have students complete a "player profile" (a copy can be found at the end of this chapter). This profile allows players to list academic and athletic honors and write about their participation in other sports and clubs. It also includes players' interests, senior essays, individual records, and post-season honors. The information in the profiles is collected and printed with pictures in a team booklet. Some varsity teams could use this as an ad book for revenue. Our focus has been to promote what is meaningful in our program and document evolving traditions. While we can't always control what is written in the local media, this program booklet creates our own media venue and serves as a way of articulating our own values and sharing memories.

SHARED VISION

A servant leader creates a shared vision, a sense of vision that people are drawn to, and united in, that enables them to be driven by motivation inside them toward achieving a common purpose.
—Robert Greenleaf, *Servant Leadership*

Additional written communication occurs when the season begins. After the team has practiced for a week or so, players are asked to submit three to five team and individual goals for the year. It is important for players to balance realistic outcome-oriented and measurable process-oriented goals. While outcome-oriented goals are easily measurable, they often overlook necessary action steps for development. Additionally, outcome-oriented goals are so measurable that they create a success/failure paradigm, ignoring the benefits of ongoing personal growth. On the other hand, process-oriented goals at times are too vague and become difficult to measure. Most importantly, players should select goals in which they have control of the outcome and are realistically attainable based on their past performances. It is recommended to avoid goals that are subjectively determined by media, coaches, and administration, such as being named to all-league or all-state teams. Below I have provided samples of individual goals from two students. It is apparent that one student is more process-oriented while the other integrates the two types of goals. Even so, both lists are realistic and well articulated. After submitting personal goals, each player meets with the coaching staff to discuss and reinforce secondary and even tertiary goals that focus on a plan of action as well as what it is that will be accomplished. Twice a year, in the mid- and post-season, we schedule follow-up meetings.

Player A
1. Develop better on-the-ball defense (active hands up in the air)
2. Improve my ball-handling skills—15 minutes of ball-handling daily
3. Improve talking on offense and defense in each drill we do at practice
4. Improve my leadership skills, cheer for everyone, and help younger players

Player B
1. Be the best rebounder on the team
2. Increase free throw percentage to 80+
3. Be more of a vocal leader
4. Improve confidence, especially on offense

Team goals, once collected, are consolidated into one list and the team meets to prioritize shared goals. Creating a shared vision empowers all participants and develops a true sense of ownership. A shared vision suggests you are going to cooperate with each other. In this structure, not all the giving is done by the leader alone.[7] As Nicole LaVoi attests in chapter 3 of this volume, while parents, coaches, and peers greatly influence the development of the athletes' assets, the role and responsibility of the athlete should not be overlooked. As players develop a sense of ownership, their accountability for personal actions becomes fine-tuned. When athletes feel empowered, they become not only more accountable to themselves but have a positive impact on others where mature behavior raises the bar for one's peers.

Below are our team goals from a few years ago. It is apparent that most of the goals are process-oriented, and we were really focused on improving team chemistry. My memory suggests that our team was very process-oriented because we were cognizant of our weaknesses and understood exactly what needed to be done in order to succeed. Initially this team's chemistry was an issue for several reasons. First, we had a wide variety of personality types, and energy was expended critiquing individual differences as opposed to focusing on team objectives. Secondly, some of the players preferred more structure, favoring scripted plays, whereas others liked to create out of the structure and needed loose reins to be creative off the dribble or to gamble on defense. Extensive communication and reassessment of team goals was required, during which patience, trust, and respect were developed. We would continually remind our captains to find their voice and express team frustrations. They would consistently bring concerns to the forefront, and together we worked toward resolution. Eventually a fine-tuned shared vision allowed the team to compete to its potential. Behind the leadership of four exceptional seniors, we posted the best record in school history and learned life lessons about collaboration and accountable actions.

Collaborative Team Goals
Out-rebound opponents
Go undefeated
Build Team Chemistry
• better communication
• build on trusting each other

- play and practice with the most intensity; be LOUD
- positive attitude with ourselves and each other
- support each other on the court/pick each other up

Defeat Peddie ["Peddie" was not our archrival but a respected program that had defeated us the previous year.]

Be the best conditioned team on the court—play the 4th quarter as good as the 1st

Offensively

- Perfect our transition game
- Share the ball with patience in 1/2 court

Defensively

- Press as a weapon
- Don't give up layups in transition
- Shut down opponents with speed and hustle
- Help and help the helper! Talk on D.

While established lines of communication are important in building healthy relationships, *how* we communicate and relate to one another is also crucial. In his book *Servant Leadership,* Robert Greenleaf explains that "leadership is not just an exercise of authority." Servant leadership focuses on a shared vision that promotes "power with" one another as opposed to "power over." Empowering the entire team with a sense of belonging and commitment to a shared vision inspires each player to reach deep within to contribute their unique gifts and be accountable in times of conflict.[8] Active listening, gentle reminders, and mutual respect are all techniques that help to validate a player's importance to the team and enhance their sense of responsibility for shared team goals.

PLAYER TESTIMONIALS

Stories that touch us in the place of common humanness awaken us and weave us together. Facts bring us to knowledge, but stories lead us to wisdom.

—Rachel Naomi Remen, *Kitchen Table Wisdom*

After four years at my current school we were invited to attend a holiday tournament in Texas where each team was asked to write an essay explaining their team's uniqueness. This exercise offered a wonderful opportunity for our players to make the connection between what we valued and how the players identified the team. One of our senior captains consulted with her teammates and wrote the essay I share below. She suggested that work ethic, close friendships, diversity of talents, and well-roundedness set our team apart from others. While she mentions that winning is important, winning did not identify what made us unique.

Why Our Team Is Unique

When asked what makes us unique, three things stood out, and although they sound cliché, they fit: teamwork, determination, and balance. We play in the Inter-Academy League and have been champions of this league for four consecutive years; so you could say that we are used to winning. However, that alone cannot make a team. There are countless teams with winning records, but there are few, if any teams that work harder than us. Looking at our team we are not very intimidating. We overcome our lack of height with speed, intellect, and, most of all, HUSTLE! In practice, we are always challenging and pushing each other to make our teammates better players. We can honestly say our practices are so tiring that our games sometimes seem easy.

Many teams rely on only a few players to carry the team. We have confidence that each player has an important role. On any given day, someone else could step up and make the difference in a game. We attribute this not only to the talent we have but also to our close relationships. Our long distance trips have enabled us to travel and mature, and we have created strong bonds. We are good friends inside and outside of basketball as well. Time spent at holiday tournaments has helped us form friendships that we otherwise might not have developed.

Finally, our team is full of multi-talented girls. We must be able to balance basketball and our rigorous academics, as well as outside activities. Every player on our team plays more than one sport. Over half of us play three sports, including cross country, field hockey, soccer, water polo, softball, tennis, track, lacrosse, and diving. Also, at our school there are many opportunities to get involved with community service. Many of our players engage in service, spending Saturdays with underprivileged children on "Buddy Day" or helping to build houses at Habitat for Humanity. While we all devote much time and effort to basketball, we also have other interests that make us unique. The GA Girls Basketball Team prides itself on being well-rounded, but when November 11 comes around, we are focused and ready to work. (Stephanie Spada '02)

In the years that followed, we have used this exercise with varying themes to elicit reflection on and exploration of the deeper meaning of sport. Thomas Merton teaches us that "quiet reflection is the necessary ground for fruitful action; otherwise life will tend to be superficial and deceptive."[9] Student reflection and stories offer a twofold affirmation of self and team. Allowing the athlete to "hear" her own story offers an opportunity to validate her experience beyond the win/loss success pyramid; at the same time, it encourages other students to seek the meaning of who they are and what they stand for. Hearing another's story can provide affirmation and meaning to one's own story and increases a sense of solidarity on the team.

Before the start of each season, seniors are asked to write an essay. Topics have included attitudes, measuring success, building character, two-sport athletes, and overcoming injuries. This short essay is published in the team's media book and sometimes in tournament programs. Seniors are asked to read their reflections to their teammates and at the preseason parents' meeting. Below is an essay of a young lady, Colleen Magarity, who was a two-year captain in high school and later captained Northwestern University's national championship lacrosse team.

Participation on a Team Develops Character
　　Character building is what happens on a good team when you think you're just learning how to play basketball. You come in as a freshman trying your best, and a senior helps you up when you fall down. This kind of thing becomes contagious, and you learn

that doing what is best for the team usually ends up being best for you. Here at Germantown Academy I am a senior, and I have been lucky enough to play with some great players and even greater people. We have pushed each other to be the best we can be day in and day out on and off the court. My team has become a second family to me, from my coaches teaching me valuable lessons every day, to my teammates with whom I have shared incredible experiences. I only hope that I can do my part to reach out to the new freshmen and help them to grow as athletes and people too. I am still learning every day, and I am extremely excited about our team this year. I know the ball will not always bounce our way, but I also know that when it does not we will just work harder and pick each other up because that is what good teams do and that is what character athletes do. It has been an honor and a privilege to be a part of Germantown Academy's basketball team and I look forward to continuing to learn and grow stronger with my teammates this year. (Colleen Magarity '07)

A more recent tradition is a Captains' Dinner at the end of the year to celebrate the season and honor our captains. On this evening, captains pass the torch of leadership with an affirmation of their experiences, which deepens friendship and enhances community. Below I share the wisdom of Maggie Ebbott, a recent graduating captain whose contributions to the meaning of *team* extended beyond the Xs and Os of basketball. She possesses a strong sense of self and always maintained a remarkable balance of fun and hard work. Her personal maturity, as displayed in her remarks, modeled respect, dedication, and gratitude.

My Advice for the Future
  Sticking with basketball all four years, even though it is not my top sport, was the best decision of my life. The friendships I've made and the life lessons I've learned have made such a big impact on my life. Since basketball has ended, I have been depressed! Not only because I will probably never play basketball competitively again but most importantly because I will not be with you every day for three months out of the year. I am so grateful to be

a part of this team. The support for the coaches and players on the team is truly incredible. One of the most significant moments in my whole life was being named captain midway through the season. The fact that you guys went out of your way to ask Coach if I could be captain is so meaningful to me. My advice to the future captains is to go with your instincts; do what you know is right and lead how you would want to be led.

And, here is some advice for everyone:

(1) Have fun. At times, we all get caught up in winning and being the best, but when it comes down to it, we all play basketball because we love the sport and we love being a part of this team. I had the most fun four years of my life on this team. Every day I looked forward to practice, a chance to run around and challenge myself athletically. I looked forward to seeing everyone that I don't get to see in school all the time.

(2) Cheer. I have spent a lot of time on the bench cheering and being a bench player is so underrated . . . it's important to know that we all play very significant roles on this team, whether it is on the court or off the court. And, whenever I get out on the court and hear all of you cheering so loud, it makes me so happy! On senior day, when I got ten points, I obviously couldn't have done it without all of you passing me the ball, but also the support and encouragement helped me keep shooting and not give up. Cheer loud because it is crucial to the outcome of the game.

(3) Friendship. This isn't really a piece of advice but it is really important. I have made the best friends on this team and I am so grateful to have all of you in my life. If it weren't for basketball, who knows if we would all be friends or even know each other. (Maggie Ebbott '10)

ACTIVE LISTENING

You never really understand a person until you consider things from his point of view . . . until you climb inside of his skin and walk around in it.
—Atticus Finch, in *To Kill a Mockingbird*

While the written word is valuable in establishing and focusing on core values, daily interactions are essential in setting the tone of right relationship between coach and player. Coach Chuck Daly, who coached the first U.S. Olympic Dream Team, nurtured his relationship with his players each day. He believed it was important to greet every player individually, every day, as they entered the gym. We also know that healthy communication allows two-way interactions. It is essential for daily communications to be framed in the positive with a foundational mutual respect for one another's intentions and investment in a shared vision. And remember, verbal interactions always include more than just our words. Our human condition has a keen sensitivity to tone, body language, and personal interpretation. Jesus tells us to "do to others as you would have them do to you" (Lk 6:31), and St. Catherine of Siena provides a solid communication strategy for difficult situations, when she writes, "speak the truth with love."

In addition to daily interactions, we frequently use off-court meetings with players to address concerns or issues. Having two coaches in attendance for all meetings with players allows for broader perspective and added clarity. Often students, when frustrated or confused, just want and need to be heard. Active listening, with appropriate body language and emotional connection, can validate a player's story. Paraphrasing and repeating what has been shared invites clarity through nonjudgment. When emotions are high, students don't always need an answer, they simply need a space to enhance trust and think rationally. Many times the invitation for the adult is to acknowledge the players' struggles and the tensions associated with life's challenges.

When giving on-court instruction, we integrate positive with constructive comments. While we all try to avoid confrontations, there have been times when my emotions have gotten the best of me. There was an incident at the end of the quarter during a playoff game where I crushed the confidence of my top defensive player when I asked too emphatically, "How does she keep getting past you?" The player looked at me and started crying. I knew at that moment I had caused her embarrassment. She was obviously working as hard as she could and was likely more frustrated than me. With a little breathing space, she regained her composure and went back on the court. Her teammates had her back and my assistant coaches were my wing pilots. After the game the tension remained thick. As soon as we broke huddle, my associate head coach said, "Let's talk tonight, don't put this off until tomorrow." Another assistant suggested we meet with all the captains and the distraught player. We spent fifteen minutes in an away locker room walking through the incident. I valued this young lady, as well as the advice of my staff, and realized I had unintentionally humiliated her in front of her teammates. Candid communication and a heartfelt apology brought reconnection and healing. I believe we were able to move forward with a deepening trust. All the members of our staff consistently offer suggestions to make our program successful. While doing what is best for the team, we always have each other's back.

STUDENT LEADERSHIP

Student leadership has been an integral part of our team's success. At the helm, my hope is to provide direction while eliciting the contagious fire of student leaders. Each year I witness our captains embrace a tradition of excellence and take ownership in their responsibility to lead. As a staff, we constantly encourage and honor strong leadership, whether from the floor, the bench, or off the court. Every Monday we carve out time before practice to meet with our captains and discuss the team's energy and chemistry. It is a quick, fifteen-minute meeting that allows us to connect and get a sense of anything from stress-related problems to heavy academic calendars to attitude issues. Most importantly we establish an open-door policy of honest, mature communication with necessary checks and balances. There are many times throughout the years that we have been faced with internal adversity, yet continual communication has been the key component to resolution.

While we have been blessed with outstanding players who are also exceptional leaders, most of them have waited their turn to hold the privileged title of captain. Our captains are selected by their peers, and the pattern has been consistently weighted toward seniors. In my tenure, underclassmen have never been recognized as a captain. Only on three occasions in the past twelve years have juniors assisted in the role. We are flexible with the number of captains selected and have had anywhere from one to four in a year. On occasion, due to exemplary leadership, captains have been appointed either by recommendation of players or coaches. The honor of being team captain also includes having your name added to the Captains' Board after graduation. Captains' Boards for all sports circle the gym walls, a tradition that dates back to 1880 . . . quite the tradition!

While our captains set the standards of ownership and responsibility, it is our hope to nurture the leadership capabilities of all players with team meetings and open dialogue. I am reminded of an incident some years ago where a preseason poll had our team ranked nationally. Such recognition placed a bull's-eye target on our backs, and every opponent would have us circled on their schedule. This was an ambiguous honor that could have easily become a distraction. When we brought the team together to discuss the recognition and a proper perspective, Joey Rhoads, our sophomore starting point guard commented, "How do we move up in this national poll?" One sentence shifted everyone's perspective. As a poised warrior, she focused our team in a very positive direction looking beyond the possible distractions. With a little luck and lots of perseverance, we did go on to move up in the rankings. Even as a young leader, Joey possessed natural leadership skills and acquired tremendous respect from her teammates.

At Germantown Academy, student leadership establishes the tone and personality of our team. Our former Associate Head Coach Tom Nerney continually reminded our captains, "When it comes to leadership, you can't have a bad day. All eyes are on you. First and foremost, maintain your composure." Fortunately our leaders hold this responsibility in high regard and work toward accountability. Upon graduation, each senior leaves a little part of themselves in the hearts of their coaches and teammates.

Like most programs, we celebrate our graduating seniors at the last home game. The tradition honors both seniors and their parents with gifts, flowers, and balloons. Additionally, all the players and coaches reflect on the impact the seniors have had on their lives and submit quotes for a Senior Day Program. Below I offer some of the quotes from recent progams. It is interesting to notice how the depth of reflections has evolved over the years.

Chelsea '00 is amazing! She always has a positive attitude, even when she's battling an injury. She's the glue to our team. (Erin Osborn '01)

Colleen Magarity '07 is the fuel that lights our fire. No matter what the circumstances, she's always giving 100%. Her intensity is contagious on the court, and the team tries to match her intensity ~ making every one of us better. She will be greatly missed next year and our team will never be the same without her. (Caroline Doty '08)

Jesse Carey '09 exemplifies what every young girl who sits in the GA stands wishes they can be when they get older. She stays collected and lives up to the responsibility of keeping the team under control in big games. She pushes everyone in practice to play better because she wants everyone to get better. She cares about the players off the court as well, always saying hi in the hallways, and asking about someone's day and how they are doing. Jesse makes the team fun and players like her are what makes being on this team a great opportunity. (Dana Lotito '11)

RITUALS AND TRADITIONS

Rituals are storehouses of meaningful symbols by which information is revealed and regarded as authoritative, as dealing with the crucial values of the community. . . .They are also transformative for human attitudes and behavior.

—Victor Turner, *The Drums of Affliction*

In addition to the many traditions discussed above, we also have additional rituals and ceremonies that nurture a sense of belonging and responsibility to the team. Rituals can transform attitudes and reinforce commitment. Some rituals are passed on year to year, while others evolve through various team personalities. I will discuss a few and am confident there are an extensive number of exciting and meaningful traditions being used in other programs.

On the first day of practice as the girls are finishing their stretching, we like to do an icebreaker. It can be as simple as inviting each player and coach to share something about her- or himself that no one else knows. We usually hear interesting stories about summer vacations, family history, or funny events. Another icebreaker would be for each player to describe herself with three facts and one lie on an index card. Coaches would then read the comments on the cards and teammates have to guess which comments belong to which player. At one gathering we had each player choose a "super power" that they would most like to have. Small, simple icebreakers elicit laughter and set the tone for players getting to know one another off the court.

One of my favorite team activities happens the second week of practice. On the Wednesday before Thanksgiving at the end of practice we have a "gratefulness circle." Players and coaches sit in a circle, take off their shoes, and place them on the floor in front of them. Everyone is asked to imagine what it would be like to walk in the shoes of the people to their immediate right and left and then mention why they are grateful for that member of the program. After quiet reflection, each player speaks about both the gifts and, perhaps, challenges of walking in the shoes of the other two individuals. This activity allows everyone to speak and be spoken of. It invites us to learn and appreciate more about how we "see" one another and how we are seen. In sharing opinions and perspectives on the contributions and challenges of various members of the program, we create awareness of teammates as people and not just athletes. When a player is coping with an injury or issues at home, teammates and coaches can speak their concern for the other's situation.

Additional traditions include class responsibilities, which suggest rites of passage. Freshmen put the balls in the rack at the end of practice and take care of team equipment for away games. Juniors organize Senior Day with gifts, balloons, flowers, and locker room decorations. Seniors are responsible for writing essays and ordering and selecting team gear. Sophomores, well . . . I guess I need to come up with an idea for them. Perhaps they can organize the "pink zone" game.

There are other small rituals that have surfaced throughout my tenure. Such rituals include game-day captains, psych bags, huddle cheers, team claps, locker decorations, and practice "shout outs." An honorary "game day captain" leads the pregame prayer and attends the pregame officials' meeting with the established captains. Since we are an independent school with various religious denominations, prayers usually focus on gratitude, blessings, and protection. At times, coaches have made "psych bags" that are filled with candies and inspirational notes for big game days. School locker decorations have appeared on the players' lockers for our games with rivals. "Hustle" awards and "shout outs" are given by both coaches and captains at the end of each practice. Positive reinforcement acknowledges an appreciation for both leadership and work ethic. One year we instituted the "Thinking Out of the Box" award because we noticed the players were becoming too structured and we wanted to encourage creativity on the court.

Team dinners have become a common tradition. Pregame pasta meals and post-game dinners are opportunities to build community, hospitality, and gratitude within the program. The team holiday dinner and end-of-the-year party includes players, parents, and siblings. This is an opportunity for parents to pause, socialize, and notice the players' "family-like" interactions off the court.

A few years ago, through the creativity of some of our upperclassmen, a more recent tradition evolved at team meals. Toward the end of a meal, there is the tapping of a glass and the presentation of a speech. Everyone quiets down and listens to the usually entertaining "reflections of the day" by one of our captains. In the first year of this tradition, Maggie Lucas wrote the speech on her cell phone while Maggie Ebbott provided the delivery. This simple tradition displays the unique team personality and was a fun activity that enhanced the bond of friendship among the players.

TEAM SELECTION

Because of the size of our school and our participation philosophy, our school has a no-cut policy. I imagine that making cuts is one of the most challenging aspects of coaching. My previous experience with team selections and decisions regarding varsity, junior varsity, and swing players suggests that establishing specific guidelines can make this process less painful for all involved. First, it is essential to set a firm timeline and use both drills and scrimmages in evaluating talent. When decisions are made, it is necessary to meet with each student in person or at least make an individual phone call. It is helpful to offer suggestions for improvement or perhaps an opportunity to participate in the program in some other capacity. In the past, we have had wonderful students hang up their basketball shoes yet stay involved in the program as team scorekeepers. I would recommend that coaches never post a team on a bulletin board or read off a list of names at the end of a practice. Team selection involves young people in a public social negotiation with their peers. They need a safe space to process their emotions. We need to be aware of the emotional impact and implicit message received when a child is cut from a team. It takes tremendous courage for a young person to try out for membership on a team; therefore coaches should go to great lengths to honor that courage with a one-on-one post tryout meeting.

PLAYING TIME

There are many variables when it comes to making decisions about playing time. Regarding youth sports, I favored a rule implemented by Biddy Basketball that requires every player to play at least a full quarter and all teams to carry a full roster of twelve players. I realize that the Play Like a Champion Today program, described in chapter 5 of this volume, believes in guaranteeing all players equal playing time through eighth grade, and it sounds as if they are achieving great progress with this proposal. In regards to high school sports, it would be a challenge to implement equal playing time for all. Playing time, like winning on the scoreboard, can often be equated with self-esteem. It is important to recognize the impact of playing time on your players' psyche as well as continually acknowledge the plethora of individual contributions to the team vision.

Some believe playing time is purely subjective; but it can, and should, be evidence based. First, it is important to establish clear criteria regarding playing time. While game substitutions can appear to be unilateral, most of our talent evaluation is done through consensus of the coaching staff and is based on performance in practice drills, game statistics, and effort/hustle contributions. Likewise, there are many evidence-based statistical analysis programs that can be implemented during practice and games. At practice, Temple University Coach John Chaney would chart player efficiency with performance scores that tracked hustle and fundamentals, for example loose ball dives, charges drawn, pivot effectiveness, timing on screens, and defensive deflections, to mention a few. Of course there is no foolproof method, and there will usually be playing time concerns from athletes and parents.

Secondly, keeping a log of minutes is helpful in monitoring playing time both during the game and in post-game meetings (see table 12.1). Such a log helps prevent a player from getting lost on the bench and also provides information as to who has been on the court the longest. While we do not discuss playing time with parents, we do encourage students to address their concerns with the coaching staff. Sometimes it is important to explain to a player that a change in playing time is not due to anything they are doing wrong but simply the result of a teammate's improved contribution. Most importantly we work to acknowledge each player's sense of contribution, regardless of the quantity of playing time.

COLLEGE RECRUITING

While we are fortunate to have had several of our Germantown Academy players recruited by some of the top colleges in the country, this is not the norm for all students, neither in our program nor for the 433,000 who play high school basketball. NCAA data indicates

Table 12.1. Time log

GA vs.						Date:					
Minutes											

Player	F	1st Q	T	2nd Q	T	Half	3rd Q	T	4th Q	T	Overall
Laura		8 —	8	8 5 3	6	14	8 2	6	8 4	4	24
Maggie		8 —	8	8 4	4	12	8 2	6	5 2	3	21
Joey		8 4	4	4 —	4	8	7 3	4	8 2	6	18
Caroline		8 2	6	8 4 2	6	12	8 —	8	8 7	1	21
Gillian		8 4	4	5 2	3	7	8 3	5	5 2	3	15
Jesse		4 —	4	8 2	6	10	8 7	1	8 5	3	14
Tory				2	2	2	3 —	3	4 —	4	9
Colleen		4	4	8 3	5	9	3 —	3	2 —	2	14
Niki							2 —	2	8 —	8	10
Chelsea							2 —	2	7 5 2	4	6
Alexa		2	2	4	4	6			2	2	8
Total			40		40			40		40	160

Note for time log: Each quarter consists of 40 minutes of play—5 positions at 8 minutes each. To use the chart, place an 8 by the name of each starter in the first quarter column to signify when they entered the game. As the starter is substituted out of the game, place the time of her exit next to the 8 which indicated the beginning of the quarter. Likewise place the same time next to the substitute's name. Find the difference between the two numbers to get the total number of minutes played in a quarter. For example, Joey started the game (8) and was substituted at (4) and played 4 minutes in the first quarter. Jesse entered the game at 4 minutes and played to (0) thus also playing 4 minutes in the first quarter. When marking substitutions, we round the number to the nearest half minute.

that there are approximately 4,600 freshman roster spots in the NCAA for the 123,000 senior high school players; thus only 3.7 percent of high school senior basketball players will go on to compete at the college level.[10] The entire recruiting process is tedious and highly subjective. Each year talented players are overlooked. Hearts are broken, limitations realized, and emotional upheaval can occur. Walking with a student as she dreams and sets goals is a privilege; it is also an opportunity to encourage her to be "her" best, not "the" best. Athletic scholarships should not be a focus of sports participation, but they often do become a distraction. This is why we consistently remind students to enjoy the experience at hand and appreciate their friendships in sport; this approach nurtures consolation in what can be a time of intense questioning of self-worth. This does not mean we don't talk about the prospect of playing basketball in college. Generally, most students have a realistic understanding of their potential to play at the next level and what level is a good fit for their skills. This is not always the case, however. Frequent conversation with prospective college student-athletes and their parents can assist with understanding the recruiting calendar and helps the athlete to interpret the subtle signals that indicate the depth of interest from college coaches. With the expansion of multiple summer national tournaments and showcases, most players have an opportunity to be seen by recruiters. However, most college recruiters are in attendance at these events to see "specific" athletes and not just survey the talent. For students on the bubble of playing college sports, it is important to be proactive in the recruiting process and initiate contact with colleges that are potentially a good fit both academically and athletically. Students should forward to these schools a simple resume with their summer team schedule.

Attending the college's basketball camp, especially for mid and low Division I programs, provides an opportunity to meet coaching staff personally. There is no script in moving through the recruiting process, and each situation is different. I have had several players fly under the radar until senior year and go on to have very successful college careers. As coaches, we don't have a crystal ball regarding our athletes' futures; however, close attention to individual patterns of recruiting can assist with the process. Some questions that we ask our players are: What type of communication is coming from the university? Are the coaches calling or texting? When was the last time they called? Who on the coaching staff is calling? How many students are in their pool of recruits? Where do you rank on their list? Have they already extended offers; if so, to how many players? Are they ready to make you a scholarship offer or confirm a place on their roster?

GAME VIDEO

While video can be a valuable tool, I practice caution when using it to evaluate high school players in a team setting. Boys tend to be less sensitive, whereas high school girls can be overly sensitive to replaying their individual mistakes in front of their teammates. Think about it: what high school student wants to be filmed in the heat of competition and have their mistakes pointed out in slow motion to the entire team? Let's walk in their shoes for a moment. Which of us coaches would want to be filmed coaching on the sideline? From another perspective, players who did not play in the game are now expected to watch the game for a second time. With today's technological advancements, a better method may be to email the digital clips of game video for personal viewing. Another alternative is to meet with individual players one on one to review correctable errors. However, on occasion we gather as a team for watching video in preparation for rival competitions. In such situations, the players often provide positive feedback on the experience.

SERVICE COMMITMENT

Service is not a relationship between an expert and a problem; it is a human relationship, a work of the heart and the soul.
—Rachel Naomi Remen, "Recapturing the Soul of Medicine"

Each season our team commits to a service project with a focus on the needs of others. Projects have included running a middle school basketball clinic, volunteering with special needs clients, dedicating a game to be a fundraiser for a charitable organization, purchasing and wearing "Hope for Haiti" shooting shirts, and hosting a tournament for victims of Katrina or other charitable organizations. I am awed not only by the opportunity to give back but also to hear how our players find meaning in these experiences. Sometimes the lessons learned extend beyond the activity itself.

Last season the optional service day was scheduled in direct conflict with the student body's powder-puff football competition between the classes. I had considered moving the activity to accommodate the players who had signed up for the football game, but after consulting with a mentor, swim coach Dick Shoulberg, I decided to go ahead as scheduled. Since the service activity was on the calendar for over a month he thought that letting the girls make a "tough choice" would give them experience for the future. Interestingly, every varsity player decided to forgo the powder-puff game. I was aware of their sacrifice and was pleased with what I perceived as the mature decision. After the event, we gathered for pizza and shared stories about their experience working with special needs students. Each player was profoundly grateful, not only "to do" for the special needs students but "to be with" them in a "truly fun" afternoon of basketball. Our players were touched by their happiness. Smiles were contagious all afternoon and the activity was a success. The seniors who had considered missing the clinic to attend the powder-puff game were humbled by the fact that they had thought of choosing otherwise. They thanked our staff profusely for the opportunity to work with these special young people. It was obvious that the memories of the afternoon would have a lasting effect on all who participated. While the event was an obvious success, I learned from my mentor Coach Shoulberg that making "tough decisions" is a valuable opportunity for our young athletes.

I can't emphasize enough the importance of having trusted mentors who provide sound advice and helpful perspectives with challenging situations. In my situation I have a wonderful coaching support staff, but none are on campus during the day. I am fortunate to have mentors on campus who are available for advice. I have tremendous respect for my mentors, Coach Shoulberg and cross country Coach Judy Krouse, for their genuine passion and care for their athletes, as well as their wisdom when decisions are unclear. They share their own stories and offer advice, but never tell me how to solve a problem. This type of mentoring allows me to chart my own course and personal growth.

While we create collaborative opportunities for our team to give back to the larger community, it is rewarding to witness our young athletes respond. A few years ago, one of our players, Maggie Lucas, had just won the three-point competition at a holiday tournament in Naples, Florida. After the competition a young girl, Andrea, asked to see Maggie's trophy. (Andrea copes with several physical disabilities and has had more than twenty surgeries.) Maggie explained to Andrea that her dad had already taken the trophy to the car, but she would go out and bring it back into the gym. Later that evening, I received a call from Andrea's dad, one of the tournament directors, explaining how meaningful it was for Maggie to give her trophy to Andrea. Maggie had not shared this with any of her teammates or coaches. I was moved beyond words when I heard about Maggie's gesture. As it turned out, later that month Andrea would be traveling to Children's Hospital in Philadelphia for another surgery. Andrea's family made a special effort to come up a day early to see our team play. For over two years, our girls have adopted Andrea and her siblings as our favorite fans. Maggie reflected,

> Andrea's perseverance has had a huge effect on my life and has inspired me greatly. It can be easy sometimes in athletics to lose perspective, or to think it is the end of the world after a loss or a bad game. But after having the opportunity to meet someone as special as Andrea, who overcomes challenges every day, you come to realize what is really important. Andrea may not know it, but her strength has taught me so much, and since I met her I have done my best to apply what I have learned from her to every aspect of my life, whether it be on or off the court. (Maggie Lucas '10)

Maggie's genuine connection with Andrea was definitely a "work of the heart and the soul."

Another extraordinary evening of community commitment occurred recently when the Germantown Academy Patriots and Archbishop Carroll Patriots united in our efforts to create awareness and raise funds for the Women's Basketball Coaches Association Pink Zone game, which supports breast cancer research. It was inspiring to see two of the top girls' high school basketball teams in the Philadelphia area, intense rivals, working together, using their basketball talents for a cause larger than basketball. Pink t-shirts were printed that read "PATRIOTS . . . United in the Fight against Breast Cancer." While the idea was proposed by the GA Patriots, the ACHS Patriots were full participants. Without solicitation, the ACHS Head Coach Chuck Creighton, upon entering the gym, presented several checks exceeding $600. Needless to say, in the standing room–only gym that evening, all were winners in a way that had little to do with the numbers on the scoreboard at the end of the game. The aforementioned events within our program resonate with Pope John Paul II's reflection on the potential of sport as "a significant vehicle for the overall development of the person and a very useful element in building a more human society."[11]

THE MOVEMENT OF PLAY

For almost three decades we have witnessed a paradigm shift in high school athletics toward early specialization, elite training, and dreams of college scholarships and professional contracts. With these changes many observers fear we are losing the play element in sport. It is important to reflect on what play is and how we can maintain the play element in high school sports.

Psychologist Donald Winnicott defines play "as a creative engagement with the world where our imagination interacts with whatever we find outside ourselves."[12] In this sense, play has a great deal to do with "connection." When I speak of play, I include sports and athletics. For me, play evolves into sport when we apply rules and regulations and an emphasis on competition. The etymology of the word competition is derived from the Latin *petere*, "to seek or desire," and *con/cum*, "together/with." Competition is basically defined as "seeking with." The "seeking with" emphasis of sport can move in two opposed directions.

The first direction has a focus on outcome alone with an emphasis on dominance or power over. When winning becomes idolatrous a power pyramid develops with a focus on survival, being the best, not just one's best. This dynamic eventually leads most to think of themselves as losers and implodes.

The second direction has an emphasis on the journey, or as mentioned in chapter 7, doing something for its own sake. In this approach, sport is experienced as a dynamic interplay, integrating the spiritual virtue of right relationship with the physical challenges of competition. It engages one's creative abilities to perform intricate tasks at ever increasing levels of complexity with reverence for self, others, and the world around us. While the scoreboard depicts winners and losers, the emphasis in this approach is less extrinsic. Theologian Jim Bacik explains that play can take us out of our ordinary time and space, remind us that our final destiny is beyond this world, and speak to us about integrated life in the Spirit. Such experiences can be integrative and transformative.[13]

While the spiritual dimension of sport is often associated with the joy of playing, it can also be experienced in difficult times of sacrifice and struggle. I specifically remember a locker room conversation after a heartfelt loss where one of my players shared, "I would rather lose with you as teammates than win with anyone else." It was obvious that to her the value of friendship far outweighed any numbers on the scoreboard. Her words shifted everyone's perspective from a sense of defeat to a reverence for one another and the opportunity to compete.

PERSPECTIVE

The most important thing in the Olympic Games is not to win but to take part, just as the most important thing in life is not the triumph but the struggle. The essential thing is not to have conquered but to have fought well.

—Baron Pierre de Coubertin, founder of the modern Olympic Games

As I mentioned in the opening pages, sports are about relationships, relationships that facilitate connection, reflection, and validation in our students' lives. I have discussed various principles, traditions, and communication techniques that support and empower relationships in our program. Within this context students and coaches are consistently invited to assume responsibility as members of the program and invest in a shared team vision. Essential to our shared vision is a structure of core values based on collaborative communication, mutual respect, and discerning integrity. While we encourage performing at "one's best" and striving for excellence, the true measure of success for our players reaches far beyond team championships or individual achievements. Our students value the opportunity to have fun, hone skills, and develop friendships. Actually, I believe these are the same values of most high school student-athletes. Yes, even in today's highly competitive culture of sports.

Most importantly, I have learned that no matter how attentive we are to details and checks and balances, there will always be times of challenge. Heeding the advice of the old Haitian proverb "We see from where we stand" and building a shared vision takes time and perseverance. Coaching is a journey on which we are all teachers and learners.

PRE-SEASON PARENTS' LETTER

Dear Parents,

It is a pleasure to be a part of the Basketball program at GA. Your daughters exhibit a superior work ethic and are gifted both in the classroom and on the court. They are loyal teammates, as evidenced in their senior captains' essays. While winning on the scoreboard is a major emphasis in our program, the desire of our educational vision is to teach through the game of basketball.

At the conclusion of our season it is my hope that our players have achieved success in the vast majority of their team and individual goals. Ideally, I hope each athlete develops a sense of contribution with an appreciation for others' talents, has opportunities to test herself in game situations, and establishes friendships for the rest of her life. It is my sincere desire that each player create cherished memories while increasing her passion and respect for the opportunity to compete. Honestly, over the past thirteen years, I think we have been extremely successful in these endeavors.

I ask your support in encouraging and modeling behavior that is conducive to success in all of our goals. Specifically, I ask for your support in the following guidelines:

* Be a positive role model at the game; respect the game, the officials, the coaches, their teammates, and the opponents.
* Support your daughter's opportunity to be a member of this team. Applaud her contributions and encourage her through adversity. Please be aware that conflict and adversity are inevitable in competition and talent development.
* Honor your daughter's friendships on this team.

I am available to discuss any growth and developmental concerns that may arise during the season. I would appreciate any communication of above matters to occur through my office phone ____ ____ ____. I do not discuss playing time with parents, but suggest that your daughter address such concerns with any of the coaches. I can easily be contacted via email with any other questions or concerns.

Warm regards,

PLAYER PROFILE

Name _____ Jersey# _____

Year_____ Height _____ Position _____

Academic honors: _____

Athletic honors:_____

Clubs & Sports: _____

Player's interests:_____

Pre-game rituals, earliest sports memory:_____

Most inspirational individual:_____

Favorite movie: _____

Must-see TV show: _____

The music I enjoy is:_____

Favorite actress/actor: _____

I would like to switch places for a day with:_____

Place I would most like to visit:_____

The best place I've visited was:_____

My favorite class at GA:_____

My most prized possession is: _____

The thing I would change about this world:_____

Birthday:_____

Middle School:_____

Siblings: _____

Daughter of:_____

NOTES

1. Nel Noddings, *Educating Moral People* (New York: Teachers College Press, 2002), 132.

2. Robert Kegan, *The Evolving Self: Problem and Process in Human Development* (Cambridge, MA: Harvard University Press, 1982).

3. Kevin Lixey, Norbert Müller, and Cornelius Shäfer, eds., *Blessed John Paul II Speaks to Athletes: Homilies, Messages and Speeches on Sport* (Blessed John Paul II Sports Foundation, 2012), 66. Available at http://www.laici.va/content/dam /laici/documenti/sport/eng/magisterium/jpii-pastoral-messages.pdf.

4. This parents' meeting is an opportunity to share the team's vision, solicit their support in achieving team goals, and address any questions. In addition, our school now uses a parents' contract that reinforces the mission statement of our athletic program.

5. Robert Evans, "Changing Families, Changing Schools," *Independent School* (Winter 1998).

6. B. W. Tuckman, "Developmental Sequence in Small Groups," *Psychological Bulletin* 63 (June 1965): 384–99.

7. Mike Krzyzewski, *Leading with the Heart* (New York: Warner Books, 2000), 39.

8. Robert Greenleaf, *Servant Leadership* (New York: Paulist Press, 1977).

9. Thomas Merton, *Contemplation in a World of Action* (Notre Dame, IN: University of Notre Dame Press, 1998), 369.

10. See https://www.ncaa.org/sites/default/files/Probability-of-going-pro -methodology_Update2013.pdf.

11. Lixey, Müller, and Shäfer, *Blessed John Paul II Speaks to Athletes*, 56.

12. Donald Woods Winnicott, *Playing and Reality* (New York: Routledge, 1989), 39.

13. James Bacik, *Spirituality in Action* (Kansas City, MO: Sheed and Ward, 1997).

CHAPTER 13

Coaching and the Ignatian Pedagogical Paradigm

JAMES CHARLES NAGGI

As teachers in Catholic schools we're allowed, obligated actually, to approach the education of our students from a set of central values articulated in the mission statements and other "vision" documents of our schools. Sometimes they are developed by the individual Catholic school; more usually they reflect a common approach to education as defined by the diocese or religious orders that run our various institutions.

Having clear values is an advantage when it comes to education. Human beings are not one dimensional. We're physical, intellectual, and spiritual in our composition. If our approach to education is only addressed to the mind (narrowly understood), with the culture of the day defining the learning environment, we miss the other dimensions of our students that need to be addressed for their education to be complete and relevant.

If what I'm saying is true—that it is an advantage to teach at schools based on values that address the whole student—we're missing the boat if we don't embrace the mission of our schools in a direct way and incorporate the values expressed there as much as we can into our coaching. As a teacher, coach, and administrator at a Jesuit high school I've come to realize the importance of doing just that, and how working with my school's mission and the teaching tradition fostered by Jesuit education has made my work more effective.

While I'm going to talk about one piece of that tradition, called the Ignatian pedagogical paradigm, or teaching strategy, such an approach is not limited to coaches at Jesuit schools. Every Catholic school in the country has its own traditions and methods. Any coach can apply what I'm going to say to his or her own situation.

The Ignatian pedagogical paradigm breaks the teaching process into five major components: context, experience, reflection, action, and evaluation. Despite an annoying similarity to graduate-level "eduspeak," it's possible for coaches to look at this way of teaching and see a huge advantage in incorporating it into their coaching technique. Many coaches and teachers already use pieces of the paradigm without recognizing that they do.

Athletic coaches, who generally favor the practical, might want to dismiss something like the Ignatian paradigm as too abstract and far too typical of the theory-laden droning of faculty in-service workshops. Or, after a quick look, they might reject it with a quick "get-it-out-of-my-face" conclusion: "We already do all that stuff anyway" —no further discussion necessary. But an out-of-hand rejection by coaches of the principles outlined in the paradigm is shortsighted.

It's shortsighted on two counts. Most importantly, understanding this approach, rooted as it is in fundamental Ignatian principles, is a legitimate way to become a better coach at any Catholic school. It's also shortsighted because given the changing ratio of religious and lay faculty, athletics can expect long-term support from a Catholic school's administration, trustees, parents, and constituency only to the extent that coaches can make the case that their programs are truly linked to Catholic teaching traditions and value systems. Moreover, by deliberately and authentically aligning oneself with his or her school's ideals, a coach can deflect easy charges of personal, player, or program "egocentricity," one of the potential pitfalls inherent in sports identified by Shields and Bredemeier in chapter 6.

If you stop reading here with the comment, "That's baloney. I'll *always* get support as long as I win!" I submit you are at a school that has lost its way, just another school with a crucifix on the wall.

We should recognize that our teams don't exist just to provide entertainment or to keep students busy or to publicize the school name or to attract college scholarship offers. Or even to win. These are all highly favorable by-products but don't in themselves justify athletic programs at Catholic schools.

The athletic experience at Catholic schools should teach student-athletes firsthand, based on active participation, as many as possible of the important character traits identified in Catholic school mission statements and other key documents presented by the religious orders or dioceses that set their standards. It is the responsibility of the coach, as a Catholic educator, to see to it that they are attained. The Ignatian paradigm can be used to help make this happen.

To be effectively used by high school sports programs, the five components of the paradigm—context, experience, reflection, action, and evaluation—must be considered as active ingredients operating throughout an entire season. What follows is a general look at these five components and their potential relationship to athletics at Catholic high schools.

CONTEXT

To establish context is to understand the personal background, goals, and hopes of student-athletes. It is to know each student better on a personal level in order to create a relationship of mutual trust and respect, essential for effectively developing both athletic talent and true teams, those whose members view the good of the whole as more significant than self.

Many coaches have devised ways to learn the goals of each athlete before the start of the season. Maybe it takes the form of a questionnaire or a face-to-face meeting, or both. Regardless of method, goal-setting is part of establishing context.

It's likewise key for the coach to know something of the personal background of students—family situations, economics, and personality strengths and weaknesses.

Context also refers to the world within which high school student-athletes operate. This world changes fast, and even young coaches are usually out of step with it. Being aware of the assumptions about sports, adults, drugs, media, money, responsibility, appearance, success, and all else that constitute modern American adolescent life will help the coach know the context of his or her athletes. It is a mistake for any coach to assume that today's athletes will be checking the pervasive influence of their teen culture at the locker room door. The question is how much of it stands diametrically opposed to what the coach is trying to teach, and how does one contradict those influences without alienating student-athletes?

The course most coaches take, perhaps without realizing they are setting up a "counterculture" to compete against the one that students carry with them, is to create a specific "context" for the team itself—one that reinforces the ethos upon which the coach seeks to build his or her team. In doing so, coaches often align their values, sometimes unwittingly, with that of the Catholic school itself. One of the starting points is establishing an environment of care for the individual—a core Catholic principle. It's important that team members know their teammates and that the staff know the players. One of the goals many coaches have for the start-of-season weeks when teams are together for much of each day during two-a-day workouts is for the athletes to become more close-knit. If a coach develops a specific format for doing this—for example, team meals, rookie shows, overnight stays, team social activities like going to the movies, and so on—that coach is helping create the "context" portion of the team. And coaches take context up a notch when they deliberately build in ways for athletes to openly talk to each other in team situations about their goals, their vision of the team and their teammates, and their common expectations in the coming weeks.

Establishing the context of a program isn't complete until the coach too shares him- or herself with athletes. Unless coaches allow their student-athletes at least a glimpse of their own inner workings, the opportunity to weave together players and staff into a cohesive, dedicated whole will probably be lost—certainly not maximized. At stake is whether or not mutual trust will be part of the program's context.

Once context is established early, coaches must continually work to sustain their grasp of it. Because a team is a dynamic entity composed of living, breathing, generally unpredictable human beings, context will inevitably undergo changes as the season progresses. By deliberately seeking out each athlete outside of instructional coaching situations on a regular basis—maybe during the school day or in warm-ups or while walking back to the locker room after practice— and making it a point to engage the athlete in even casual conversation, coaches signal their interest in every individual and in staying up with any contextual adjustments going on within the team.

EXPERIENCE

"Experience" refers to the learning process that takes place under the direction of the coach. In Ignatian paradigm terms, learning is not limited to just what's absorbed by the brain. Catholic education is supposed to engage the whole person—body, mind, heart, and will.

Athletics encompass this combination naturally. Being effective in competitive sports demands consistent physical effort and mental concentration simultaneously. This is a difficult combination for high school athletes, with plenty of room to fall short. Only a keen desire to take on the challenge in the first place and the absolute determination to work through difficulties until it gets done right will lead to fulfilling one's potential as an athlete. Because athletics require desire and determination, or heart and will, coupled with the requirement to think and make decisions under pressure, they fulfill the expectations of the Catholic learning "experience" of engaging the full person.

An aside here. Not listed among the Ignatian paradigm ingredients is "content," probably because there are too many subjects to reach any kind of consistency. Nonetheless, it seems appropriate to take a moment to relate the learning experience in sports to what it is that's being learned.

The learning experience in athletics obviously includes physical skills and the systems being used by the sport for competition. Certainly the Xs and Os are crucial. But in Catholic school athletics it is essential that certain virtues promoted by Catholic education be part of the lesson. In Jesuit schools specifically, and typically within other Catholic schools and their individual traditions, there are resources that articulate a number of educational virtues that happen to be very relevant to athletics. It's up to coaches to work out the exact language, but a short list of examples provides an idea of the possibilities: seeking human excellence, handling criticism, developing full potential, overcoming selfishness, taking pride in accomplishments, valuing integrity, sharing talents with the community, recognizing that God is active in all things, developing self-confidence as well as self-discipline, dealing with others honestly and fairly. Even a cursory overview suggests the impact athletics can have if the Catholic school coach has the wisdom to help players apply their "whole person—minds, hearts, and wills" toward such virtues.

One way to do this is to write a team "code" and present it to athletes. Many coaches already employ such a code in various forms. It is basically a list of those qualities that the coach considers important for the student-athlete to be successful. Commonly, coaches will name "commitment," "coachability," "personal pride," "unselfishness," and similar virtues, and it's not hard to see how close these are to characteristics that Catholic education promotes.

But if the coach's list is only based on some handout picked up at a coaching clinic two years earlier, no matter how worthwhile the points listed, it will only randomly connect with the school's priorities. That's why a head coach who claims to promote lasting Catholic education principles must develop such a code with a copy of the school's mission statement in hand.

It is unlikely that a coach will set up team expectations quoting exactly the mission statement's descriptors. The descriptors usually need to be adapted to an athletic frame of reference. But it is essential that the coach can actually relate the points of a team code to those that a given Catholic school has identified as qualities it seeks to have its graduates model.

And, of course, the coach needs to believe in them. In chapter 4, McNamee suggests that "the habits that are fostered by the sports coach are as good and as bad as the coach." He's right. No code at all is preferable to one that the coach preaches but fails to personally model.

It is also essential that the coach work with athletes to help them recognize how practice and competition bring forth the ideals contained in such a code. The coach as an educator must be able to teach that the goal-line stand in the last game was as much about developing confidence and brotherhood as it was about everybody plugging the right gap. The coach has to have the insight to recognize the charitable and humble heart of the third-stringer who goes all out at every practice—and find a way to let the team recognize it too. In short, the coach must be someone who can continually show athletes how moral ideals on a sheet of paper are in fact real entities that relate directly to their lives.

If a coach can make those values come alive for athletes during the high school years, graduates will trust their worth and power in the post–high school world as well. Moreover, when a Catholic high school pushes its mission statement goals as blueprints for student development while the coach teaches how athletic standards and the school's standards interlock, both coach and school reinforce each other as they create a uniquely Catholic educational "experience" for students. Also, in this way, the critical role that athletics play within a Catholic high school becomes readily apparent.

REFLECTION

Most coaches I know, myself included, recoil at the thought of huggy-touchy sharing sessions where people bare their souls to the rest of an embarrassed discussion group. The word "reflection" may unfortunately conjure up such a vision. Coaches have to get past that knee-jerk assumption if they hope to take advantage of this part of the paradigm.

"Reflection" as used by the Ignatian paradigm means to clarify the meaning and essential value of what is being experienced—that is, learned. On the technical level in athletics, this clarification occurs every day at practice as athletes repeat what they have to do to execute the sport successfully. In fact, "repetition" has been identified as one way reflection occurs. Clarification also takes place in meetings, in one-on-one instructional sessions with coaches, and even pregame warm-ups. Thus, technically, there's no lack of clarification or "reflection" provided within the teaching approach of most coaches.

Regarding the larger lessons taught by sports, reflection takes a different form. For example, some coaches at Catholic schools have their teams attend Mass together. Even within the structure of a liturgy, there is opportunity—perhaps guided by the coach, perhaps by a priest, perhaps student-driven—for athletes to clarify for themselves the larger meanings contained within the experiences they are going through during the season.

The process becomes even more focused when the coach recognizes that when players talk together about what being on the team means to them, a sense of ownership is built that no number of technique drills can ever produce. Such ownership helps create genuine loyalty and commitment and becomes a major part of the team's context. Moreover, the benefit to athletes in the way of personal growth is tremendous.

Realizing this, a coach may set aside time each week for the team to come together, for example, in a chapel setting. Weekly chapel could allow players to share prayers and for them to talk openly about matters important to them personally, thoughts related to the season and their fellowship with teammates, thoughts also perhaps about anxieties outside the sport, such as those having to do with illness or a death in the family, for example, which allows teammates to rally in support, demonstrating a viable community.

Such a discussion in a chapel is obviously serious and intense. It only works if there is absolute trust and acceptance by those gathered. It doesn't have to be particularly long or cover every topic under the sun. It doesn't even have to take place in a chapel. In such sessions, the coach has to steer athletes away from talking about the immediate game or opponent—psyching up for competition is better done at a different time and place. The environment for such a team meeting has to be comfortable, quiet, and out of the campus mainstream of action, a place where athletes can drop their pretensions and talk straight from the heart. By identifying certain athletes each week to address various kinds of topics—without writing a script for the students—a coach can assure that the tone and direction of the session are the proper ones.

While feeling free to occasionally offer personal thoughts, the coach needs to back off during chapel sessions and let the athletes lead the way. The coach has to fight the urge to preach and trust that players can handle it. Early preparatory work with seniors and team leaders about the intent of such sessions helps assure success in that regard.

The coach will probably be surprised and moved by what is said by players on these occasions—as long as the coach enters into the experience sincerely, sold on its importance. High school athletes can almost always tell when they're being manipulated.

Thus, the third component of the paradigm, reflection, can occur in sports both on the physical, technical level as well as on the discernment level. Certainly there are several ways to accomplish the latter, with liturgies or chapels being just two examples. The Catholic school coach must not use such methods as motivational ploys for improving short-term performance but instead personally embrace them as a natural and essential piece of the "education of the whole person" promised by Catholic schools.

ACTION

Since "action" and the playing of sports are inseparable, the connection between this element of the Ignatian paradigm and high school athletics seems obvious. But the paradigm takes the definition of action beyond just the physical. In the Ignatian learning process, "action" is defined as internal human growth based on experience that has been reflected upon, as well as its manifestation externally.

This latter part, the "manifestation externally" of what student-athletes have experienced in the way of knowledge, is easily evident in sports. Blocking the shot, hitting the ball, serving with power, handing off the baton—athletic actions like these reveal how much or how little the athlete has mastered the skills and techniques taught by the coach. For St. Ignatius, learning is shown in deeds, not words—pretty close to the coaching credo that it takes more than lip service to get the job done well.

The other part of the definition that refers to "internal human growth" is also at the heart of the high school athletic experience, and is an example of what Nicole LaVoi calls "asset development," which can happen for young people through participation in sports. As skills are being demonstrated in practice and competition, the growth of personal insight and understanding within the participants often simultaneously occurs.

Growth continues to take place even as spectators watch. Pushing past previous levels of endurance, confronting pressure with poise and control, pulling together with teammates against daunting adversity, demonstrating courage in the face of pain, self-respect despite heart-breaking defeat, calm modesty when blessed with success—what are any of these if not the "actions" of adolescents becoming more than what they were before they stepped into the arena? If the Catholic school coach has done the job right, what's revealed through situations like these will be the blend of athletic values and school ideals that the effective coach always keeps somewhere close to team consciousness. Will every moment in every game and practice always reflect leaps of inner development within the student-athlete involved? No. In fact most won't. But with patience, over time, and with perhaps full results not blossoming until years after graduation, guiding students to such "action" will rank among the coach's greatest accomplishments.

EVALUATION

No official high school activity in which students take part receives as much continual evaluation as their athletic performance. Nothing else a group of students does together in any school program is subject to the critical scrutiny devoted to teams during a season by their coaches.

In some sports, evaluation is done on the basis of graded film analysis; in others it's a matter of times, statistics, and other cut-and-dried data; in still others the coach's evaluation has less to do with raw numbers than it has to do with his or her own "gut" response to the athlete's efforts. Moreover, students are expected to absorb and incorporate into their next actions the continual stream of evaluation directed at them throughout every workout.

The Ignatian paradigm defines evaluation as determining what has been learned as well as what needs to be learned. It is aimed at pointing out the need to always do more with one's talents.

Identifying the "more" that must be done by athletes is a basic part of the job of every coach, many of whom instinctively measure performance against perfection. But while making certain that the athlete is fully aware of his or her shortcomings, the Catholic school coach must also pay heed to the first part of the definition—identifying what has been learned. The constant feedback provided athletes during practice and after contests needs to also cover improvement that has happened, not just the improvement that should happen. After all, perfection remains beyond human reach. "More" doesn't imply comparison against an absolute standard but against the individual's full personal potential, whatever that might be.

While true perfection is impossible, personal excellence can be attained regularly. When a coach consistently blends acknowledgement of progress with demanding challenge, evaluation itself becomes a motivational tool for helping make excellence a reality for adolescents. And excellence offered to God is a worthy form of gratitude for the blessings of ability and opportunity.

Evaluation of internal growth is also necessary. It is more difficult to do than evaluating physical action but ultimately of more importance. The Ignatian coach must hold athletes as accountable in this area as they do in that of skill execution.

The measuring here isn't done with a tape or a computer or a clock. It's based on the moral compass of the coach. For the coach at a Catholic school, that moral compass must include an understanding of, and strong commitment to, the characteristics so clearly fostered by the traditions of Catholic education.

Whenever there's a breakdown of the inner development of Catholic school values within an athlete or team, the coach must forcefully respond. Whether it is talking trash, throwing punches, or criticizing teammates, primary Catholic principles, for which the athletic program at every Catholic school must stand, have been violated. Proper evaluation requires that student-athletes are called to account for such breakdowns, just as they are for dropping a pass or overthrowing first base. And if the trash-talker is the leading scorer, it cannot make a difference to the coach.

IN SUMMARY

The five components of the Ignatian pedagogical paradigm compose a process absolutely compatible with coaching athletics at Catholic schools. First, context is established as coach and athletes learn about each other and develop an environment of mutual respect, leading to what the paradigm describes as a "readiness to begin." Then meetings and practices constitute the learning experience, which exposes student-athletes to the physical skills and inherent principles cultivated by the program and closely identified with Ignatian learning goals. Next, experience enters into reflection as repetition occurs physically and mentally and as players take time to share and internalize the larger meanings of their athletic and team commitments. Action crystallizes all that came before into a demonstration of what has been mastered under the guidance of the coach. Finally, evaluation identifies achievement and shortcomings for the purpose of always moving students closer to becoming more.

Once the general usefulness of a Catholic teaching methodology like the Ignatian paradigm is acknowledged, it's necessary for athletic departments to put it into practice. Whether it's within a school, on a regional basis, or at the national level, Catholic coaches should begin to fill out its precepts with some practical detail. What does one coach do to create a context of unity among his athletes early in the season?

How does another coach set goals and objectives that deliberately challenge an athlete's mind, heart, and will, so that the learning experience becomes complete? What about coaches who use liturgies, chapels, or other means whereby teams share reflections about themselves and each other? Is there a coach who emphasizes the "action" of *internal* growth as much as physical performance by student-athletes? What are the evaluation methods coaches use for either? And, in the area of content, what codes of values have coaches developed for their teams, and are they in any way actually connected to the Catholic mission of their schools?

The answers to all these questions are available from Catholic high schools around the country. They are spread out. Probably no school possesses them all, but they're all out there. It only remains for athletic coaches to get off the bench and actively assume a leadership role in the ongoing examination of the Catholic vision of education through sports.

The benefit to tomorrow's leaders will be significant.

NOTE

For further reading, see International Commission of the Apostolate of Jesuit Education (ICAJE), *Ignatian Pedagogy: A Practical Approach* (Rome, 1993); and Sharon J. Korth, "Precis of Ignatian Pedagogy: A Practical Approach," in *A Jesuit Education Reader*, ed. George W. Traub, 280–84 (Chicago: Loyola Press, 2008).

CHAPTER 14

Parents as Partners
in Youth Sport

NICOLE M. LAVOI

While the coach is arguably the most important influence *during* the sport event, parents also influence the sport experiences of their children. Parents' beliefs and values about sport and their child's sport competence create a climate at home that influences the child in many ways. Many parents take on important roles in youth sport—such as coach, manager, "team mom," or youth sport board member—that impact their child's sport experience. Parents are also the majority of "fans" on youth sport sidelines. Clearly, parents play a central and important role in youth sports and in the lives of their children. In this chapter the evidence pertaining to the influences of parents in youth sport involvement will be summarized and some suggestions will be made on how to include parents as partners in creating a climate where positive youth development through sports is more likely to occur.

THE INFLUENCE OF PARENTS

Based on the evidence, parents are the most critical sport socialization agents for youth, especially in childhood. As children move into adolescence, parents are replaced by peers and peer groups as the primary socialization influence. Mothers and fathers serve as models for observational learning, provide experiences, encourage participation in a variety of ways, and help to interpret experiences for their children. As a result, children develop beliefs in their abilities, create and maintain certain expectations of themselves, and acquire sport-related value systems based primarily on the influence of their parents. When children perceive that their parents believe in and support their athletic competence, it has been shown to lead to increased positive self-perceptions of the child, as well as child enjoyment, interest in sport, and sustained involvement and participation. Given that many children drop out of sport around adolescence, approximately one in three children are completely sedentary, and childhood obesity continues to be a national public health issue, adopting strategies to ensure children remain in sport as a source of physical activity is imperative. The key take home or lesson for parents: if the child perceives parents believe in and value sport and, better yet, actively participate in sport or physical activity, children are more likely to participate. Conversely, when children perceive parents to be disinterested and feel parents don't value sport—or feel sport involvement is unimportant—children are less likely to participate. Additionally, when children perceive parents to be primarily focused on winning and outperforming others (rather than doing one's personal best and giving effort), overinvolved, critical, or possessing unrealistic expectations, evidence suggests it can lead to lower belief in sport competencies, lower sport enjoyment, added stress, anxiety, and less intrinsic motivation for the child—all outcomes that parents would likely choose to avoid!

DIFFERENTIAL PERCEPTIONS OF MOTHERS' AND FATHERS' INFLUENCE

Based on the data, differential perceptions of mothers' and fathers' influence appear to vary depending on the specific dimension or type of parental influence assessed. Variables typically assessed include belief in child sport competence, parental pressure, involvement, support, beliefs, expectations, reactions to performance, and values. Whether or not mothers and fathers affect children differently, both are important social influences. Children's perceptions of their parents' beliefs and values are influential predictors of child outcomes such as enjoyment, intrinsic motivation, good and poor sport behavior, anxiety, and other positive psychosocial outcomes. Therefore parents should be aware of how their thoughts, emotions, and behaviors are being interpreted by their children. Most parents assume the messages they intend are being clearly communicated and received, but according to the children's perceptions this is not always true. What parents *think* they do and say and what they *actually* do and say is often different. For example, parents perceive they yell from the sidelines far less frequently than is reported by children. Why is this important? Data indicate that children's perceptions of parental sideline behaviors is the biggest predictor of poor sport behavior during competition. If dad is yelling at the referee, the child believes it is acceptable for him to do the same. Similarly as previously stated, if the child perceives the parents value physical activity as a lifelong endeavor, the child is more likely to be physically active. To help ensure the "right" messages are being communicated to children, parents should engage in self-reflection in addition to communicating openly and bidirectionally with children. Another message communicated indirectly to children pertains to who is seen (and not seen) in positions of power in sport contexts.

GENDERED ROLES IN YOUTH SPORT

Available research illustrates a clear gendered division of labor exists in youth sports. Males occupy a majority of coaching roles and other visible positions of power (e.g., league president, head coach, coaching director). At the same time females fill most of the "helping" positions, such as team manager; likewise they engage in significantly more logistic support (e.g., enroll child, transport child, buy equipment, make snacks, etc.). The gendered division of labor and the absence of women in positions of power in youth sport are likely to affect children's beliefs, values, and expectations related to the role of women not only in sport but also in contexts outside of sport. Children need to see both males and females in a variety of roles if stereotypical notions of gender and leadership are to be challenged and ultimately changed. Sport leaders hold a great deal of power and importance in the lives of millions of children and youth, and when females occupy those positions in equal numbers it will provide evidence, for boys and girls, that women can succeed and be powerful.

PARENT-CREATED CLIMATE

In addition to children's perception about individual parental variables discussed in the previous section, children also perceive and interpret situational cues. In the literature this is often called the "parent-created motivational climate" and is defined by an athlete's perceptions of parental cues pertaining to success, failure, winning, and performance; these in turn influence athletes' achievement-related cognitions and subsequent behaviors. When parents focus on intrinsic motives for sport participation such as learning, skill mastery, enjoyment, and making friends, in addition to providing support and encouraging effort and self-referenced improvement, children are more likely to reap positive outcomes. Conversely, when parents create a motivational climate in which love, care, and attention is contingent on performance, children worry about making mistakes, believe success comes without practice and effort and is constructed primarily around winning and outperforming others, and will be less likely to attain positive youth development outcomes. Practically speaking, parents should strive to construct a motivational climate in which they encourage children to persist in the face of failure, focus on what can be controlled, learn from mistakes, and feel good about their effort regardless of the outcome.

PARENTAL SIDELINE BEHAVIORS

Another aspect of the parent-created sport climate pertains to parents' behaviors on youth sport sidelines, and how the child perceives and is influenced by those behaviors. Research on sport parents is not new, nor are the problems associated with overzealous parents on the sidelines. With the growing popularity of social media and the speed with which news and video can go viral, the perception is constructed that "bad" sport parent behavior is more prevalent and more egregious today than ever before. Longitudinal empirical data to substantiate this popular perception does not exist, but many anecdotes corroborate the phenomenon. In the 1976 book *Sports in America*, novelist James Michener wrote, "Youth leagues have been severely criticized because of the misbehavior of parents."[1] Unarguably, a subset of misbehaving parents on youth sport sidelines who create a toxic climate for everyone has always existed.

Survey, observational, and interview data support the existence of background anger on youth sport sidelines. The two most common background anger behaviors reported by athletes, coaches, and parents emanating from youth sport sidelines are yelling at the referee and coaching from the sidelines. Other background anger behavior includes yelling racial slurs, physical and verbal fighting between spectators, and yelling at the coach. Based on the data, background anger increases with the age of the athlete, peaking around sixteen to seventeen years of age; it is more prevalent in team sports and at the travel level rather than in-house competitive levels and individual sports. Background anger happens with similar occurrence regardless of the sex of the athlete. Interestingly, the peak in the reported frequency of background anger on the sidelines corresponds with the age when many young people drop out of organized sport. Future research should examine the cause and effect relationship between background anger and drop-out rates, as well as related negative outcomes for youth athletes.

When children experience background anger between parents within the home, it results in negative outcomes such as stress, increased aggressive behaviors, negative emotion, sadness, increased heart rate, depression, self-blame, and interpersonal, academic, and health problems. It is likely that exposure to background anger within the youth sport setting is the origin of some negative outcomes of youth athletes. Not all parents act egregiously all the time on youth sport sidelines, but background anger does occur with enough frequency that room for improvement does exist. Most parents do not set out to ruin or destroy their child's sport experience, but many do so nonetheless or inadvertently. The good news is that background anger is a set of controllable behaviors. Parents can learn, for example, how not to yell at the referee. Yelling at the referee is not a requisite behavior of "how to be a good sport parent," and when parents are taught how that behavior is perceived by their children, it can be an eye-opening revelation. One way to help parents examine their own sideline behaviors is to help them see their behaviors through the eyes of the child. Children are very clear about how they prefer their parents to behave in youth sport contexts.

When asked, children explained three roles pertaining to sport parents. Children preferred the *supportive parent* role, described as a parent who shows up to the competitive event, sits silently until someone (anyone, a player on their team or the opposing team) does something good, and encourages with positive support at appropriate times (e.g., time outs, after the game). Children do not like when parents act like a *crazed fan* or *demanding coach*. A crazed fan acts angrily, yells, argues, belittles, distracts, and embarrasses the athletes with disruptive and loud cheering. A demanding coach yells unsolicited advice, commands, and instructions at inappropriate times and this is perceived by the child to be delivered in a disapproving tone. The parental behaviors that youth athletes do *not* prefer fall neatly into the definition of background anger. Researchers have found that youth athletes' perceptions of parental background anger on the sidelines is predictive of athlete poor sportsmanship on the field. Emerging evidence suggests that sideline behaviors of adults affect the sport experience and perhaps the sport performance of youth athletes.

Youth sport stakeholders have the responsibility to work together to reduce youth sport background anger. One way to create a positive and growth-promoting youth sport climate is to use evidence-based educational programming.

Whaen parents are given evidence about what works and what does not in terms of their children, they will likely respond. Many parents simply don't realize, or are not aware of, what they are doing, how their actions are being perceived, or the potential negative impact of their actions on children and others in the sport environment. Inviting parents to see youth sport through the eyes of their child is a worthwhile endeavor. Parents can employ the "ABC" model to increase understanding of how children see their sporting world and the behavior of the parent. First, *Ask* the child how he or she prefers the parent to act or what the child sees. Second, *Believe* the child when he or she tells you something. For example a parent might ask, "What do I do on the sidelines that you wish I wouldn't do?" If the child replies, "I don't like it when you yell out my name and cheer loudly, it is embarrassing," then believe the child! Resist the temptation to explain it away such as, "Oh, you like it when I cheer! I just can't help myself!" Last, *Change* behavior according to what the child prefers. Another tool is to have discussions amongst parents about what kind of environment should be created for children in sport. Set expectations and norms together, and then work together to create accountability and responsibility around those norms. These simple tools can start an honest dialogue which may enlist parents as partners and help make sport a more enjoyable experience for everyone.

ADDITIONAL READING

Jennifer Fredricks and Jacquelynne Eccles, "Parental Influences on Youth Involvement in Sports," in *Developmental Sport and Exercise Psychology: A Lifespan Perspective*, ed. M. R. Weiss, 165–96 (Morgantown, WV: Fitness Information Technology, 2004).

Nicole LaVoi, "Occupational Sex Segregation in Youth Soccer Organization: Females in Positions of Power," *Women in Sport and Physical Activity Journal* 18, no. 2 (2009): 25–37.

Nicole LaVoi and Megan Babkes Stellino, "The Relation between Perceived Parent-Created Sport Climate and Competitive Male Youth Hockey Players' Good and Poor Sport Behaviors," *Journal of Psychology: Interdisciplinary & Applied* 142, no. 5 (2008): 471–95.

Nicole LaVoi, Jens Omli, and Diane Wiese-Bjornstal, "Minnesota PLAYS™ (Parents Learning About Youth Sports): A Research-Based Parent Education Solution," *Journal of Youth Sports* 3, no. 2 (2008): 14–16.

Jens Omli and Nicole LaVoi, "The Perfect Storm: Background Anger in Youth Sports," *Journal of Sport Behavior* 32, no. 2 (2009): 242–60.

Jens Omli, Nicole LaVoi, and Diane Wiese-Bjornstal, "Towards an Understanding of Parent Spectator Behavior at Youth Sport Events," *Journal of Youth Sports* 3, no. 2 (2008): 30–33.

Jens Omli and Diane Wiese-Bjornstal, "Kids Speak: Children's Preferences for Coach and Parent Behavior" (paper presented at the meeting of the Association for the Advancement of Applied Sport Psychology, Miami, Florida, September 2006).

David Shields, Brenda Bredemeier, Nicole LaVoi, and Clark Power, "The Behavior of Youth, Parents, and Coaches: The Good, the Bad, and the Ugly," *Journal of Research on Character Education* 3, no. 1 (2005): 43–59.

David Shields, Nicole LaVoi, Brenda Bredemeier, and Clark Power, "Predictors of Poor Sportspersonship in Youth Sports: An Examination of Personal Attitudes and Social Influences," *Journal of Sport and Exercise Psychology* 29 (2007): 747–62.

Sally White, "The Parent-Created Motivational Climate," in *Social Psychology in Sport*, ed. Sophia Jowett and David Lavallee, 131–43 (Champaign, IL: Human Kinetics, 2007).

NOTE

1. James Michener, *Sports in America* (New York: Random House, 1976), 97.

CHAPTER 15

The Examen of Consciousness for Coaches and Parents

EDWARD HASTINGS

I do the Examen all the time during the season. That helps me put things into perspective—how grateful I should be for the life I've been blessed with. Sometimes I write my Examen down with my iPad. I have pages and pages and pages during the season. So I think it's just the overall appreciation of understanding your purpose in life, understanding God's will for you.
—John Beilein, University of Michigan basketball coach

I was at a meeting the other day and I noticed several people from time to time picking up their BlackBerries and checking their messages and texting back. Trying not to be judgmental and not really into the multitasking thing, I wondered how present and attentive they could be to the meeting if these kind of distractions were occurring. And I thought about how intrusive some of our communication "advancements" can be on our ordinary lives—iPhones, Facebook, Twitter. These new devices and forms of communication can render us unavailable not only to those around us but also to our God who is trying desperately to connect with us.

God reaches out to us all the time and wants to meet us in our own lived experience. If we are so distracted in our ordinary, everyday experience, we will not be able to listen for God calling out to us. The insightful spiritual writer Ronald Rolheiser says that we are far too busy these days from what he calls "unbridled restlessness" to notice a felt presence of God.[1] He asks the thoughtful question, "Can we murder God's presence simply by the way we live?"[2] I think it is definitely possible to do this.

We are not available to hear because we have too many distractions, too many other things competing for our attention. We are texting or on our cell phones or tweeting or plugged into iPods while sitting directly across from people, so we are not available to listen to them, let alone listen for a message from God. We are not ready to be "hearers of the Word," because we are *homo distractus* (distracted humans).

Long before our modern, sophisticated forms of technology, St. Ignatius of Loyola came up with a method designed to help us become aware of the presence of God. He called this the Examen of Conscience. In our own time it has become commonplace to refer to this as the Examen of Consciousness. (The English word "conscience" tends to refer to the capacity that we use when making moral decisions, which is narrower than the analogous word in Spanish and the other Romance languages.)

WHAT IS THE EXAMEN OF CONSCIOUSNESS?

Jesuit George Aschenbrenner considers the Examen a daily exercise of discernment in a person's life.[3] It is meant to help us, at the end of the day, to notice the Spirit working in our daily experiences, thoughts, feelings, and actions. It could typically take anywhere from three minutes to fifteen minutes or more. There are five steps of the Examen: (1) prayer for enlightenment, (2) reflective thanksgiving, (3) review of the day, (4) contrition and sorrow, (5) hopeful resolution for the future.

The prayer for enlightenment is asking the Spirit to shed light upon our life this particular day. Asking the Spirit for enlightenment reminds us that the exercise ahead is to be a prayerful reflection back on the day's experiences, not an analysis, judgment, or merely introspection. This gentle reflection is not meant to provoke unhealthy guilt but a deeper awareness of God's presence.

The second step, reflective thanksgiving, is meant to offer a moment of gratitude for all that has happened in our day, good or bad. The Spirit can teach us as much through painful or difficult experiences as through joyful experiences. All that happens to us can be considered a gift. Brother David Steindl-Rast believes that gratitude is the heart of prayer.[4] Indeed, this is so much the case that Meister Eckhart once wrote, "If the only prayer you say in your whole life is 'thank you,' that would suffice."[5]

The third element of the Examen is the review of the day. In this part we ask the Spirit to help us look back over the day for the high and the low moments. Initially this entails asking the questions, "What has been happening in us? How has the Spirit been working in our lives?" Here we are called to notice our interior moods, feelings, urges, and movements, as well as their relationship to the day's activities. This part is not meant to help us to move toward or attain perfection; it is meant to assess the quality of our response to the Spirit's presence in our lives.

The fourth part is contrition and sorrow. While not always, at times while doing the Examen we may recognize that we have not been responding to the workings of the Spirit in our lives the way we would like to. Perhaps we were impatient with a loved one or said something hurtful, for example. On such occasions, we express our sorrow and ask God for forgiveness and healing. This part of the prayer is not meant to generate unhealthy shame for our weaknesses and failures but a deeper appreciation of our need for God's grace.

In the fifth part, hopeful resolution for the future, we look forward to the next day and pray for a deeper sensitivity to the Spirit working in our lives. We look ahead to the people we will meet, the events that will take place, and what we will be doing, and we pray for the Spirit's guidance in all these moments.

In short, the Examen is an aid to help us attend to the Word spoken to us in our daily life. God tries to get our attention all the time in a myriad of ways: through other people, through scripture, through nature, to mention a few. In her own way, the poet Elizabeth Barrett Browning reflects upon an experience of noticing God communicating to her through nature.

> Earth's crammed with heaven,
> And every common bush afire with God;
> But only he who sees, takes off his shoes—
> The rest sit round it and pluck blackberries.

Browning is aware that earth is full of revelations from God if we can pay attention. Alluding to Moses's experience of the burning bush, she points out that if we have our eyes open, we can realize that all ordinary bushes or parts of nature have the potential of exploding with God's presence. Practicing the Examen can help us to see, to notice God at work in our daily experiences as does the poet Elizabeth Barrett Browning.[6]

WHY THE EXAMEN FOR COACHES AND PARENTS?

Jesus used the ordinary experiences of life and significant aspects of his culture to teach about God and the reign of God. In his attempt to relate the love of God to the people around him, he used what was available to them: birds, seeds, wheat, water, wine, bread, and so forth. The apostle Paul knew that athletics were important to the people of Greece, and so he used athletic metaphors to describe the dynamics of the Christian life.

The spiritual writer and abbot Thomas Keating says, "Every human pleasure is meant to be a stepping stone to knowing God better or discovering some new aspect of God. . . . Everything in the universe is meant to be a reminder of God's presence."[7] Experiences of play and sports are pleasurable and so can be a stepping stone in the sense that Keating describes.

And yet, sports and spirituality are not usually associated with one another. Given the problems with steroids and the prevalence of violence and domestic abuse amongst athletes and the selfishness and shallowness of many of our sports figures, the last place many people would tend to look for deeper spiritual meaning is sports. If, however, we believe God is in all things, God is also in sports. It is just that we don't always recognize this presence.

One of the ways we can recognize God's presence is by attending to how our young people grow and flourish while participating in sports. After all, "the glory of God is the human being fully alive," as Irenaeus taught.[8] In sports, young people can experience the joy of play, make friendships, learn the value of commitment, how to be a part of something larger than themselves, how to cope with losing and failure, and how to be good, gracious winners. As we have seen in other chapters of this book, under the direction of a thoughtful coach young people can also learn about the relationship between these experiences and core themes in Christian spirituality.

The Examen is one aid that can help coaches and parents recognize the presence of God working in their lives. The Examen does not make God appear magically in youth sport but can shine light on or call attention to our God always already there waiting for us to notice. The appendix to this chapter offers some examples of questions that can help facilitate the Examen for coaches and parents.

COMMON EXPERIENCES THAT REVEAL SOMETHING DEEPER

Because all of the above can sound a bit ethereal or esoteric, I have identified a few things to look for with the Examen that could reveal the presence of God in our day. The first one is an experience of joy. Teilhard de Chardin said, "Joy is the most infallible sign of the presence of God."[9] A coach can look back on a day for times when he or she felt a deep sense of joy or contentment, satisfaction or fulfillment. Perhaps this was experienced simply by spending time with young people at practice on a given day. Or maybe a bench player made a significant play to win a game or a player consoled a teammate after a costly mistake. The experience of joy is an important indication that we have discovered our vocation, and somebody who is called to work with young people in sports should experience a kind of joy that comes from the Lord.

The second sign is an experience of awe or wonder. This would be the jaw dropping moment where we are moved to say, "Oh my God!" The spiritual writer Adrian van Kaam said, "An experience of awe is the beginning of spirituality."[10] The sense of amazement at the gracefulness of an athlete or a sense of awe at the talent of a player can move us to gratitude to God, who is the giver of all gifts. We could also be amazed by the commitment and perseverance of an athlete who returns to play after a serious injury or even a disease. I am thinking here of a Boston College star football player who came back to play after a bout with cancer. Because of the intense nature of sports, there are also many circumstances that call out for forgiveness. When a coach or parent witnesses forgiveness in action among young people, this too can be awe inspiring.

A third sign of the presence of God are goose bumps. Medical doctor and spiritual writer Rachel Naomi Remen says, "Goose bumps happen when your soul comes close to you, breathes lightly on the back of your neck, and wakes you up."[11] The thing about goose bumps is that we can't force them; they just happen and we can't fake them. I got goose bumps when I heard the story about the college softball player from Western Oregon who hit a home run but tore her ACL as she turned from first toward second. She could not run the bases and her teammates were not allowed to help her. So two opponents carried her around the bases so she could complete her home run.

A fourth sign is a spontaneous tearing up that comes when we are deeply touched or moved by an emotion. Tears have a way of sneaking up on us and can be gifts from God. Tears can occur when we witness children experiencing the pure fun of playing sports. Here it is their sense of belonging, their sense of friendship, their sense of joy in participating that can move us to tears. Or we might be moved to tears as we witness the depth of sharing that occurs in a chapel session, as the members of the team begin to form a genuine community.

Besides these four "revelations of God," it can be helpful to be aware of any sort of strong emotion. Attended to properly, such feelings can help awaken us to new directions, growth, and depth.

AN EXAMPLE OF THE USE OF THE EXAMEN

At one point I was the chaplain for the men's basketball team at Neumann University. During one game our team was losing by thirty-seven points to one of our archrivals with two seconds to go in the half. The other team threw up a half-court shot that banked in and put us down by forty. To say the least, I was not happy as I stood up and headed to the locker room. As I was crossing the court moving toward the locker room, my eyes caught sight of one of the opposing coaches laughing as he approached the scorer's table. This made me even more angry. It took everything in me not to go directly over to him and say, "What are you laughing about? Wipe that smile off your face!" I put my head down and headed over to join our team.

Later that night as I was falling asleep, I got to thinking about the game. I recalled the strong feeling of pain and anger. I asked myself, "Why was I so upset?" I started thinking about why winning is so important to me. I also reflected that I did not really know why the coach was laughing—it could have been at something entirely different. I became aware of the affection I felt for our team and did not enjoy them being laughed at (or so I thought) by the coach. My reflection helped me to gain some perspective (*per-spect*—to see clearly) and some insight into myself. The Spirit guided me to a new awareness about myself and helped me to consider how I can sometimes rush to judge another person.

The Examen of Consciousness is a way of praying designed by St. Ignatius of Loyola to foster a greater awareness of how God is present and working in our lives. Coaches and parents can utilize this aid not only to enrich their own spiritual lives but also those of the young people with whom they work. The Examen inspires an attitude of gratitude for these young people and provokes an appreciation for the hope they bring to the future.[12]

APPENDIX

Examen Questions for Coaches

1. What was I most grateful to God for today at practice or the game?
2. Did I experience joy, tears, turmoil, or other particularly strong feelings today? What were these?
3. When did I experience the "life to the full" that Jesus invites us to today as a coach?
4. Have I noticed any changes in the attitude of the players? (failed an exam, distracted, quiet, possibly hurt and not telling anyone, upset, etc.)
5. Are my expectations too high for some of the players?
6. Did I miss an opportunity to compliment a player, assistant coach, official, or opposing player today?
7. Did I notice when I was impatient at practice or the game?
8. Did I notice how my bad attitude before the practice/game carried over to the practice/game?
9. Are there certain players that I respond to better or worse?
   —the whiner   —the trouble maker   —the hard worker
   —the comic   —the scorer   —the loud mouth
10. Am I aware of how my response to a player might influence his or her self-confidence?
11. Would I be able to apologize to the players or coaches for something I did or did not do?

Examen Questions for Parents

1. What was I most grateful to God for today as a parent?
2. Did I experience joy, tears, turmoil or other particularly strong feelings today? What were these?
3. When did I experience the "life to the full" that Jesus invites us to today as a parent?
4. Have I noticed if my child is enjoying playing sports?
5. Have I noticed if I tried to overprotect my child today?
6. Have my expectations for my child overburdened him or her today?
7. Did I do any comparing of my child today?
8. Was my treatment of my child dependent upon their performance or achievement today?

9. Have I paid attention to my child's body language today?
10. Did I notice if my child was frustrated on the ride home after the game or practice?
11. Have I noticed myself being negative about the coach or my child's teammates when talking to my child?
12. Have I noticed when my child is uncharacteristically or inappropriately upset?

NOTES

1. Ronald Rohlheiser, *The Shattered Lantern* (New York: Crossroad, 2001), 42.

2. Ibid., 11.

3. George Aschenbrenner, "Consciousness Examen," *Review for Religious* 31 (1972): 14–21.

4. David Steindl-Rast, *Gratefulness, the Heart of Prayer* (Ramsey, NJ: Paulist Press, 1984).

5. Quoted in Nick Young, "Meister Eckhart," *Contemplative Catholic* (blog), July 10, 2009, http://contemplativecatholicuk.blogspot.com/2009/07/meister-eckhart.html.

6. Quoted in Elizabeth A. Dreyer, *Earth Crammed with Heaven* (Mahwah, NJ: Paulist Press, 1994), vi.

7. Thomas Keating, *The Human Condition: Contemplation and Transformation* (Mahwah, NJ: Paulist Press, 1990), 27.

8. Quoted in Michael Himes, *The Mystery of Faith* (Cincinnati: St. Anthony's Press, 2004), 26.

9. Quoted in James Martin, "The Most Infallible Sign," *America*, April 2, 2007, 10–12.

10. Adrian van Kaam, *Human Formation* (New York: Crossroad, 1985) 177.

11. Quoted in Sue Bender, *Stretching Lessons* (New York: HarperCollins, 2001), xi.

12. For additional understanding of the Examen, see the following: George Ganss, ed., *Ignatius of Loyola: The Spiritual Exercises and Selected Works* (New York: Paulist Press, 1991); Sheila Dennis and Matthew Linn, *Sleeping with Bread* (Ramsey, NJ: Paulist Press, 1995); Ronald Rolheiser, *The Holy Longing: The Search for a Christian Spirituality* (New York: Doubleday, 1999); Dennis Hamm, "Rummaging for God: Praying Backwards Through Your Day," *America*, May 14, 1994, 22–24; and John Govan, SJ, "The Examen: A Tool for Holistic Growth," *Review for Religious*, May/Jun 1986, 394–400.

Conclusion

PATRICK KELLY, SJ

YOUTH SPORT AND SELF-TRANSCENDENCE

The reader will recall from the Introduction that the human capacity for self-transcendence is fundamental to spirituality. As David Perrin put it, "Spirituality, as an innate human characteristic, involves the capacity for self-transcendence: being meaningfully involved in, and personally committed to, the world beyond an individual's personal boundaries."[1] It is significant, then, that so many of the authors in this book focused on the experience of self-transcendence in youth sport.

For Michael McNamee, the process of initiation into youth sport itself involves self-transcendence. Young people first find the sport attractive and take delight in it; they are willing to forego other pleasures because of the enjoyment experienced while immersed in sport. They develop a passion for the sport. Only after some time do they realize that there are standards of excellence, which will require new skills and abilities that they will need to dedicate time and energy to developing. It is in this context, while trying to meet the standards of excellence, that young people have the opportunity to grow in the virtues.

Kelly writes about a similar dynamic, making use of the flow theory of Mihaly Csikszentmihalyi. Csikszentmihalyi arrived at his original insights into the dynamics of the flow experience *when he was studying people at play*. When engaged in sports and other forms of play, people described themselves as fully immersed in what they were doing, with a one-pointedness of mind. They also described experiencing a sense of egolessness, where they weren't thinking about themselves during the activity. After the activity, however, they had a fuller sense of self, as though the boundaries of their being had been pushed forward. It is when people were "pushing the envelope" or going beyond where they were in the domain in which they were participating that they experienced self-transcendence.

This way of understanding self-transcendence in youth sport correlates well with the way Dombrowski, Shields, and Bredemeier understand competition as a "seeking-with." As was mentioned, the word competition is taken from the Latin prefix *com* (in English *with*), and the Latin verb *petere* (in English *to seek*). In this understanding, competition is a search for excellence that is done in *cooperation* with another person or team. As these authors emphasize, competition in youth sport can stretch young people beyond their current level of skills and abilities. And in team sports the demands of competition make it all the more necessary for young people to work together— and give themselves to something larger than themselves.

YOUTH COACHES AND SPECIALISTS

Youth sport, then, is a context where self-transcendence can occur and where young people can experience being a part of something larger than themselves. Such experiences can have an impact on their lives outside of sport, even long after their playing days are over. The lessons learned in sport will have the most impact, however, if coaches and others provide young people with opportunities to reflect together on the meaning of their experiences. In the context of Catholic schools and parishes, coaches and others will also want to provide ways for young people to explicitly connect their experiences to their Christian faith.

In the second half of this book, coaches have written about how they have provided young people with the opportunity to reflect on such topics as what they are grateful for, attitudes, building character, and community. By doing so the coaches helped the bond between the young people to deepen, because they were now connecting to one another at the level of the meaning of their involvement in sport and the meaning of their lives. Some coaches provided their players with opportunities to serve those in need in the broader community, along with focused reflection on these experiences. Several coaches also mentioned the importance of praying as a team at practices and games or at weekly chapel sessions or team Masses. In such contexts, coaches encouraged their players to speak "heart to heart" with one another. Such activities helped the young people to realize that their bond has a spiritual dimension, rooted in God.

It is important to recall that the coaches are assuming implicitly the traditional Christian understanding of the human person as a *unity* of body, mind, and spirit. In this understanding, embodied activities young people engage in, such as sport, necessarily impact their minds (in the sense of their understanding of themselves, others, and their place in the world) and spirit (their relationship with God). Because the coaches provide young people with the opportunity to reflect on the meaning of their experiences in sport and to pray together, they help the youth sport experience to be what John Paul II has called a "gymnastics of body and spirit."[2]

Edward Hastings encourages youth coaches and parents themselves to engage in the same kind of reflection that we are discussing by making use of Ignatius of Loyola's Examen of Consciousness. He points out that it requires disciplined attention to become aware of the way God's love is present in our daily lives and the ways we are responding to or resisting this love. Ignatius's Examen provides a tried and true way to become aware of these dynamics. The Examen is especially important to make use of in the context of youth sport in the United States today, because coaches and parents often experience so many strong and, at times, conflicting thoughts and feelings during their involvement in it. These thoughts and feelings need to be discerned in the light of our faith commitments and relationship with God.

If one of the main lessons young people learn from youth sport is how to cooperate with others and be a part of something larger than themselves, the adults who run youth sport programs and leagues should also take this lesson to heart. This is true of adults in any youth sport league. Adults who work with teams in CYO and Catholic high school leagues have even more reason to cooperate with each other, given the emphasis in the Catholic tradition on commitment to the common good and our shared life as members of the body of Christ. Indeed, Catholic parishes and schools should excel in cooperating with each other and working together to shape league policies and processes that recognize the dignity of young people and have an impact in fostering their integral development as persons.

In this book we have learned that such development happens when youth sport retains its play dimension. In other words, there is a both/and relationship between *playing* sport and integral human development. And when the play dimension is lost, so too are many of the potential developmental benefits for young people. Much remains to be done to rescue the notion of play from the realm of the trivial and insignificant, even spiritually dangerous, that it fell into early in our country's history. An important part of this rescue mission will be to show that play can be compatible with competition (that is to say, it is not only "frolicking") and that it has an important relationship to spiritual values (it is not necessarily the opposite of seriousness). Several of the authors in this volume have helped us to start this project of reconceptualizing play.

If you are a coach and you think there is too much at stake for youth sport to be considered play any longer, I would refer you to Phil Jackson, one of the most successful professional coaches of all time in the United States. In his book *Sacred Hoops: Spiritual Lessons of a Hardwood Warrior*, Jackson writes about the importance of basketball retaining its play dimension. When he was a player for the New York Knicks he taped a slogan to his mirror that read, "Make your work play and your play work," which reminded him of this point. He later reflected on this theme in his role as a coach, saying:

> Basketball is a form of play, of course, but it's easy for players to lose sight of this because of the pressures of the job. As a result, my primary goal during practice is to get the players to reconnect with the intrinsic joy of the game.[3]

According to Jackson, when players get distracted by money and fame they can lose touch with the deeper meaning of their participation in sport. As he put it,

Whether they're willing to acknowledge it or not, what drives most basketball players is not the money or the adulation, but their love of the game. They live for moments when they can lose themselves completely in the action and experience the pure joy of competition. . . . One of the main jobs of a coach is to reawaken that spirit.[4]

Pope Francis would likely agree with Phil Jackson. As he put it in a recent talk to the European Olympic Committee:

When sports is considered only within economic parameters or for the sake of victory at any cost, one runs the risk of reducing athletes to mere merchandise for the increasing of profit. These same athletes enter into a system that sweeps them away, they lose the true meaning of their activity, the joy of playing that attracted them as children and that inspired them to make many real sacrifices and become champions.[5]

If it is possible for sport even at the most elite levels to retain the play element and its connection to joy, then maybe the time has arrived for CYO leagues, Catholic high schools, and other youth sport organizations to reclaim play and recover the joy that should rightly be a part of youth sport.

NOTES

1. David Perrin, *Studying Christian Spirituality* (New York: Routledge, 2007), 20.

2. Pope John Paul II, "Pope to Milan Football Team," *L'Osservatore Romano*, May 28, 1979, 4. The traditional Christian understanding of the person, following St. Paul, includes other dimensions of the person as well, such as "heart" and "soul." I am focusing on the dimensions of body, *mind*, and spirit, in part, because this is a book that will be used widely by people working in Catholic schools, where the development of the mind is front and center.

3. Phil Jackson and Hugh Delehanty, *Sacred Hoops: Spiritual Lessons of a Hardwood Warrior* (New York: Hyperion, 1995) 123.

4. Ibid., 79.

5. Pope Francis, "Address of Pope Francis to Members of the European Olympic Committee," Clementine Hall Saturday, November 23, 2013, available at http://www.cultura.va/content/cultura/en/dipartimenti/sport/risorse/messaggio delpapa/europeanolimpiccommittee.html.

CONTRIBUTORS

Brenda Light Bredemeier, Ph.D., is an associate professor in the College of Education, University of Missouri–St. Louis. Her primary research interests are in character education, moral development, and sports. In addition to publishing dozens of research articles and book chapters in these areas, she is co-author of *Character Development and Physical Activity* and *True Competition: A Guide to Pursuing Excellence in Sport and Society*. Doctor Bredemeier was a founding board member of the Association for the Advancement of Applied Sport Psychology and served on its board for four years as the section head of Social Psychology.

Daniel A. Dombrowski, Ph.D., is professor of philosophy at Seattle University. He is the author of seventeen books and over a hundred articles in scholarly journals in philosophy, theology, classics, and literature. One of his latest books is *Contemporary Athletics and Ancient Greek Ideals* (University of Chicago Press, 2009). His main areas of intellectual interest are history of philosophy, philosophy of religion, and ethics. He is a former baseball and basketball player in high school and college. Since that time he has been an unrelenting gym rat.

Richard R. Gaillardetz, Ph.D., is currently the Joseph Professor of Catholic Theology at Boston College. From 2001 to 2011 he was the Thomas and Margaret Murray and James J. Bacik Professor of Catholic Studies at the University of Toledo. Doctor Gaillardetz's research interests include topics in ecclesiology: Vatican II, ecumenism, authority, and ministry. One of his recent books is *Ecclesiology for a Global Church* (Orbis, 2008). In 2000 he received the Sophia Award from the faculty of the Washington Theological Union in recognition of "theological excellence in service to ministry," and he has received numerous awards from the Catholic Press Association for his occasional pieces. Doctor Gaillardetz has served as the president of the Catholic Theological Society of America.

Edward Hastings, Ph.D., was the director of the Center for Sport, Spirituality, and Character Development at Neumann University from 1999 to 2011. He received his doctorate from Duquesne University and wrote his dissertation on "A Spirituality of Competition." He also received a master's degree in systematic theology from the Washington Theological Union. He played and coached basketball at Villanova University and was a co-captain his senior year. Currently Dr. Hastings teaches theology and spirituality at Villanova.

Patrick Kelly, SJ, Ph.D., is a Jesuit priest and associate professor of theology and religious studies at Seattle University, where he teaches classes about the history of sport and sport as it relates to human development and spirituality. Father Kelly played CYO football, basketball, baseball, and track in elementary school, three sports at Bishop Borgess High School, and football at Grand Valley State University in Michigan. After graduating from college, he taught theology at a Catholic high school in Michigan and coached basketball and football. Father Kelly holds a B.A. in religious studies from the University of Detroit (1983), a Masters of Theological Studies from Harvard Divinity School (1989), a Licentiate in Sacred Theology from Weston Jesuit School of Theology (1999), and a Ph.D. from Claremont Graduate University's School of Religion (2005) in the area of theology, ethics, and culture. He is the author, most recently, of *Catholic Perspectives on Sports: From Medieval to Modern Times* (Paulist, 2012).

Nicole M. LaVoi, Ph.D., teaches in the area of social and behavioral sciences in the School of Kinesiology at the University of Minnesota where she is also the associate director of the Tucker Center for Research on Girls & Women in Sport (www.tuckercenter.org). She is also the co-founder of the Minnesota Youth Sport Research Consortium (www.MNYSRC.org). LaVoi's research interests include the physical activity of girls and women in sport, media portrayals of females in sport, the lack of females in coaching, and the influence of sideline parent behaviors at youth sport events. She strives to answer critical questions that can make a difference in the lives of youth athletes—particularly girls. She continues to deliver research-based coach and parent education workshops in the U.S. and abroad, and helped develop and launch the Play Like a Champion Educational Series with colleagues at the University of Notre Dame. As a public scholar she maintains a blog, One Sport Voice (www.nicolemlavoi.com).

Mike McNamee, Ph.D., is professor of applied ethics at Swansea University, Wales, UK. His teaching and research interests are in medical ethics, research ethics, and sports ethics. He is a former president of the International Association for the Philosophy of Sport and the founding chair of the British Philosophy of Sport Association. He has served on numerous national and international committees of sports organizations, and editorial boards of scholarly journals. He is the founding editor of the international journal *Sport, Ethics and Philosophy* and co-editor of the Routledge twenty-volume book series Ethics and Sports. Mike played and coached various sports at college and recreational levels. He and his wife, Cheryl, a qualified high school physical education teacher, have two daughters: Megan and Ffion.

Greg "Dobie" Moser is the executive director of Youth and Young Adult Ministry and CYO for Catholic Charities in the Cleveland diocese. Dobie played tennis in high school and college before becoming a teaching pro and coach in the U.S. and Canada. He has an undergraduate degree in education from Indiana University of Pennsylvania, an M.A. in family systems counseling from Mount Saint Joseph University, and a Doctorate in Ministry Leadership from the Graduate Theological Foundation. Dobie was a member of the U.S. Olympic Committee and was on the design team for the Play Like a Champion Today program and ND Vision program at the University of Notre Dame. Dobie has trained thousands of coaches and educational leaders around the U.S. and Canada and has authored many sports and ministry resources. He and his wife, Lisa, volunteer extensively with refugees and with young adults suffering with mental illness.

James Charles Naggi is vice principal for administrative services at Jesuit High School, Portland, Oregon, where he has been employed for the past eighteen years. His entire career has been as an educator at three different Catholic secondary schools: Jesuit High School in

Portland, Oregon, Marist High School in Eugene, Oregon, and Notre Dame High School in Riverside, California. His varied duties have included sixteen years as an athletic director and forty-two seasons as a football coach. He is a past national chairman of the Jesuit Schools Education Association's athletic directors conference, has been a guest panelist on the topic of character development through sports at the National Catholic Educational Association national convention, and over the years has authored a number of articles on athletics for various publications. He graduated from University of California, Riverside, in 1973, majoring in English. He and his wife, Donna, have been married since 1970, and have a grown daughter and son, Erika and Nathan.

Clark Power, Ph.D., is a professor of psychology and education at the University of Notre Dame. He received his doctoral degree in moral education under the direction of Lawrence Kohlberg. He is a past president of the Association for Moral Education and a recipient of the Kuhmerker Award for his contributions to the field of moral education, the Ganey Award for community-based research, and the Reinhold Niebuhr Award for his work on behalf of social justice. He is the co-director of the Play Like a Champion Program. His publications focus on moral development and education, civic engagement, and youth sport. He is a co-author of *The Measurement of Moral Judgment* and *Lawrence Kohlberg's Approach to Moral Education* and a co-editor of *The Handbook of Moral Education.*

Sherri Retif is a teacher, coach, and parent at Germantown Academy in Ft. Washington, Pennsylvania. A native of New Orleans, she attended and played basketball at Tulane University and has coached high school basketball for twenty-five years. She is a practicing spiritual director and received her M.A. in holistic spirituality at Chestnut Hill College. Sherri is currently pursuing her D.Min. in spirituality at Fordham University. She co-authored the book *More Than a Game* (St. Mary's Press, 2006). While she has been invited to coach at the highest levels, including USA Basketball's Sports Fest in Colorado Springs and the McDonald's All-American game, her core values remain grounded in her relationship with God.

Kristin Komyatte Sheehan, M.A., serves as the program director for Play Like a Champion Today. She coordinates educational programs and teaches a course on coaching and ministry for Notre Dame's Education, Schools, and Society undergraduate program in education. Kristin has co-authored several articles and presentations with Clark Power on youth sport and moral development. She is a two-time graduate of the University of Notre Dame, earning a B.A. in theology with concentrations in gender studies and peace studies and an M.A. in counseling psychology. While an undergraduate, Kristin was a Division I varsity cheerleader for three years, a career highlighted by cheering for the 1988 National Championship Irish Football Team. Kristin and her husband, Dan, have been blessed with three children. In addition to her collegiate athletic experience, Kristin's role as a parent-coach for her children in gymnastics, soccer, and baseball helps her bring a unique combination of skills and perspective to development of the Play Like a Champion Today initiatives.

David Light Shields, Ph.D., is an associate professor in the College of Education at the University of Missouri–St. Louis. Doctor Shields's research has focused on social and moral development, especially in the context of sport and physical activity. He is the author, co-author, or editor of four books, including most recently, *True Competition: A Guide to Pursuing Excellence in Sport and Society* (Human Kinetics, 2009). From 1999 to 2004, Dr. Shields served as co-director of the Mendelson Center for Sports, Character, and Community at the University of Notre Dame. He is the founder and executive director of TrueCompetition.Org, a nonprofit organization dedicated to reclaiming competition for excellence, ethics, and enjoyment.

Jim Yerkovich recently completed his forty-fifth year as head basketball coach at Judge Memorial Catholic High School in Salt Lake City, Utah. Coach Yerkovich has been the driving force behind the development of the National Catholic Educational Association (NCEA) program "Activities/Athletics: Classroom for Values." At the 2000 NCEA convention, Coach Yerkovich spearheaded a national symposium on "Athletics, Activities, and the Mission of the Catholic School." In the spring of 2003 his book *WE: A Model for Coaching and Christian*

Living, with Patrick Kelly, SJ, was published (National Catholic Educational Association, 2003). This book is the formal presentation of Coach Yerkovich's "WE" philosophy. The book has enjoyed great popularity and is a resource now in over eight hundred high schools. Coach Yerkovich was honored in the spring of 2007 by the NCEA for "Outstanding Contributions to Secondary Catholic Education in the Field of Sports and Catholic Values." His basketball teams at Judge have participated in thirty-six state tournaments, reaching the final four fifteen times, highlighted by three state championships.

INDEX

PATRICK KELLY, SJ,

is associate professor of theology and religious studies
at Seattle University. He is the author of
Catholic Perspectives on Sports:
From Medieval to Modern Times.

CPSIA information can be obtained
at www.ICGtesting.com
Printed in the USA
LVHW071207230719
624999LV00020B/573/P